2004

MACROMEDIA® FIREWORKS® MX
DESIGN PROFESSIONAL

Barbara M. Waxer

THOMSON
COURSE TECHNOLOGY

Macromedia® Fireworks® MX—Design Professional

Barbara M. Waxer

Managing Editor:
Nicole Jones Pinard

Product Manager:
Jane Hosie-Bounar

Associate Product Manager:
Christina Kling Garrett

Editorial Assistant:
Elizabeth Harris

Production Editor:
Anne Valsangiacomo

Development Editor:
Jane Hosie-Bounar

Composition House:
GEX Publishing Services

QA Manuscript Reviewers:
Harris Bierhoff, Chris Carvalho, Stephen Connor, Vitaly Davidovich, Christian Kunciw, Jeff Schwartz, Danielle Shaw, Burt LaFountain, and Susan Whalan

Text Designer:
Ann Small

Illustrator:
Philip Brooker

Cover Design:
Philip Brooker

Design Professional Series Vision

The Design Professional Series is your guide to today's hottest multimedia applications. These comprehensive books teach the skills behind the application, showing you how to apply smart design principles to multimedia products, such as dynamic graphics, animation, Web sites, software authoring tools, and video.

A team of design professionals including multimedia instructors, students, authors, and editors worked together to create this series. We recognized the unique learning environment of the digital media or multimedia classroom and have created a series that:

- Gives you comprehensive step-by-step instructions
- Offers in-depth explanation of the "why" behind a skill
- Includes creative projects for additional practice
- Explains concepts clearly using full-color visuals

It was our goal to create a book that speaks directly to the multimedia and design community—one of the most rapidly growing computer fields today.

This series was designed to appeal to the creative spirit. We would like to thank Philip Brooker for developing the inspirational artwork found on each unit opener and book cover. We would also like to give special thanks to Ann Small of A Small Design Studio for developing a sophisticated and instructive book design.
—The Design Professional Series

Author Vision

The Design Professional series and Fireworks MX are a perfect match. By combining unique educational construction with students' creativity, we have made the process of learning to use Fireworks fun. Because the Web continues to be fresh, nearly any Web-based application can provide the basic motivation for learning. This book provides comprehensive conceptual information, directed but interesting lessons, and appealing projects—a solid recipe for inspired study in this exciting field.

My ongoing thanks and appreciation to Nicole Pinard and Rebecca Berardy for their early and unswerving support for this project. This book and my sanity are the humble beneficiaries of Rebecca's wise counsel and guidance. I also thank everyone at Course

Technology and the Illustrated Team for their assistance.

A very special acknowledgment to Jane Hosie-Bounar, who made this book editorially richer and managed it perfectly.

I happily acknowledge the graphic contributions of Anita Quintana and Laura Gutman. Thanks also to the reviewers, Chris Carvalho, Jeff Schwartz, Susan Whalan, Vitaly Davidovich, Harris Bierhoff, Stephen Connor, Christian Kunciw, Danielle Shaw, and Burt LaFountain. And thanks also to Ashlee Welz, who scheduled the reviews. Thanks also to our table of contents and manuscript reviewers, Sister Mary Juliano of Caldwell College, Jeff Kushner of James Madison University, Bruce Neubauer of Pittsburg State University, and Piyush Patel of Northern Oklahoma College. We are also grateful to Alisse Berger and Mark Haynes at Macromedia for ensuring a smooth review and adding technical expertise.

I would like to give special thanks to my partner, Lindy, who can now reclaim the words "Just one more thing" as her own. A final note for my mom, Ruth Goodman Waxer, who passed on her love of things new and different. May her memory be a blessing.

Introduction

Welcome to *Macromedia® Fireworks® MX—Design Professional*. This book offers creative projects, concise instructions, and complete coverage of basic to intermediate Fireworks MX skills, helping you to create and publish Fireworks documents. Use this book both in the classroom and as your own reference guide.

This text is organized into eight units. In these units, you will learn many skills to create interesting graphics that also include interactivity and animation. In addition, you will learn how to use Fireworks to import and export files.

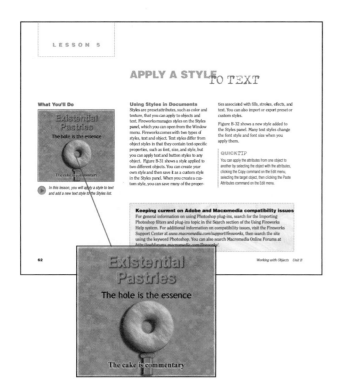

What You'll Do

A What You'll Do figure begins every lesson. This figure gives you an at-a-glance look at the skills covered in the unit and shows you the completed data file for that lesson. Before you start the lesson, you will know—both on a technical and artistic level—what you will be creating.

Comprehensive Conceptual Lessons

Before jumping into instructions, in-depth conceptual information tells you "why" skills are applied. This book provides the "how" and "why" through the use of professional examples. Also included in the text are tips and sidebars to help you work more efficiently and creatively, or to teach you a bit about the history behind the skill you are using.

Step-by-Step Instructions

This book combines in-depth conceptual information with concise steps to help you learn Fireworks MX. Each set of steps guides you through a lesson where you will apply tasks to a Fireworks MX data file. Step references to large colorful images and quick step summaries round out the lessons.

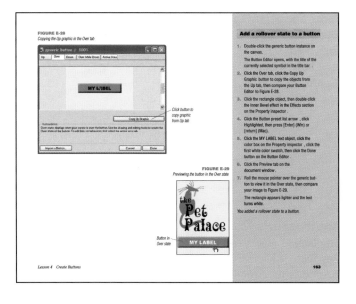

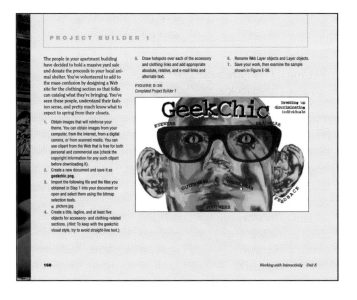

Projects

This book contains a variety of end-of-unit materials for additional practice and reinforcement. The Skills Review contains hands-on practice exercises that mirror the progressive nature of the lesson material. The unit concludes with four projects: two Project Builders, one Design Project, and one Group Project. The Project Builders require you to apply the skills you've learned in the unit to create powerful graphics. Design Projects explore design principles by sending you to the Web to view Fireworks in action. Group Projects encourage group activity as students use the resources of a team to create a project.

What Instructor Resources are Available with this Book?

The Instructor's Resource CD-ROM is Course Technology's way of putting the resources and information needed to teach and learn effectively into your hands. All the resources are available for both Macintosh and Windows operating systems, and many of the resources can be downloaded from *www.course.com*.

Instructor's Manual

Available as an electronic file, the Instructor's Manual is quality-assurance tested and includes unit overviews and detailed lecture topics for each unit, with teaching tips. The Instructor's Manual is available on the Instructor's Resource CD-ROM, or you can download it from *www.course.com*.

Syllabus

Prepare and customize your course easily using this sample course outline (available on the Instructor's Resource CD-ROM).

PowerPoint Presentations

Each unit has a corresponding PowerPoint presentation that you can use in lectures, distribute to your students, or customize to suit your course.

Figure Files

Figure Files contain all the figures from the book in bitmap format. Use the figure files to create transparency masters or use them in a PowerPoint presentation.

Data Files for Students

To complete most of the units in this book, your students will need Data Files. Put them on a file server for students to copy. The Data Files are available on the Instructor's Resource CD-ROM, the Review Pack, and can also be downloaded from *www.course.com*. Instruct students to use the Data Files List at the end of this book. This list gives instructions on copying and organizing files.

Solutions to Exercises

Solution Files are Data Files completed with comprehensive sample answers. Use these files to evaluate your students' work. Or, distribute them electronically or in hard copy so students can verify their work. Sample solutions to all lessons and end-of-unit material are provided.

Test Bank and Test Engine

ExamView is a powerful testing software package that allows instructors to create and administer printed, computer (LAN-based), and Internet exams. ExamView includes hundreds of questions that correspond to the topics covered in this text, enabling students to generate detailed study guides that include page references for further review. The computer-based and Internet testing components allow students to take exams at their computers, and also save the instructor time by grading each exam automatically.

Additional Activities for Students

We have included **Macromedia Fundamentals** interactive training tutorials to help students learn the basics of each of the applications in Macromedia Studio MX.

BRIEF CONTENTS

UNIT A GETTING STARTED WITH MACROMEDIA FIREWORKS MX

UNIT B WORKING WITH OBJECTS

UNIT D — MODIFYING PIXELS AND MANIPULATING IMAGES

UNIT E **WORKING WITH INTERACTIVITY**

UNIT F   CREATING ANIMATION

UNIT G   CREATING SOPHISTICATED WEB PAGE NAVIGATION

UNIT H   ENHANCING PRODUCTIVITY

Intended Audience

This text is designed for the beginner or intermediate student who wants to learn how to use Fireworks MX. The book is designed to provide basic and in-depth material that not only educates, but also encourages the student to explore the nuances of this exciting program.

Approach

The text allows you to work at your own pace through step-by-step tutorials. A concept is presented and the process is explained, followed by the actual steps. To learn the most from the use of the text, you should adopt the following habits:

- Make sure you understand the skill being taught in each step before you move on to the next step.
- After finishing a skill, ask yourself if you could do it on your own, without referring to the steps. If the answer is no, review the steps.

Icons, Buttons, and Pointers

Symbols for icons, buttons, and pointers are shown in the step each time they are used.

Fonts

Data and solution files contain a variety of commonly used fonts, but there is no guarantee that these fonts will be available on your computer. In a few cases, fonts other than those common to a PC or a Macintosh are used. If any of the fonts in use is not available on your computer, you can make a substitution, realizing that the results may vary from those in the book.

Creating a Portfolio

The Group Project and the Project Builders allow students to use their creativity to come up with original Fireworks designs. You might suggest that students create a portfolio in which they can store their original work.

Windows and Macintosh

Fireworks MX works virtually the same on Windows and Macintosh operating systems. In those cases where there is a significant difference, the abbreviations (Win) and (Mac) are used.

The nature of working with graphics requires detailed work. In Fireworks, this means that you will need to magnify areas of an image. Because monitor sizes vary, be sure to set the magnification to the setting that allows you to work comfortably.

Windows System Requirements

Fireworks MX runs under Windows 98 SE, Windows ME, Windows NT® 4.0 (Service Pack 6), Windows 2000, and Windows XP. For a Windows operating system, Fireworks MX requires an Intel 300 MHz Pentium II or equivalent processor, 64 MB of RAM (128 recommended), 80 MB of disk space, an 8-bit (256 colors) color monitor capable of displaying a resolution at 800 x 600 or better, Adobe Type Manager Version 4 or later for use with Type 1 fonts, and a CD-ROM drive.

Macintosh System Requirements

Fireworks MX runs under Mac OS 9.1 (or later) and Mac OS X version 10.1 (or later). For Macintosh operating systems, Fireworks MX requires a Power Macintosh G3 processor, 64 MB of RAM (128 MB recommended), 80 MB of disk space, an 8-bit color (256 colors) monitor capable of displaying a resolution at 800 x 600 or better, Adobe Type Manager Version 4 or later for use with Type 1 fonts (OS 9.x), and a CD-ROM drive.

Data Files

To complete the lessons and end-of-unit material in this book, you need to obtain the necessary Data Files. Please refer to the directions on the inside back cover for various methods to obtain these files. Once obtained, select where to store the files, such as the hard drive, a network server, or a zip drive. The instructions in the lessons will refer to "the drive and folder where your Data Files are stored" when referring to the Data Files for the book.

Projects

Several projects are presented at the end of each unit that allow students to apply the skills they have learned in the unit.

GETTING STARTED
WITH MACROMEDIA
FIREWORKS MX

1. Understand the Fireworks work environment.

2. Work with new and existing documents.

3. Work with bitmap images.

4. Create shapes.

5. Create and modify text.

UNIT A
GETTING STARTED WITH MACROMEDIA FIREWORKS MX

Understanding Fireworks MX

Fireworks is a graphics program intended specifically for the Web. Both Web enthusiasts and professionals can create, edit, and optimize files, and then add animation and JavaScript-enabled interactivity to those optimized files. Many Fireworks tasks are compartmentalized so that graphic artists can enhance or create designs without disturbing the programming added by developers, and vice versa.

In Fireworks, you can also work with files created by other graphic design programs, and save and export files you create in Fireworks to other programs. Fireworks is an integral component of the Macromedia MX Suite, and integrates seamlessly with other Macromedia applications, including Macromedia Flash, Dreamweaver, FreeHand, ColdFusion, and Director Shockwave Studio. In addition, you can use other applications, such as Macromedia Flash or Dreamweaver, to edit Fireworks images using the Fireworks interface from within the host application. Fireworks also allows file sharing with other applications, such as Adobe Photoshop and Microsoft FrontPage.

In this book, you will learn to use the tools and apply the concepts that make Fireworks a comprehensive Web graphics program. In addition to creating files that can be used in other programs, you will create sample Web pages and animated graphics.

Tools You'll Use

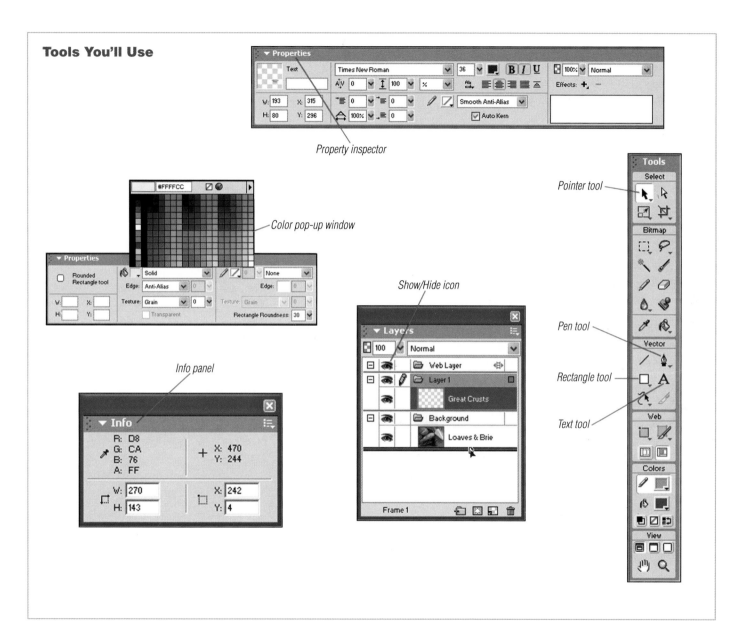

Property inspector

Color pop-up window

Info panel

Show/Hide icon

Pointer tool

Pen tool

Rectangle tool

Text tool

UNDERSTAND THE FIREWORKS WORK ENVIRONMENT

What You'll Do

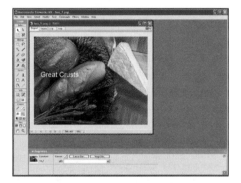

 In this lesson, you will start Fireworks, open a file, and adjust panels, including undocking and collapsing them.

Viewing the Macromedia Fireworks Window

The Fireworks window contains the space where you work with documents, tools, and panels. The overall Fireworks environment emulates the familiar interface in other Macromedia MX applications. When you open or create a document, the document window contains display tabs, known as document window tabs, and a canvas. The **canvas** is the area where you draw and manipulate objects and images. The four display tabs afford you different views of the document: Original, Preview, 2-Up, and 4-Up. When you select the 2-Up tab or 4-Up tab, you can select different optimization settings and evaluate them side-by-side. You work in your document in Original view.

QUICKTIP

The bottom of each document window also contains VCR buttons for playing animation.

Tools are housed in the **Tools panel**; other functions are contained in panels such as the Optimize and Layers panels. The Tools panel is separated into **tool groups**: Select, Bitmap, Vector, Web, Colors, and View, so you can easily locate the tool you need. You can modify selected objects and set tool properties and other options using the **Property inspector**. Depending on the action you are performing, information on the Property inspector changes. For example, when you select a tool or an object, properties specific to the selection appear on the Property inspector.

Opening Windows-specific toolbars

If you are using Windows, you can open the Main and Modify toolbars from the Window menu. The Main toolbar includes buttons for common tasks, while the Modify toolbar contains buttons for modifying objects. You can open the status bar, which displays tips and other information about selected tools, from the View menu.

You can rearrange panels in the Fireworks window based on your work preferences. Fireworks allows you to dock, undock, regroup, collapse, expand, and close panels or panel groups. If you want to move or resize a panel, you must first undock it.

Figure A-1 and Figure A-2 show the main components in the Fireworks window in Windows and Macintosh, respectively. Note that displaying all of the panels at one time can obscure your view of the document window.

panel gripper left hand corner

QUICKTIP

You can customize panel groupings by moving individual panel tabs to other panels or by creating new panels. To regroup a panel, click the Options menu icon on a panel, point to Group *Panel Name* With, then click the name of the panel where you want to move the panel. You can quickly hide and show all open panels by pressing [Tab].

FIGURE A-1
Fireworks window (Windows)

Document window tabs

Tools panel

Canvas

Property inspector

Docked panel

Undocked panel has blue bar

Collapse arrow icon

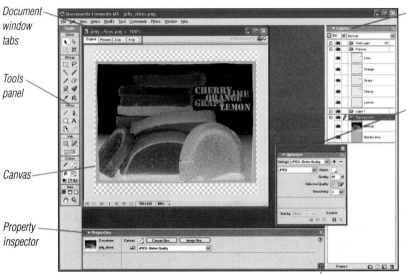

FIGURE A-2
Fireworks window (Macintosh)

Start Fireworks and open a Fireworks document

1. Click the Start button on the taskbar, point to All Programs, point to the Macromedia folder, then click the Macromedia Fireworks MX program icon (Win).

   TIP   To start Fireworks on a Macintosh, double-click the hard drive icon, double-click the Applications folder, double-click the Macromedia Fireworks MX folder, then double-click the Macromedia Fireworks program icon.

2. If necessary, close the Welcome dialog box.

3. Click File on the menu bar, then click Open.

4. Navigate to the drive and folder where your data files are stored, click fwa_1.png, then click Open.

   TIP   If the drive containing your data files is not displayed, click the Look in list arrow.

5. Compare your default work area to Figure A-3.

You started Fireworks and opened a file.

FIGURE A-3
Newly opened document

Your default colors
may vary

Your open panels and
their location may vary

FIGURE A-4

Opening panels from the Window menu

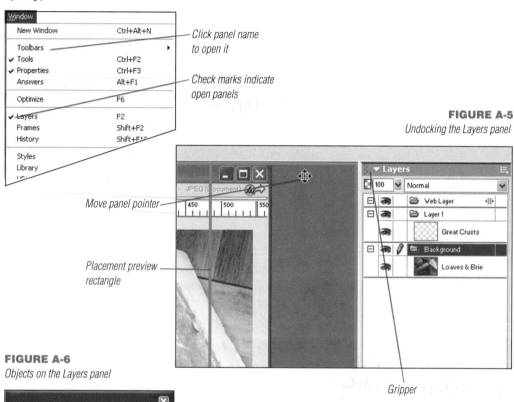

Window	
New Window	Ctrl+Alt+N
Toolbars	▶
✔ Tools	Ctrl+F2
✔ Properties	Ctrl+F3
Answers	Alt+F1
Optimize	F6
✔ Layers	F2
Frames	Shift+F2
History	Shift+F1°
Styles	
Library	

— Click panel name to open it

— Check marks indicate open panels

FIGURE A-5

Undocking the Layers panel

Move panel pointer —

Placement preview rectangle —

Gripper

FIGURE A-6

Objects on the Layers panel

Lesson 1   Understand the Fireworks Work Environment

1. Click Window on the menu bar, then click the panel names until your menu resembles Figure A-4.

2. Position the mouse on the top of the Layers panel, drag the gripper down and to the left until you see the placement preview rectangle shown in Figure A-5, then release the mouse button.

   TIP   On a Macintosh, the gripper has 15 dots.

3. Click and drag the bottom edge of the Layers panel down, if necessary, until all of the objects are visible, as shown in Figure A-6.

4. Click the panel name to collapse the panel, then click the Close button to close the panel.

5. Click the Collapse arrow ▼ in the bottom right corner of the Property inspector, then click the Expander arrow to expand it. ▶

6. Click File on the menu bar, then click Close.

You adjusted panels in the Fireworks window, and opened and closed a document.

9

WORK WITH NEW AND EXISTING DOCUMENTS

What You'll Do

In this lesson, you will set document properties, use the Index and Search tabs of Help, add a layer, and copy an object between documents.

Working with Files

Fireworks files are known as **documents**. When you create a new document, you can set properties such as the document's size, resolution, and canvas color. Fireworks will retain the changes you make to document properties as the default settings for new documents. A Fireworks document consists of many **layers**, which you can use to organize the elements of your document. A layer can contain multiple objects, all of which are managed on the Layers panel.

Although you can open or import a wide range of file formats, the files you create in Macromedia Fireworks are PNG files and have a .png extension. PNG files have unique characteristics that afford you considerable flexibility in working with images. Different file formats support images differently. You can divide a document or image into parts and then individually optimize and export them in the format that best supports the image. For example, you can save a photograph in your document as a JPEG and a cartoon

automatic - .PNG
photograph   .JPG
Cartoon   .GIF
Line art

Duplicating options in Fireworks

You can duplicate an object within a document by selecting the object on the canvas, pressing and holding [Alt] (Win) or [option] (Mac), and then dragging the object to a new location. However, if you open a document immediately after copying an object to the clipboard, Fireworks automatically sets the size of a new document to those dimensions.

illustration as a GIF. JPEG format compresses color well, and is thus best suited for photographs, while GIF format is suitable for line art.

QUICKTIP

QUICK**TIP**

You can change canvas settings by clicking one of the choices under the Canvas command on the Modify menu.

You can also open an existing file or import a file into a Fireworks document. You can copy and paste or drag and drop images or text into a Fireworks document from other documents or applications, or from a scanner or digital camera. Figure A-7 shows an object copied from a source document to a target document.

Accessing Help

The Fireworks Help system consists of several tabs that you can use to access Help topics: Contents, Index, and Search. The Contents tab lists various topics by subject matter. You can type a keyword on the Index tab and access all the topics that begin with that keyword. You can also enter a keyword on the Search tab, and retrieve a listing of the topics that contain the keyword.

QUICK**TIP**

You can save Help topics of interest on the Favorites tab by displaying the topic, clicking the Favorites tab (Win), and then clicking the Add button.

In Help, commands on the menu bar help you navigate and print topics. In Fireworks, other commands on the Help menu link you to online support, such as the Fireworks Support Center and Macromedia Online Forums. You can also obtain updates and tips and search for information on the Fireworks MX Web site: *www.macromedia.com/ software/fireworks*, or by clicking links in the Answers panel.

FIGURE A-7
Object copied between documents

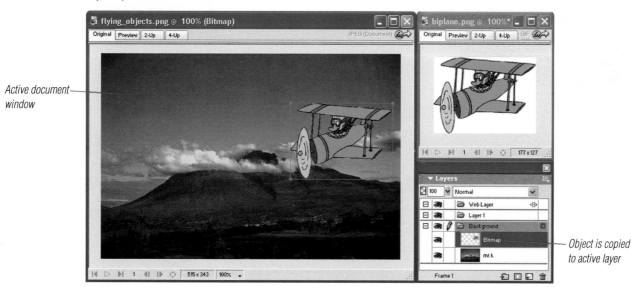

Active document window

Object is copied to active layer

Create and save a new document

1. Click File on the menu bar, then click New.

2. Type **325** in the Width text box, double-click the value in the Height text box, type **275**, then verify that the resolution is 72.

3. Click the Custom option in the Canvas Color section of the New Document dialog box, then click the Canvas Color box. ■

4. Double-click (Win) or click (Mac) the hexadecimal text box, type **#0099FF**, as shown in Figure A-8, press [Enter] (Win) or [return] (Mac), then click OK.

    A new document window appears in the Fireworks window.

    > TIP   You can click a color swatch in the color pop-up window or type a color's hexadecimal value in the text box.

5. Click File on the menu bar, click Save, type **my_blue_heaven** in the File name text box (Win) or Save As text box (Mac), click the Save in list arrow (Win) or Where box list arrow (Mac) to choose your destination drive and folder, then click Save.

6. Compare your document to Figure A-9.

You created, modified, and named a new document.

FIGURE A-8
Selecting a color on the color pop-up window

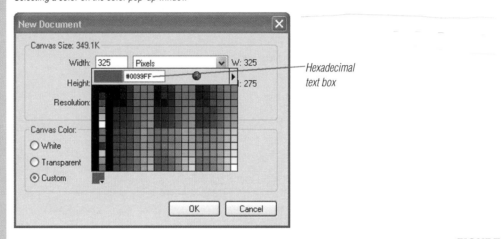

Hexadecimal text box

FIGURE A-9
Newly created document

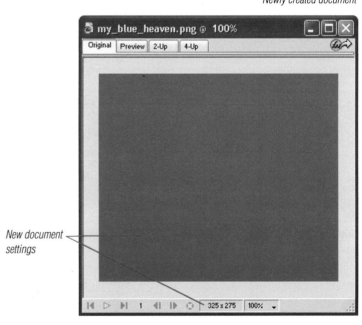

New document settings

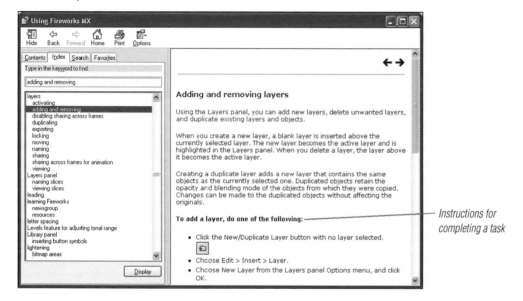

Adding and removing layers

Using the Layers panel, you can add new layers, delete unwanted layers, and duplicate existing layers and objects.

When you create a new layer, a blank layer is inserted above the currently selected layer. The new layer becomes the active layer and is highlighted in the Layers panel. When you delete a layer, the layer above it becomes the active layer.

Creating a duplicate layer adds a new layer that contains the same objects as the currently selected one. Duplicated objects retain the opacity and blending mode of the objects from which they were copied. Changes can be made to the duplicated objects without affecting the originals.

To add a layer, do one of the following: —————— *Instructions for completing a task*

- Click the New/Duplicate Layer button with no layer selected.
- Choose Edit > Insert > Layer.
- Choose New Layer from the Layers panel Options menu, and click OK.

FIGURE A-11
Layer added to Layers panel

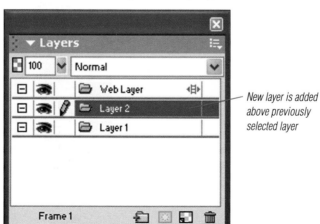

New layer is added above previously selected layer

Use the Index tab of Help and add a layer

1. Click Help on the menu bar, click Using Fireworks (Win) or Fireworks Help (Mac), then click the Index tab (Win), if necessary.

   TIP   You can also open the Help system by pressing [F1].

2. Type **layers** in the Type in the keyword to find text box (Win) or in the dialog box at the top of the Help window, click Ask (Mac), then double-click adding and removing in the topic list.

3. Read the instructions on adding a layer, compare your Help window to Figure A-10, then click the Help window Close button.

4. Click Window on the menu bar, click Layers, click the New/Duplicate Layer button on the Layers panel, then compare your Layers panel to Figure A-11.

   A new layer, Layer 2, appears on the Layers panel above the active layer.

   TIP   Expand the Layers panel, if necessary, to see all the layers.

5. Click File on the menu bar, then click Save.

You entered a keyword in the Index tab of Help and added a layer to the Layers panel.

Use the Search tab of Help

1. Open pool.png.

   TIP   If the .png extension is not visible, Windows users can open the file management tool that is on your operating system, then adjust the settings to display extensions.

2. Drag the pool.png document to a blank part of the Fireworks window, then make sure that your view of the documents is unobstructed, as shown in Figure A-12.

   TIP   You can resize the document window by dragging any edge or the bottom right corner. Be sure to move undocked panels that obstruct your view.

3. Click Help on the menu bar, click Using Fireworks, then click the Search tab (Win).

4. Type **Inserting objects into documents** in the Type in the keyword to find text box, then click List Topics (Win) or Ask (Mac).

5. Double-click the Inserting objects into a Fireworks document topic, then compare your Help window (Win) to Figure A-13.

6. Read the instructions for inserting objects, then close the Help window.

You entered a search topic in Help.

FIGURE A-12
Open documents in the work area

FIGURE A-13
Search tab in Help

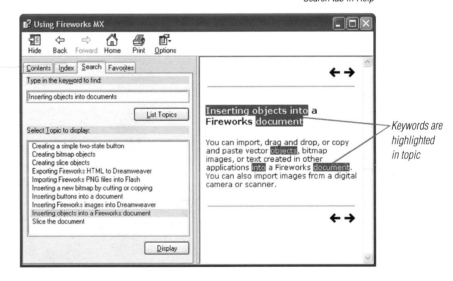

Keywords are highlighted in topic

FIGURE A-14
Object being copied

Blue line indicates
image area of object
being moved

FIGURE A-15
Object centered in document

1. Make sure that the Pointer tool is selected on the Tools panel.

2. Click the mouse anywhere on the pool image, drag it to the my_blue_heaven document, then compare your image to Figure A-14.

   TIP You can also select the object, click Edit on the menu bar, click Copy, position the pointer in the target document, click Edit on the menu bar, and then click Paste.

3. Use the arrow keys to center the image on the canvas.

   TIP The arrow keys move an object in 1-pixel increments; press and hold [Shift] to move 10 pixels.

4. Click pool.png, click File on the menu bar, then click Close.

   TIP If you are prompted to save changes, click No.

5. Click the blank area around the canvas to deselect the object, then compare your document to Figure A-15.

6. Click File on the menu bar, click Close, then click Yes (Win) or Save (Mac) to save changes.

You dragged an image from one file to another.

WORK WITH BITMAP IMAGES

What You'll Do

In this lesson, you will modify a bitmap image and create and lock a layer.

Understanding the Layers Panel

Although *layer* is a common term in graphic design applications, a layer's function varies depending on the program. In other applications, such as Adobe Photoshop, you use layers to manipulate pixels, discrete squares of color values that can be drawn in a document. In Fireworks, you use layers to position objects, which are the individual elements in your document. One function of the Layers panel is to arrange the elements in your document in a logical design order. For example, you can place related elements on the same layer, such as the design elements of a logo, or all the buttons for a Web page. The position of objects/layers in the Layers panel affects their appearance in your document. Each object is akin to an image on a clear piece of acetate—you can stack them on top of each other and view them from the top. The artwork on the bottom may be obscured by the layers above it, but you can adjust visibility by making some pieces more transparent.

You can place as many objects as you wish on a layer, arrange them in any order, and select one or more of them at a time. A document can easily accumulate numerous layers and objects, which can make it difficult to quickly find the ones with which you want to work. You can collapse or expand layers to show all or none of the objects. Figure A-16 shows components of the Layers panel.

Customizing your view of the Layers panel
You can select the size of the thumbnails that are displayed in the Layers panel or choose not to display them at all. To change thumbnail size, click the Options menu icon on the Layers panel, point to Thumbnail Options, and then select the option you want.

Understanding Bitmap Images and Vector Objects

Fireworks allows you to work with both bitmap and vector graphic images in your document. A bitmap graphic represents a picture image as a matrix of dots, or pixels, on a grid. Bitmaps allow your computer screen to realistically depict the pixel colors in a photographic image. In contrast, vector graphics are mathematically calculated objects composed of anchor points and straight or curved line segments, which you can fill with color or a pattern and outline with a stroke.

Because a bitmap image is defined pixel by pixel, when you scale a bitmap graphic, you lose the sharpness of the original image. Resolution refers to the number of pixels in an image (print graphics require greater resolution). Resolution also refers to an image's clarity and fineness of detail. Onscreen resolution is usually 72 or 96 pixels per inch (ppi). Bitmap images are, therefore, resolution-dependent—resizing results in a loss of image quality. The most visible evidence is the all-too-familiar jagged appearance in the edges of an image.

Because they retain their appearance regardless of how you resize or skew them, vector graphics offer far more flexibility than bitmap images. They are resolution-independent—enlarging retains a crisp edge. Figure A-17 compares the image quality of enlarged vector and bitmap images.

> **QUICKTIP**
>
> An object in Fireworks corresponds to a layer in Photoshop.

FIGURE A-16
The Layers panel

Pencil icon

Collapsed layer

Expanded layer

Show/Hide Layer icon

Lock/Unlock Layer icon

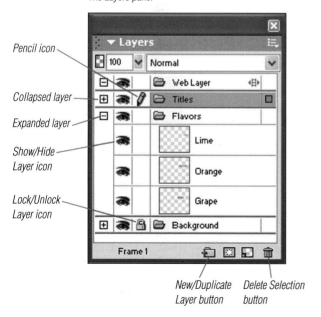

New/Duplicate Layer button   Delete Selection button

FIGURE A-17
Comparing vector and bitmap graphics

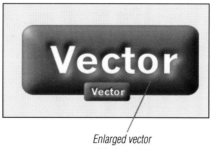

Enlarged vector object remains crisp

Enlarged bitmap image appears jagged and blurry

Bitmap
picture = pixel

Vector
math calculated
more "flexible"

Resolution
clarity
pixels (72×96)

Open a document and display the Layers panel

1. Open fwa_1.png, then save it as **breads**.

   TIP You can also access the Open dialog box by pressing [Ctrl] O (Win) or [command] O (Mac).

2. Make sure that the Layers panel is displayed and expanded to show all the layers.

3. Click the Show/Hide Layer icon next to the Great Crusts object in Layer 1 on the Layers panel to hide the layer. 👁

   Notice that the Show/Hide Layer icon toggles between an eye icon and a blank box, depending on whether the layer is hidden or visible.

   TIP If you do not see an object in a layer, click the Expand Layer icon. ⊞

4. Compare your image to Figure A-18, then click the Show/Hide Layer icon next to the Great Crusts object in Layer 1. ▢

5. Click the Great Crusts object in Layer 1 on the Layers panel, then drag it beneath the Background layer until a double line appears beneath the Loaves & Brie layer, as shown in Figure A-19. 🖐

   The Great Crusts object has become the bottom-most object in the Background layer, and is no longer visible in the document.

6. Verify that the Great Crusts object is still selected, then click the Delete Selection button on the Layers panel. 🗑

You hid and displayed an object in a layer on the Layers panel and moved and deleted an object.

Object hidden on the Layers panel

Text is no longer visible

Show/Hide Layer icon (blank box) indicates object is hidden

Show/Hide Layer icon hides object or layer

FIGURE A-19
Object moved between layers

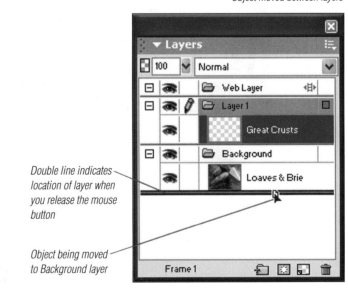

Double line indicates location of layer when you release the mouse button

Object being moved to Background layer

FIGURE A-20
Brightness/Contrast dialog box

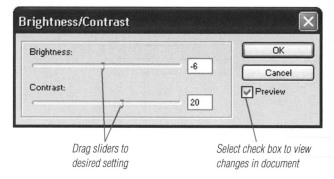

Drag sliders to
desired setting

Select check box to view
changes in document

FIGURE A-21
Layer locked on Layers panel

Click pencil icon or
blank box in column
to lock layer

Click padlock icon to
unlock layer

1. Click the Loaves & Brie object on the Background layer to select it (if necessary).

2. Click Filters on the menu bar, point to Adjust Color, then click Brightness/Contrast.

3. Drag the Brightness slider to **–6**, then drag the Contrast slider to **20**.

   TIP   You can also enter values in the text boxes.

4. Compare your Brightness/Contrast dialog box to Figure A-20, then click OK.

   The colors in the image appear richer.

5. Click the pencil icon in the column next to the Background folder icon to lock the layer.

   The padlock icon replaces the pencil icon in the column.

   TIP   While it is locked, you cannot edit a layer or its objects.

6. Compare your Layers panel to Figure A-21, then save your work.

You adjusted the brightness and contrast of the Loaves & Brie object and then locked the layer.

CREATE SHAPES

What You'll Do

 In this lesson, you will display rulers and guides, and create and modify a vector object.

Using Rulers, Guides, and the Grid

Rulers, guides, and the grid are design aides that help you precisely align and position objects in your document. Because Fireworks graphics are Web-oriented, where the rule of measurement is in pixels, ruler units are always in pixels. You insert guides from the rulers by dragging them onto your canvas. Guides do not print or export, although you can save them in the original .png document. If you want to specify an exact location, you can double-click a guide and then enter a coordinate. For each open document you can adjust the grid size to create squares or rectangles and snap objects directly to guides and the grid at any time.

QUICKTIP

To change guide and grid line colors, point to the Grid or Guides command on the View menu, then click Edit Grid or Edit Guides, respectively.

Sizing and Moving Objects

You can use the Info panel to view information about the position of the pointer on the canvas and selected objects. The R, G, B, and A color values and the X and Y coordinate values correspond to the area of the canvas where the pointer is positioned. You can use the color values to view the values of the selected pixel. You can use the coordinate values to position an object in a precise location.

Using the Tools Panel

Although you can use many tools on both bitmap and vector graphics, graphic mode-specific tools are housed in separate sections of the Tools panel. Based on the object, layer, or tool, Fireworks automatically determines whether you are editing a bitmap or a vector graphic, and activates or nullifies the tool appropriately. Figure A-22 shows the Blur tool (a bitmap tool) actively blurring the floral bitmap image, but the tool can't blur the text because text is a vector object. You can create vector

Vector tools

objects using several tools, including the basic shape tools: the Rectangle, Rounded Rectangle, Ellipse, and Polygon tools. Bitmap selection tools modify the pixels in a bitmap image, which makes them useful for retouching photographic images.

Some tools have multiple tools associated with them. A small arrow in the bottom right corner of the tool button indicates that more tools are available. To select additional tools, press and hold the tool, then click the tool you want from the list, as shown in Figure A-23. The properties

associated with a selected tool are displayed on the Property inspector, although not all tools have properties associated with them. For example, when you select one of the basic shape tools, such as the Ellipse tool, you can adjust an object's fill and stroke settings on the Property inspector.

Applying Fills and Strokes

You can fill an object with a solid color, texture, or pattern. When you apply a fill, you can adjust the following attributes: its color and category (such as solid, gradient, or pattern), and the type and amount of edge

of the fill. You can apply a border, known as a stroke, to an object's edge. You can set several stroke attributes, including color, tip size (the size of the stroke), softness, and texture. Anti-aliasing blends the edges of a stroke or text with surrounding pixels so that the edges blend into the background. When editing text, you can select one of four anti-alias settings: No, Crisp, Strong, or Smooth, which make the edges look smoother or crisper. If you are working with a rectangle or rounded rectangle, you can also adjust the degree of roundness of the stroke.

FIGURE A-22
Using a bitmap tool on different graphic types

FIGURE A-23
Selecting tools on the Tools panel

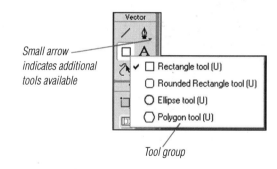

Small arrow indicates additional tools available

Tool group

Blur tool pointer is active on bitmap image

Blur tool is inactive on vector object

Display the guides

1. Verify that Layer 1 is active, then click the New/Duplicate Layer button on the Layers panel to create a new layer, Layer 2.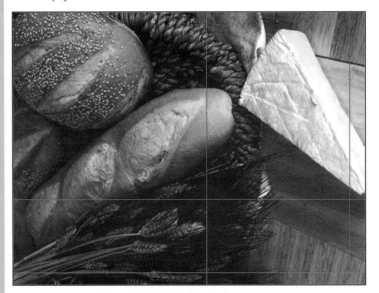

2. Double-click Layer 2, type **Ad Copy** in the Layer Name text box, then press [Enter] (Win) or [return] (Mac).

3. Click View on the menu bar, point to Guides, then click Show Guides.

4. Compare your image to Figure A-24.

You named a layer and displayed guides.

Create a vector object

1. Press and hold the Rectangle tool on the Tools panel, then click the Rounded Rectangle tool. ⬜

2. Click the Fill category list arrow on the Property inspector, click Solid (if necessary), then click the Fill Color box 🖌🟦 to open the color pop-up window.

3. Click the right-most swatch in the second row from the bottom (#FFFFCC), as shown in Figure A-25. 🖊

4. Click the Edge of fills list arrow, click Anti-Alias (if necessary), click the Texture name list arrow, click Grain (if necessary), click the Amount of texture list arrow, drag the slider to **10**, then click the Transparent check box to select it.

> TIP Fireworks automatically applies the last selected stroke and fill to an object.

(continued)

FIGURE A-24
Guides displayed

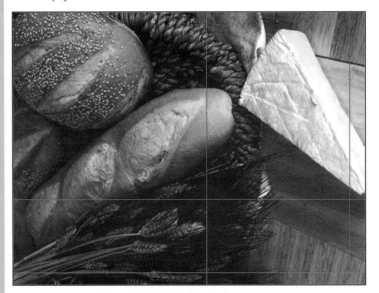

FIGURE A-25
Selecting the fill color

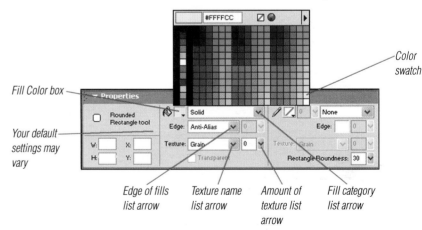

Fill Color box

Your default settings may vary

Color swatch

Edge of fills list arrow

Texture name list arrow

Amount of texture list arrow

Fill category list arrow

FIGURE A-26
Creating a rectangle

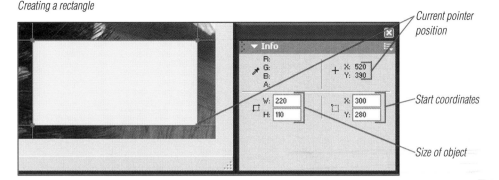

Current pointer position

Start coordinates

Size of object

FIGURE A-27
Stroke properties

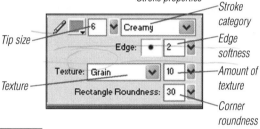

Stroke category

Tip size

Edge softness

Amount of texture

Texture

Corner roundness

FIGURE A-28
Stroke applied to rectangle

5. Click Window on the menu bar, then click Info to open the Info panel.

6. Position the pointer at approximately 300 X/280 Y, click, then drag the pointer to 520 X/390 Y, noticing the changing coordinates in the Info panel. ┼

7. Click Edit on the menu bar, then click Undo Rounded Rectangle tool.

   The rectangle disappears.

8. Click Edit on the menu bar, click Redo Rounded Rectangle tool, compare your image to Figure A-26, then save your work.

You set properties for the Rounded Rectangle tool, opened the Info panel, and created a rectangle.

Apply a stroke to an object

1. Click the Stroke Color box 🖉■ on the Property inspector, type **#FF9900** in the hexadecimal text box, then press [Enter] (Win) or [return] (Mac).

2. Click the Stroke category list arrow, point to Charcoal, then click Creamy.

3. Click the Tip size list arrow, then drag the slider to **6**.

4. Enter the remaining stroke values shown in Figure A-27, then click a blank area of the document window.

   TIP Drag the Rectangle Roundness slider to 0 for square corners and to 100 to create an ellipse.

5. Click Select on the menu bar, click Deselect, then compare your image to Figure A-28.

6. Save your work.

You selected stroke properties and applied a stroke to the rectangle.

CREATE AND MODIFY TEXT

What You'll Do

 In this lesson, you will create text and a path, attach the text to the path, save your document, and then exit the program.

Using Text in a Document

The text features in Macromedia Fireworks are typical of most desktop publishing programs—once you select the Text tool, you can preview the font family and modify properties including size, color, style, kerning, leading, alignment, text flow, offset, and anti-alias properties. Kerning adjusts the spacing between adjacent letters or a range of letters, while **leading** adjusts the amount of space between lines of text. You can set other text attributes, such as indent, alignment, the space before and after a paragraph, and baseline shift, on the Property inspector. Figure A-29 shows Text

tool properties on the Property inspector You can automatically preview in your document the changes you make to Text tool properties.

Once you create text, you can edit the text block as a whole, or edit just a range of text. When you create text, you can create auto-sizing or fixed-width text blocks. Auto-sizing means that the text block expands to accommodate the text you enter. If you delete text, the text block contracts. You can spell check text at any time, including selecting multiple text blocks to check their spelling.

Using the Text Editor panel

You can use the Text Editor panel to preview fonts and view and modify text that may be difficult to see in your document. To open the Text Editor panel, select a text block or a range of text, click Text on the menu bar, then click Editor. You can also copy text from the text editor and paste it as text into other applications.

Attaching Text to a Path

You can manipulate text by creating a path, and then attaching text to it. A path is an open or closed vector consisting of a series of anchor points. Anchor points join path segments—they delineate changes in direction, whether a corner or a curve. To create a path, you use the Pen tool to define points in your document, then attach the text to it. You can edit text after you've attached it to a path. You can also edit the path, but only if it is not attached to text. Figure A-30 shows text attached to paths.

To edit a path, you adjust the anchor points. To adjust the anchor points, select the path, select the Subselection tool on the Tools panel, and then drag points to new locations on the path as desired. You can also modify the appearance of text on a path by changing its alignment, orientation, and direction. By combining the shape of the path with the text alignment, orientation, and direction, you can create unique-looking text objects that convey the exact message you want.

FIGURE A-29
Text properties on the Property inspector

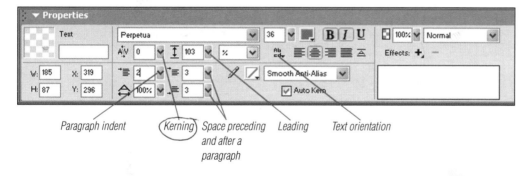

Paragraph indent   Kerning   Space preceding and after a paragraph   Leading   Text orientation

FIGURE A-30
Sample text on a path

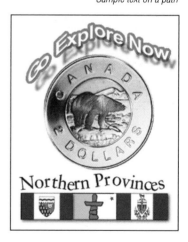

Create text using the Text tool

1. Verify that the Ad Copy layer is selected on the Layers panel, then click the Text tool on the Tools panel. A
2. Click the Font list arrow on the Property inspector, click Times New Roman, double-click the Size text box, then type **36**.
3. Click the Fill color box, type **#663300** in the hexadecimal text box, then press [Enter] (Win) or [return] (Mac).
4. Click the Bold button to select it. **B**
5. Click the Italic button to select it. *I*
6. Verify that the Center alignment button and Smooth Anti-Alias option are selected, then compare your Property inspector to Figure A-31.

(continued)

FIGURE A-31
Setting Text tool properties

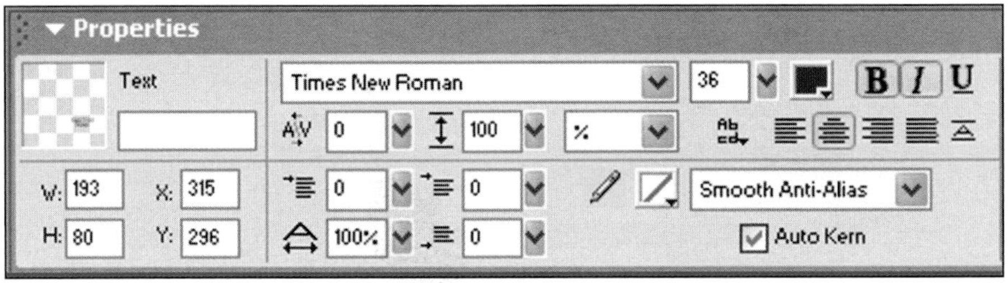

7. Click the middle of the rectangle, type **Upper Crust**, press [Enter] (Win) or [return] (Mac), then type **Shoppe**.

8. Click the Pointer tool on the Tools panel, then center the text by dragging it in the rectangle, if necessary.

9. Click Select on the menu bar, then click Deselect.

> TIP You can also press [Ctrl] D (Win) or [command] D (Mac) to deselect an object.

10. Compare your image to Figure A-32.

FIGURE A-32
Newly created text

Upper Crust Shoppe

Spell check text

1. Click the Text tool **A** on the Tools panel, double-click the Size text box on the Property inspector, type **24**, then verify that the Bold **B** and Italic *I* buttons are selected.

2. Click the top of the cheese wedge, type **Frehs Daily**, then compare your image to Figure A-33.

3. Click Text on the menu bar, click Check Spelling, then click Change.

   The word "Fresh" is spelled correctly.

   > TIP   If prompted to continue checking the current document, click Cancel. If prompted to select a dictionary, choose an appropriate language.

You checked the spelling of the text.

Misspelled word

FIGURE A-34
Path created in document

Last/selected
path point
created is solid

1. Click the Pen tool on the Tools panel. 🖋

2. Click the document in the locations shown in
   Figure A-34.

   A path appears in the document.

3. Click the Pointer tool on the Tools panel,
   press and hold [Shift], then click the
   Fresh Daily text to select both the path and
   the text. ➤

4. Click Text on the menu bar, then click Attach
   to Path.

5. Click Text on the menu bar, point to Align,
   then click Stretched.

6. Click a blank part of the document window,
   then compare your image to Figure A-35.

7. Save your work.

8. Click File on the menu bar, then click Exit
   (Win) or click Fireworks, then click Quit
   Fireworks (Mac).

You created a path using the Pen tool, attached
text to it, then saved the document and exited the
program.

FIGURE A-35
Text on path

Text follows
points on path

Lesson 5   Create and Modify Text

Start Fireworks and open a document.

1. Start Fireworks.
2. Open fwa_2.png.
3. Undock the Tools panel.
4. Collapse and expand the Property inspector.
5. Close fwa_2.png without saving changes.

Create a new document and use Help.

1. Create a new document and set the Width to **200**, the Height to **150**, and the Canvas Color to **#FF6633**.
2. Save the document as **pasta_1.png**.
3. Access the Index tab of Help and search for **layers**. (*Hint*: Click the Work with layers and objects topic in the Topics found dialog box.)
4. Read the topic on duplicating, then close the Help window.
5. Add a layer to the Layers panel.
6. Access the Search tab of Help and search for **creating bitmap objects**.
7. Read the topic on creating bitmaps, then close the Help window.
8. Open elbow.gif.
9. Drag the object to pasta_1.png.
10. Center the object on the canvas.

11. Close elbow.gif without saving changes.
12. Compare your document to Figure A-36.
13. Save and close pasta_1.png.

Work with the Layers panel and edit a bitmap image.

1. Open fwa_2.png.
2. Save the file as **pasta_2.png**.
3. Select the Varieties object on the Background layer of the Layers panel.
4. Hide and display the Varieties object on the Layers panel.
5. Move the Ingredients object from Layer 1 above the Varieties object so that it is now in the Background layer.
6. Delete the Ingredients object.
7. Select the Varieties object.
8. Open the Brightness/Contrast dialog box, and set the Brightness to **5** and the Contrast to **25**. (*Hint*: Use the Adjust Color command on the Filters menu.)
9. Lock the Background layer.
10. Save your work.

Create a vector object.

1. Display the guides.

2. Create a new layer above Layer 1.
3. Rename the newly created layer **Proper Names**. (*Hint*: Double-click the layer name.)
4. Select the Rounded Rectangle tool.
5. Enter the following fill color properties on the Property inspector: Color: **#66CC00**, Fill category: **Solid**, Edge: **Feather**, Feather amount: **4**, Texture: **Burlap**, and Texture amount: **20%**.
6. Open the Info panel.
7. Drag the pointer from approximately 10 X/250 Y to 90 X/300 Y.
8. Apply a stroke with the following properties: Color: **#339900**, Tip size: **2**, Category: **Air Brush Basic**, Edge: **100**, Texture amount: **0**, and Rectangle Roundess: **20**.
9. Save your work.

Create and modify text.

1. Select the Text tool.
2. Enter the following properties in the Property inspector: Font: **Times New Roman**, Size: **22** pt, Color: **#000000**, Bold, and Left alignment.

3. Click the pointer at 20 H/280 V, then type **Rotelie**.
4. Center the text in the rectangle, if necessary, then deselect it.
5. Make sure that the Text tool is selected, then enter the following properties: Font: **Impact**, Size: **65** pt, Color: **#990000**, Bold, and Center alignment.
6. Click the pointer above the jars, then type **Pasta Shapes**.
7. Deselect the Pasta Shapes text.
8. Select the Pen tool, then create a path at 250 X/80 Y, 300 X/70 Y, 350 X/60 Y, 400 X/50 Y, 450 X/70 Y, 500 X/80 Y. (*Hint*: Use the Info panel.)
9. Attach the Pasta Shapes text to the path.
10. Change the alignment setting of the text on the path to Stretched.
11. Deselect the text on the path.
12. Turn off the guides.
13. Save your work, then compare your document to Figure A-36.

FIGURE A-36
Completed Skills Review

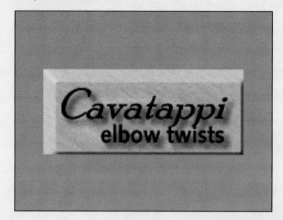

You are in charge of new services at Crystal Clear Consulting. You're preparing to roll out a new Crisis Solutions division, designed to help companies that are experiencing management or financial difficulties. You plan to brief your coworkers on the services at an upcoming company lunch. Each department head—including you— is going to submit a sample introductory Web ad announcing the division. You'll use your Fireworks skills to design a simple ad.

1. Obtain images that symbolize the new consulting service. You will import and copy these images to a layer in the document. You can obtain an image from your computer, from the Internet, from a digital camera, or from scanned media. You can use clipart from the Web that is free for both personal and commercial use (check the copyright information for any such clipart before downloading it).

2. Create a new document and save it as **crystal.png**.

3. Access Help, then search for and read a topic on importing.

4. Import one of the images you obtained in Step 1 so that it serves as the background.

5. Rename Layer 1 **Background**.

6. Create a new layer and give it an appropriate name.

7. Open another image that you obtained in Step 1 and copy it to the document.

8. Create a new layer and name it **Text Objects**.

9. Create at least one vector object and apply a fill to it.

10. Create at least two text objects. (*Hint*: The font in the sample is Matisse ITC and Eras Demi ITC. You can substitute these fonts with other fonts on your computer.)

11. Attach at least one text object to a path, then rename the object on the Layers panel.

12. Save your work, then examine the sample shown in Figure A-37.

FIGURE A-37
Completed Project Builder 1

You've just completed your first class in Fireworks. Afterwards, you meet with your boss to summarize some of the neat features. She is intrigued by the various ways you can change the alignment of text in Fireworks and has asked you to prepare a few samples for the next staff meeting.

1. Create a new document and name it **meandering_paths**.
2. Create a text object that is at least 20 characters long (you can use the font of your choice and as many words as you like).
3. Create a simple path, then attach the text to it.
4. Create text that describes the path alignment and the orientation settings. (*Hint*: Refer to Figure A-38.)
5. Add a new layer, then copy the text on the path and the descriptive text from the old layer to the new one. (*Hint*: Press and hold [Alt] (Win) or [options] (Mac), then drag the object.)
6. Change the alignment and orientation settings and update the descriptive text accordingly.
7. Repeat Step 5.
8. Save your work, then examine the sample shown in Figure A-38.

FIGURE A-38
Completed Project Builder 2

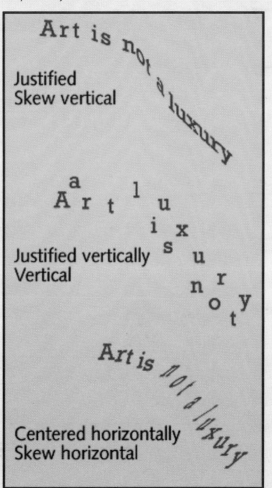

You can develop your design and planning skills by analyzing Web sites. Figure A-39 shows a page from the Rock and Roll Hall of Fame Web site. Study the image and answer the following questions. Because dynamic Web sites are updated frequently to reflect current trends, this page may be different from Figure A-39 when you open it online.

1. Connect to the Internet and go to *www.course.com*. Navigate to the page for this book, click the Student Online Companion, then click the link for this unit.
2. Open a document in a word processor, or open a new Fireworks document, then save the file as **rocknroll**. (*Hint*: Use the Text tool in Fireworks.)
3. Explore the site and answer the following questions. For each question, indicate how you determined your answer.
   ■ What vector shapes does the page contain?
   ■ What fills or strokes have been added to vector shapes?
   ■ Do objects appear to have been manipulated in some manner? If so, how?
   ■ Do objects or text overlap? If so, list the order in which the objects could appear in the Layers panel.
   ■ Has text been attached to a path?
   ■ What is the overall effect of the text?

FIGURE A-39
Design Project

Your group can assign elements of the project to individual members, or work collectively to create the finished product.

Your team serves on the Education Committee for Cultural Consequence, a cultural anthropology group. The group is constructing a Web site that examines facial expressions and moods in people around the world. The committee is in charge of developing emoticons—a short-hand method of expressing moods—for the Web site. The images will be in the style of the smiley face. You can use the facial expression of your choice in developing the emoticon.

1. Choose an emotion and the emoticon that conveys that feeling.
2. Obtain at least two images for the expression you've chosen. You can obtain images from your computer, from the Internet, from a digital camera, or from scanned media. You can use clipart from the Web that is free for both personal and commercial use (check the copyright information for any such clipart before downloading it).
3. Create a new document, then save it as **emoticon.png**.
4. Choose a canvas color other than white.
5. Create a new layer named **Faces** and copy the images you've obtained to the new layer.

6. Create a new layer and name it with the emotion you selected in Step 1.
7. Create the emoticon on the layer created in Step 6 using tools on the Tools panel, and apply fills and strokes to them as desired. (*Hint*: The emoticon in the sample was created with the Ellipse tool and the Pencil tool with a Basic Soft Rounded tip setting.)

FIGURE A-40
Completed Group Project

8. Create a text object that identifies the expression. (*Hint*: The text in the sample is Pristina.)
9. Save your work, then examine the sample shown in Figure A-40.

B

WORKING WITH OBJECTS

1. Work with vector tools.

2. Modify multiple vector objects.

3. Modify color.

4. Apply effects to objects and text.

5. Apply a style to text.

UNIT B
WORKING WITH OBJECTS

Understanding Vector Objects

Fireworks offers a number of vector tools you can use to create vector objects. There are many benefits to working with vector objects. For example, you can modify the properties of a vector path at any time—its shape, size, fill, and stroke—without affecting the quality of the image. This editability makes vector objects easy to work with and adds flexibility to your Web graphics.

Once you create an object, you can use a variety of features to transform it into a visually interesting graphic. Many of the tools in Fireworks let you alter or enhance the object. You can combine multiple objects to create entirely new shapes using various Combine Path commands. You can also modify a graphic's appearance by adjusting the alignment and grouping of multiple objects. You can change a path's color by filling it with a solid color, gradient color, or a texture, or by adjusting the stroke appearance.

The Stroke, Fill, and Effects sections on the Property inspector maximize your ability to experiment. You can create various combinations of strokes, fills, and effects, and turn them on or off in your document at will. An object's overall appearance will vary depending on the order in which effects appear in the Effects list on the Property inspector.

Tools You'll Use

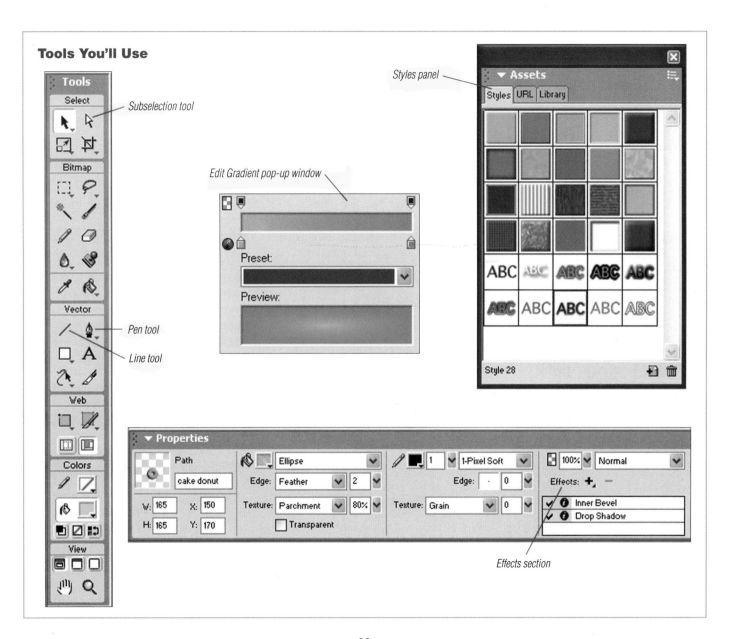

Tools

Select

Subselection tool

Bitmap

Edit Gradient pop-up window

Styles panel

Assets

Styles | URL | Library

Preset:

Preview:

Vector

Pen tool

Line tool

ABC ABC ABC **ABC** ABC

ABC ABC **ABC** ABC ABC

Style 28

Web

Colors

View

▼ Properties

Path
cake donut

Ellipse

Edge: Feather 2

Texture: Parchment 80%

Transparent

W: 165   X: 150

H: 165   Y: 170

1   1-Pixel Soft

Edge: · 0

Texture: Grain 0

100% Normal

Effects: + −

✔ ❶ Inner Bevel
✔ ❶ Drop Shadow

Effects section

WORK WITH VECTOR TOOLS

What You'll Do

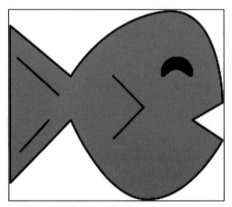

In this lesson, you will create and modify paths and objects using vector tools.

Understanding Vector Tools and Paths

A vector object can be a straight or curved path, or a group or combination of open, closed, straight, or curved paths. When you create a vector object, path segments connect the anchor points of a path. You can draw basic vector shapes using the Rectangle, Rounded Rectangle, Ellipse, and Polygon tools. (The Polygon tool has a star shape option; you can adjust the number of sides and the angles of any polygon.) You can draw free-form paths using the Vector Path and Pen tools. The Pen tool creates a path one point at a time. The Vector Path tool creates paths in one

motion. Fireworks automatically inserts anchor points as you drag the pointer on the canvas. Regardless of its initial shape, a vector object's path is always editable.

If the path of an object has curves, such as a circle, ellipse, or rounded rectangle, the circular points are known as **curve points**. If the path has angles or is linear, such as a square, star, or a straight line, the square points are known as **corner points**. Figure B-1 shows points selected for various objects. When you edit a vector object, you add, delete, or move points along the path; adjust the point handles; or change the shape of the path segment.

Using the Pen Tool and the Subselection Tool

You can add or delete points on a segment using the Pen tool. Modifying the number of points on a path allows you to manipulate it until you have created the exact shape you want. For example, adding points allows you to maneuver the path with great precision, while deleting points simplifies the path's editability. If you want to move points on a path, you can use the **Subselection tool**. You can also use the Subselection tool to select the points of an individual object that has been grouped.

Each anchor point has one or more **point handles**; point handles are visible when you edit a curved path segment, but not when you edit a straight path segment. You can modify the size and angle of a curve by adjusting the length and position of the point handles. You can use both the Pen tool and the Subselection tool to create and modify point handles on curved paths, or to convert curve points into corner points and vice versa.

FIGURE B-1
Points on paths

Curve points

Drag point handles to change amount of curve

Corner points

You can add points to an existing path by selecting the Pen tool and then clicking the path; to delete a point, double-click it.

The two-dimensional curves in a vector object are known as Bézier curves, named after the French engineer who developed the mathematical formulas to represent 3-D automobile shapes. Figure B-2 shows how you can manipulate a vector object by dragging its point handles.

As you become more familiar with using vector objects, you can experiment with more intricate vector modifications using the **Path scrubber tools**, which alter a path's appearance based on the pressure and speed with which you apply the stroke, and the **Reshape Area tool**, which pulls areas of the path to a boundary.

FIGURE B-2
Modifying a vector path

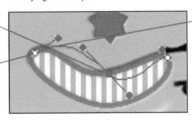

Selected point is solid

Drag point handle to modify curve

Blue outline shows preview of new path

New path

Stroke properties on the Property inspector

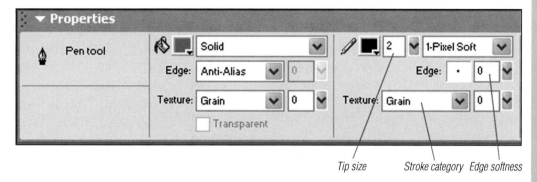

Tip size   Stroke category   Edge softness

FIGURE B-4
Creating a shape using the Pen tool

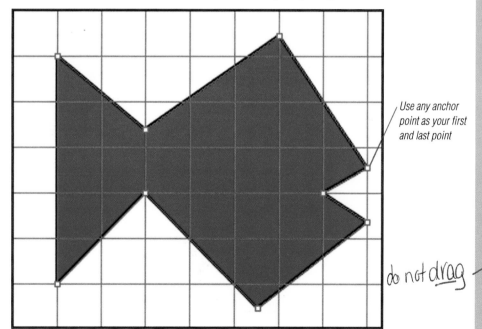

Use any anchor
point as your first
and last point

do not drag

Create an object using the Pen tool

1. Create a new document, set the Width to **300**, the Height to **275**, verify that the canvas color is white, then save it as **fish.png**.

2. Click View on the menu bar, point to Grid, click Edit Grid, click the Show Grid check box, then click OK.

   TIP You can use the grid to help align objects on the canvas.

3. Click the Fill Color box ■ on the Property inspector, double-click the hexadecimal text box, type **#999999**, then press [Enter] (Win) or [return] (Mac).

4. Click the Pen tool on the Tools panel. ♠

5. Click the Fill Color box ◈■ on the Property inspector, double-click the hexadecimal text box, type **#3399FF**, then press [Enter] (Win) or [return] (Mac).

6. Click the Stroke Color box ✎■ on the Property inspector, double-click the hexadecimal text box, type **#000000**, then press [Enter] (Win) or [return] (Mac).

7. Verify that the Stroke category is Pencil, 1-Pixel Soft, that Tip size is 2, Edge settings and Texture are 0, then compare your Stroke properties to Figure B-3.

   TIP Each stroke has a default size, edge, and texture.

8. Click the canvas in the locations shown in Figure B-4.

   TIP Close the path by clicking your first anchor point.

You created a new document, set properties for the Pen tool, and created a closed path.

Use the Pen tool and the Line tool to modify a path

1. Position the Pen tool over the top corner point, then click and drag the point to create a smooth curve, as shown in Figure B-5. 🖊

   The sharp point smoothes into a curve, and the point handles are visible.

2. Repeat Step 1, but click and drag the bottom corner point.

3. Press and hold the Rectangle tool 🔲 on the Tools panel, then click the Ellipse tool. ⭕

4. Click the Fill Color box 🎨🔲 on the Property inspector, then click the top left black color swatch in the color pop-up window.

5. Press and hold [Shift], then draw the circle shown in Figure B-6.

   | TIP   Press and hold [Shift] to draw a perfect square or circle.

6. Click the Line tool on the Tools panel, then drag the pointer on the canvas to create the lines shown in Figure B-7. ╱

You modified an object using the Pen tool and the Line tool.

FIGURE B-5
Converting a corner point to a curve point

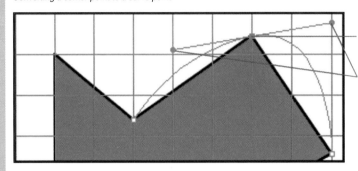

Click corner point and drag handles
to create a smooth curve

Point handles

FIGURE B-6
Circle object

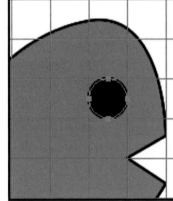

FIGURE B-7
Creating lines using the Line tool

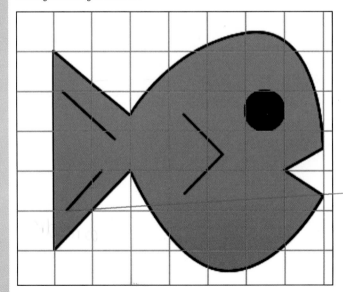

Click and drag the Line tool
to create a line

Drag point handle up

Use the Subselection tool to modify an object

1. Click the Subselection tool on the Tools panel, position the pointer over the lower center point of the black circle, then click the point. ⟨

2. Drag the point to the position shown in Figure B-8, then click a blank part of the document window.

   TIP You can also press [Ctrl] D (Win) or [command] D (Mac) to deselect an object.

3. Click View on the menu bar, point to Grid, then click Show Grid to turn off the grid.

4. Compare your image to Figure B-9, then save your work

5. Close fish.png.

You modified an object using the Subselection tool, and then closed the document.

FIGURE B-9
Modified object

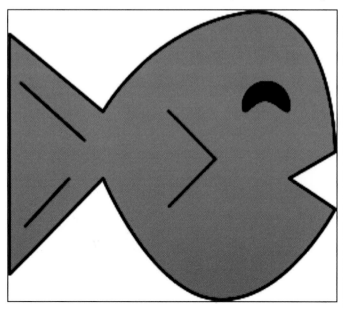

MODIFY MULTIPLE VECTOR OBJECTS

What You'll Do

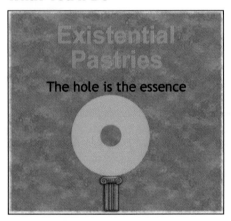

 In this lesson, you will create, copy, align, and combine paths of vector objects using the Punch command. You will also group objects.

Aligning and Grouping Objects

Using vector shapes allows you to work with many individual objects at the same time. The Align commands on the Modify menu allow you to align two or more objects with each other: left, centered vertically, and so on. You can open the Align panel to further align, distribute, size, and space multiple objects or to align a vector object's anchor points.

You can also use the Group command on the Modify menu to configure objects on the canvas. The Group command allows you to combine two or more objects to make a single object. You can group any objects in your document: vector images, bitmap images, text, and so on. Fireworks preserves each individual object's shape and its placement in relation to the other objects. Once you group objects, you can modify properties of the group as a whole; for example, by changing fill color or applying a stroke. If you want

to change any one of the objects, you can ungroup the objects, apply the change, and then regroup them. For example, if want to change the stroke of one object in a group of vector shapes, you must first ungroup the objects before you can modify the individual stroke. However, if the grouped object consists of text and another vector object or bitmap image, you do not need to ungroup the objects in order to edit the text.

Combining the Paths of Multiple Objects

Fireworks offers six commands for combining paths: Join, Split, Union, Intersect, Punch, and Crop. Each command produces a different result. You must select two or more ungrouped vector objects before you can apply a combination command to them. The Combine Paths commands are described below and most are illustrated in Figure B-10.

Join—The Join command allows you to combine the paths of two or more objects to create a single merged object that includes all the points of both paths. If the two objects are both closed, the new path is a composite path; if the objects are open, the new path is a continuous path. You can also use the Join command to join two open selected points. In Figure B-10, the two hash marks of the "X" are joined.

Split—You can split apart the paths of two or more objects that had been combined using the Join command. The Split command creates two or more simple objects and paths. Because the Split command is based on the joined path, and not the original objects, it is not the same as performing Undo.

Union—The Union command creates a path that is the sum total of all the selected paths. If two paths overlap, the non-intersecting areas will also be included. If the selected paths have different fill, stroke, or effects properties, the new path will assume the properties of the object that appears in back in the document, or as the lowest layer on the Layers panel. In Figure B-10, the union includes the upper points of the blue pointer, the wrist that extends beyond the border of the wood polygon, and the entire polygon. The properties are the same as the wood object's properties.

FIGURE B-10
Sample Combine Path commands

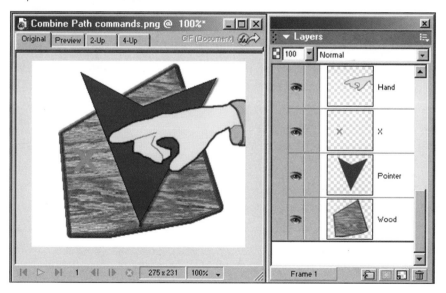

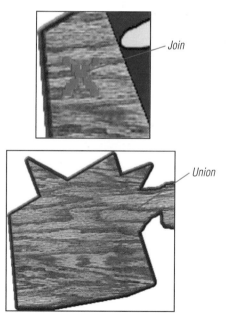

Intersect—The Intersect command creates an object consisting of the area that is common to all of the selected paths. If the selected paths have different fill, stroke, or effects properties, the new path will assume the properties of the object that appears in back in the document or as the lowest layer on the Layers panel. In Figure B-10, the intersection is the area shared by the hand, pointer, and wood objects. The properties are the same as the wood object's properties.

Punch—The outline of the topmost object carves through all of the lower selected images. In Figure B-10, the *shape* of the hand appears to slice through the objects below it. The fill, stroke, and effects properties are unaffected in the areas not being punched.

Crop—The area of the topmost path is used to remove the areas of the paths beneath it. While the area of the topmost object defines the object's shape, the fill, stroke, and effects properties of the objects placed further back

are retained. In Figure B-10, the shape of the top object, the hand, has the properties of both selected paths beneath it, the blue pointer and the wood polygon.

QUICKTIP

Use the Group command if you want your objects to maintain independent fill, stroke, and effect settings. If you want to be able to manipulate the paths of two or more objects after you combine them, use the Join command instead of the Group command.

FIGURE B-10
Sample Combine Path commands (continued)

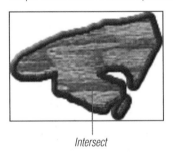

Intersect

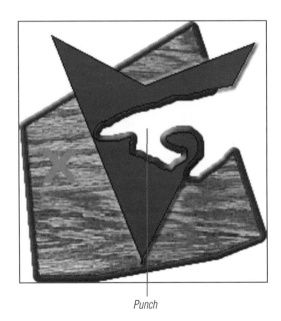

Punch

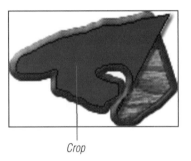

Crop

FIGURE B-11

Info panel

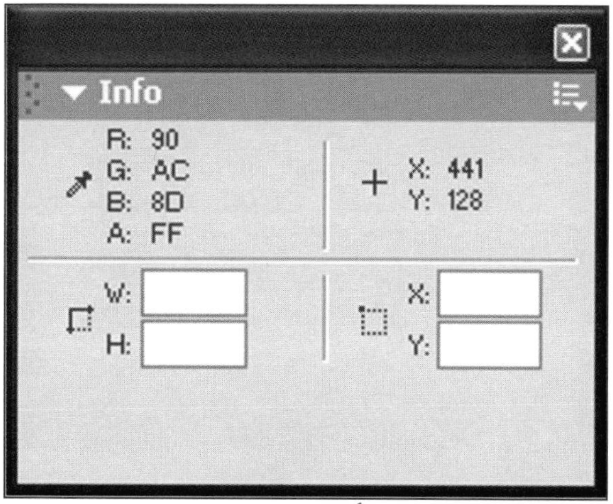

[handwritten annotations: Rt click on canvas, F12 Alt Shift, F15 matches + speckle]

R: 90
G: AC
B: 8D
A: FF

X: 441
Y: 128

W:
H:

X:
Y:

Drag border to reveal coordinate section

Create a vector shape to an exact size

1. Open fwb_1.png, then save it as **pastries.png**.

2. Insert a layer above the Text layer on the Layers panel, double-click the layer name, then type **Doughnut**.

   > TIP You can name other objects on the Layers panel in the same manner, or you can name selected objects on the Property inspector.

3. Click the Ellipse tool on the Tools panel.

4. Click the Stroke Color box on the Tools panel, then click the Transparent button on the top of the color pop-up window.

5. Click the Fill Color box on the Tools panel, double-click (Win) or click (Mac) the hexadecimal text box, type **#E8B900**, then press [Enter] (Win) or [return] (Mac).

6. Make sure that the Info panel and the Property inspector are open and that the Edge and Texture values in the Fill section are 0, then compare your Info panel to Figure B-11.

   You use the Info panel to view the dimensions of a currently selected object, including its size and position on the canvas.

   (continued)

7. Position the pointer on the canvas at approximately 130 X/170 Y, press and hold [Shift], then drag the pointer until both W and H text boxes on the Info panel display 165. ✛

> TIP If necessary, you can enter 165 in the width and height text boxes on the Info panel or on the Property inspector after you create the circle.

8. Compare your image to Figure B-11.

You created a circle and set its diameter.

Copy an object

1. Verify that the circle is selected, click Edit on the menu bar, then click Copy.

2. Click Edit on the menu bar, then click Paste.

   A duplicate Path object appears on the Layers panel.

   > TIP You can also press [Ctrl] C or [Ctrl] V (Win) or [command] C or [command] V (Mac) to copy and paste a selection.

3. Click the Fill Color box ◾ on the Property inspector, then click the top left black color swatch in the color pop-up window.

4. Double-click the W text box on the Property inspector, type **44**, repeat for the H text box, then press [Enter] (Win) or [return] (Mac).

5. Compare your image to Figure B-13.

You copied an object and changed its properties.

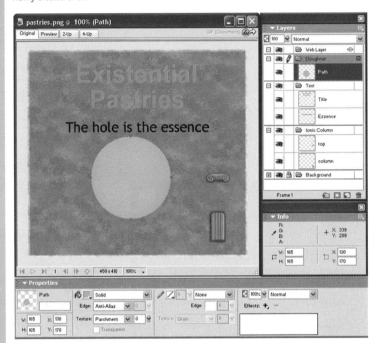

FIGURE B-13
Modified object

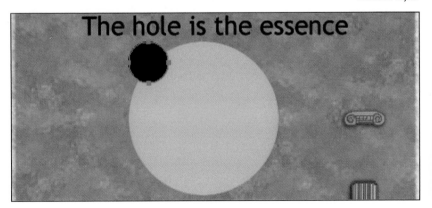

FIGURE B-14

Aligned objects

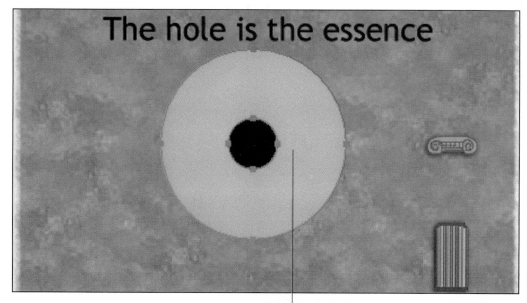

The hole is the essence

*Objects are aligned vertically
and horizontally*

1. Click the Pointer tool on the Tools panel, then verify that the black circle is selected. ⬉

2. Press and hold [Shift], then click the yellow circle to select both objects.

3. Click Modify on the menu bar, point to Align, then click Center Vertical.

4. Click Modify on the menu bar, point to Align, click Center Horizontal, then compare your image to Figure B-14.

   The black circle is perfectly centered on the yellow circle.

   (continued)

5. Click Modify on the menu bar, point to Combine Paths, click Union, then notice the combined object.

   The black circle is no longer visible.

6. Click Edit on the menu bar, then click Undo Union Paths.

7. Click Modify on the menu bar, point to Combine Paths, click Punch, then compare your image to Figure B-15.

8. Click the Edit the object name text box on the left side of the Property inspector, then type **cake donut**, then press [Enter] (Win) or [return] (Mac).

You aligned two objects and then combined their paths. You also undid a Combine Paths command.

FIGURE B-15
Objects combined by Punch command

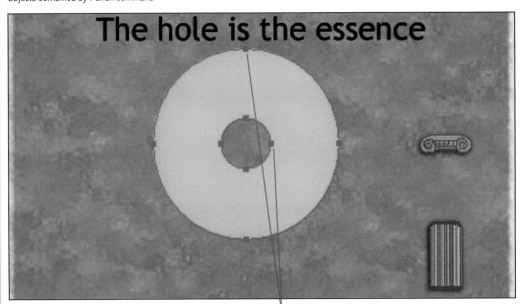

Paths of both objects are
still visible and editable

Object being moved

FIGURE B-17

Grouped objects

Selection handles for ⎯
single grouped object

Group objects

1. Verify that the Pointer tool is selected, then click the top object on the Ionic Column layer on the Layers panel.

2. Drag the top object on top of the column object, as shown in Figure B-16.

3. Press and hold [Shift], then click the column object to select both objects.

   The selection handles for both objects are visible.

4. Click Modify on the menu bar, click Group, then notice that the object on the Layers panel is renamed Group: 2 objects.

   TIP   You can also press [Ctrl] G (Win) or [command] G (Mac) to group objects.

5. Drag the grouped object under the circle, as shown in Figure B-17.

   The selection handles for a single object are visible.

6. Change the name Group: 2 objects to **full column**.

7. Save your work.

You grouped and moved objects.

MODIFY COLOR

What You'll Do

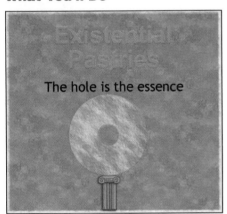

The hole is the essence

▶ *In this lesson, you will apply a gradient fill to the cake donut object, and then modify the fill.*

Understanding Fills and Gradients

After you create a vector shape, you can modify its appearance by changing its interior, or fill. The Property inspector provides powerful tools for enhancing fills in objects. You can apply several kinds of fills to an object, including solid, gradient, web dither, and pattern. The available fill, pattern, and gradient categories are shown in Figure B-18.

A **solid fill** is the color swatch or hexadecimal value that you specify in the color pop-up window or in the Color Mixer. If you want to ensure that the colors in your document are websafe, you can use a **Web Dither** fill. A Web Dither fill approximates the color of a non-websafe color by combining two websafe colors. **Pattern fills** are bitmap images that have complex color schemes and textures. Fireworks offers dozens of preset patterns from which to choose, or you can create a pattern in Fireworks or another program and then add it to the list. A **gradient** consists of two or more colors that blend into each other in a fixed design. You can select from several preset gradient fills, which you can apply to an object by choosing a fill category or by selecting the Gradient tool on the Tools panel. The Gradient tool, located as a tool option under the Paint Bucket tool, fills an object with the selected gradient, just as the Paint Bucket tool fills an object with the selected color.

QUICKTIP
You can transform or skew a fill's pattern or gradient by adjusting the width, position, rotation, and angle of the fill handles.

Whether you select a pattern or gradient as a fill, it becomes the active fill color visible on the Tools panel and on the Property inspector. There may be times when you apply a pattern or a gradient and instantly attain the look you want. You can also experiment by modifying the pattern or gradient, for example by adding a transparent gradient, adding an edge or texture, and adjusting the respective amounts of each.

The sophisticated styling you add to objects when you choose to a pattern fill type can mimic real-world lighting, surface, and depth, and can have quite a dramatic result, as shown in Figure B-19.

You can change gradient colors, including preset gradient colors, at any time without affecting the appearance of the gradient. The Edit Gradient pop-up window allows you to modify gradient colors and the transition from one color to the next by manipulating the color swatches beneath the **color ramp**. The color ramp creates and displays the range of colors in a gradient, including their transparency.

FIGURE B-18
Pattern categories

FIGURE B-19
Combining pattern and texture

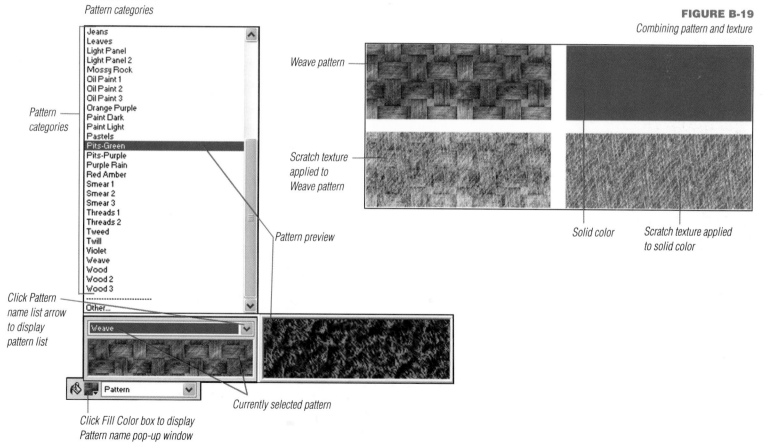

Pattern categories

Click Pattern name list arrow to display pattern list

Pattern preview

Currently selected pattern

Click Fill Color box to display Pattern name pop-up window

Weave pattern

Scratch texture applied to Weave pattern

Solid color

Scratch texture applied to solid color

Apply a gradient to an object

1. Verify that the Pointer tool is selected on the Tools panel, then click the cake donut object to select it. ▶

2. Click the Fill category list arrow on the Property inspector, then click Ellipse, as shown in Figure B-20.

    An ellipse gradient is applied to the object. It consists of the yellow solid fill color and the default gradient color, black. Gradient fill handles also appear on the gradient.

3. Click the Fill Color box on the Property inspector to open the Edit Gradient pop-up window. 🎨🔳

4. Click the left color swatch beneath the color ramp, type **#E8B900** in the hexadecimal text box, then press [Enter] (Win) or [return] (Mac) to close the color pop-up window.

5. Repeat Step 4 for the right color swatch, but type **#FF8000** in the hexadecimal text box, press [Enter] (Win) or [return] (Mac) to close the color pop-up window, then compare your color ramp to Figure B-21.

6. Click a blank part of the Fireworks window to close the color ramp.

7. Click the Edge list arrow, click Feather, double-click the Amount of feather text box, then type **2**.

8. Click the Texture list arrow, click Parchment, click the Amount of texture list arrow, drag the slider to **80**, then verify that the Transparent check box is not selected.

(continued)

FIGURE B-20
Fill and gradient categories

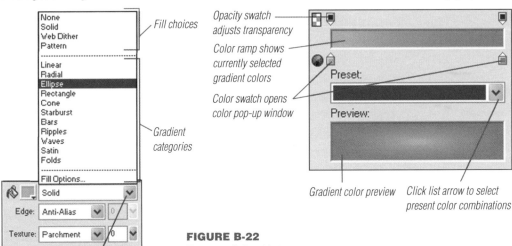

Fill choices

Gradient categories

Click Fill category list arrow to display pop-up list

FIGURE B-21
Edit Gradient pop-up window

Opacity swatch adjusts transparency

Color ramp shows currently selected gradient colors

Color swatch opens color pop-up window

Gradient color preview

Click list arrow to select present color combinations

FIGURE B-22
Texture applied to object

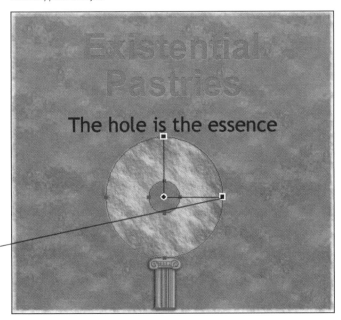

The hole is the essence

Gradient fill handle

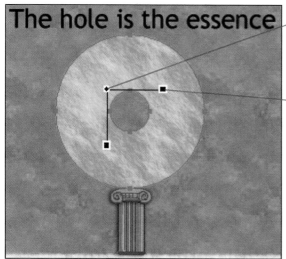

The hole is the essence

Drag round handle to adjust
gradient placement

Drag square handle to
adjust gradient width

FIGURE B-24

Modified gradient

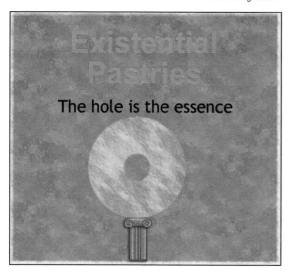

The hole is the essence

9. Compare your image to Figure B-22.

   The new gradient colors and texture are
   applied to the object.

   *You selected and modified gradient colors, and
   applied a texture to an object.*

Transform an object and its gradient

1. Verify that the cake donut object is selected.
2. Click Modify on the menu bar, point to
   Transform, then click Rotate 90° CW to
   rotate the object.

   Note that the gradient rotates with the object.
3. Drag the fill handles to the positions shown
   in Figure B-23.

   The placement and shading of the gradient
   is altered.
4. Click a blank part of the document window
   to deselect the cake donut object, then compare your image to Figure B-24.
5. Save your work.

   *You rotated the object and adjusted the fill
   handles to change the gradient.*

Understanding basic colors in the Color Mixer

The Color Mixer displays the color palette of the values of the active solid color, which
you can also view in the Fill Color box or Stroke Color box on the Tools panel or on the
Property inspector. You can edit color values to create new colors by changing the values for each color component of a color model. You can define colors in five different
models: RGB (red, green, blue); Hexadecimal (Fireworks default), which has values
similar to RGB; HSB (hue, saturation, and brightness); CMY (cyan, magenta, yellow);
and Grayscale. The color model you choose depends on the medium in which the
graphic will appear. Generally, the models Fireworks offers are geared toward screen-
based and Web-based computer graphics, with the exception of the CMY or Grayscale
models. If you want to use a Fireworks-created graphic in print media, you might want
to export the graphic into another program that has additional print-specific color
models, such as Macromedia Freehand or Adobe Photoshop. All file formats exported
by Fireworks are based on the RGB color model.

APPLY EFFECTS TO OBJECTS AND TEXT

What You'll Do

 In this lesson, you will add effects to objects, including text, and change the order of effects in the Effects list.

Understanding Effects

In addition to using the Fill and Stroke sections of the Property inspector, you can use the Effects section to customize the appearance of objects in your document. The Effects section includes the effects found on the Filters menu, as well as bevel, emboss, shadow, and glow effects. For example, you can sharpen, blur, and add the appearance of depth or dimension to an image. The features in the Effects section are similar to filters, labs, or renders used by other graphics programs, such as Adobe Photoshop or advanced 3-D landscaping programs, such as Corel Bryce. Fireworks refers to effects as **Live Effects** because you can always edit and preview changes to them even after you have saved, closed, and reopened the document. The Effects section lets you experiment with multiple effects. You can add, edit, delete, or hide effects in the Effects list at your convenience. Figure B-25 shows the options available in the Effects section.

QUICK**TIP**

To edit an effect, select the object(s) to which the effect is applied, then click the Info icon or double-click the effect name in the Effects list to open its pop-up window or dialog box.

Just as you can move objects on the Layers panel to change their appearance in your document, you can modify the overall look of an object by changing the order of effects. Figure B-26 shows how changing the stacking order of effects in the Effects list can produce very different results. Each macaw has the same settings and effects applied to it, but in a different order

QUICK**TIP**

To move an effect, drag it to a new position in the Effects list.

Using the Filters Menu

The Filters menu contains commands that correspond to many of the features found in the Effects section. However, be aware that the effects you add from the Filters menu do not appear in the Effects section of the Property inspector and you cannot alter their settings after you apply them. You can edit or remove filters only in the current work session—more precisely, you can *undo* a filter, not edit it. Once you save or close the document, the Undo actions are lost, and the filter you applied is permanently a part of your document.

Effects and File Size

Although enabled effects generally contribute to increased file size, disabling an effect instead of deleting it does not significantly add to file size. Some effects, such as the Blur, Blur More, and Gaussian Blur effects, may actually decrease file size, because blurring an object decreases the total number of colors in the graphic. The fewer colors used in your document, the less storage space required—hence, smaller file size.

Understanding Transparency

You can adjust the transparency of an image or effect in your document by varying its opacity settings. Fireworks adjusts transparency in terms of percentage, just as it uses percentage settings to adjust the amount of texture in strokes and fills. The **opacity setting** determines if your image is completely opaque (100%), or completely transparent (0%).

FIGURE B-25

Effects categories

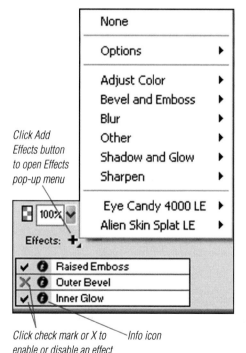

Click Add Effects button to open Effects pop-up menu

Click check mark or X to enable or disable an effect   Info icon

FIGURE B-26

Rearranged effects in the Effects list

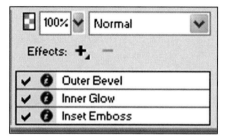

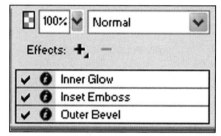

Apply effects to objects

1. Select the cake donut object, then click the Add Effects button on the Property inspector. **+**

2. Point to Bevel and Emboss, then click Inner Bevel.

   The Inner Bevel pop-up window opens.

3. Enter the values shown in Figure B-27, then click a blank part of the Fireworks window.

4. Select the cake donut object, then click the Add Effects button on the Property inspector. **+**

5. Point to Shadow and Glow, then click Drop Shadow.

6. Enter the values shown in Figure B-28, then click a blank part of the Fireworks window.

   The cake donut object appears to have depth and dimension.

7. Click the column object, then repeat Steps 4, 5, and 6.

   TIP To delete an effect, select the effect in the Effects list in the Effects section of the Property inspector, then click the Delete Effects button. **—**

8. Click a blank part of the Fireworks window, then compare your image to Figure B-29.

You applied effects to the column and cake donut objects.

FIGURE B-27
Inner Bevel pop-up window

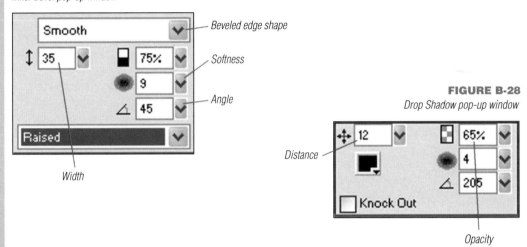

Beveled edge shape

Softness

Angle

Width

FIGURE B-28
Drop Shadow pop-up window

Distance

Opacity

FIGURE B-29
Effects added to objects

Rearranged effects

The Drop Shadow effect
appears more subtle

Apply effects to text

1. Click the Existential Pastries text, click the Add Effects button on the Property inspector, point to Bevel and Emboss, then click Raised Emboss. ➕

2. Press [Enter] (Win) or [return] (Mac) to accept the default settings in the Raised Emboss pop-up window, then click a blank part of the Fireworks window.

3. Verify that the title text is selected, click the Add Effects button on the Property inspector, point to Shadow and Glow, then click Drop Shadow. ➕

4. Double-click the Distance text box, type **2**, accept the remaining default settings, then click a blank part of the Fireworks window.

5. Drag the Drop Shadow effect to the top of the Effects list, click a blank part of the Fireworks window, then notice the difference in the text.

6. Compare your image to Figure B-30, then save your work.

You added effects to a text object, and then rearranged the effects in the Effects list.

APPLY A STYLE TO TEXT

What You'll Do

In this lesson, you will apply a style to text and add a new text style to the Styles list.

Using Styles in Documents

Styles are preset attributes, such as color and texture, that you can apply to objects and text. Fireworks manages styles on the **Styles panel**, which you can open from the Window menu. Fireworks comes with two types of styles, text and object. Text styles differ from object styles in that they contain text-specific properties, such as font, size, and style, but you can apply text and button styles to any object. Figure B-31 shows a style applied to two different objects. You can create your own style and then save it as a custom style in the Styles panel. When you create a custom style, you can save many of the properties associated with fills, strokes, effects, and text. You can also import or export preset or custom styles.

Figure B-32 shows a new style added to the Styles panel. Many text styles change the font style and font size when you apply them.

QUICKTIP

You can apply the attributes from one object to another by selecting the object with the attributes, clicking the Copy command on the Edit menu, selecting the target object, then clicking the Paste Attributes command on the Edit menu.

Keeping current on Adobe and Macromedia compatibility issues
For general information on using Photoshop plug-ins, search for the Importing Photoshop filters and plug-ins topic in the Search section of the Using Fireworks Help system. For additional information on compatibility issues, visit the Fireworks Support Center at *www.macromedia.com/support/fireworks*, then search the site using the keyword Photoshop. You can also search Macromedia Online Forums at *http://webforums.macromedia.com/fireworks/*.

Using Plug-ins

A **plug-in** adds features to an application. You can install plug-ins from other software applications into Fireworks. Some plug-ins augment existing features. For example, Fireworks includes a sampling of effects from two Alien Skin products: Eye Candy 4000 LE and Alien Skin Splat LE. (Additional information about Alien Skin plug-ins is available at *www.alienskin.com*.) You need to install the correct plug-ins, software drivers, and modules before you can import files from scanned or digital cameras. Note that plug-ins are platform-specific: for example, the TWAIN module (Win) or Photoshop Acquire plug-in.32 (Mac) are needed in order to import images from a scanner or digital camera.

Using Adobe Photoshop Plug-ins and Features

Adobe Photoshop plug-ins and other import features are often of interest to Fireworks users. The Fireworks Preferences dialog box allows you to extend the functionality of the program by accessing certain Photoshop features. For example, the Folders tab of the Preferences dialog box contains options for Photoshop plug-ins, textures, and patterns. The Import tab allows you to determine how Fireworks translates Photoshop layers and text—by sharing layers across frames or allowing you to edit text after you import it.

Plug-ins and text features from Photoshop 5.5 translate smoothly into Fireworks MX, as do text features from Photoshop 6 and 7. However, Photoshop 6 and 7 plug-ins are incompatible with Fireworks MX.

FIGURE B-31
Style samples

Style applied to object —

Your list of styles may vary

Options menu icon

Style name appears when you hold the mouse pointer over a style

FIGURE B-32
New style added to Styles panel

Preset styles

New Style button

New style

Apply a style to text

1. Click Window on the menu bar, then click Styles.

   TIP Make sure that the Styles panel is undocked.

2. Click the Text tool on the Tools panel, then enter the values shown in Figure B-33. **A**

3. Click the middle of the column, then type **The cake is commentary**.

   TIP If your text block does not automatically resize to fit the text, drag a blue sizing handle until the words fit.

4. Click Style 28 in the Styles panel, as shown in Figure B-34.

   The text changes size, color, and has an effect applied to it.

5. Compare your text to Figure B-35.

You applied a style to a text object.

FIGURE B-33
Text properties

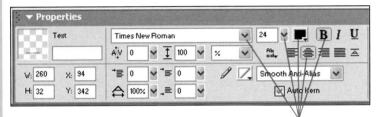

Change these properties

FIGURE B-34
Selecting a style in the Styles panel

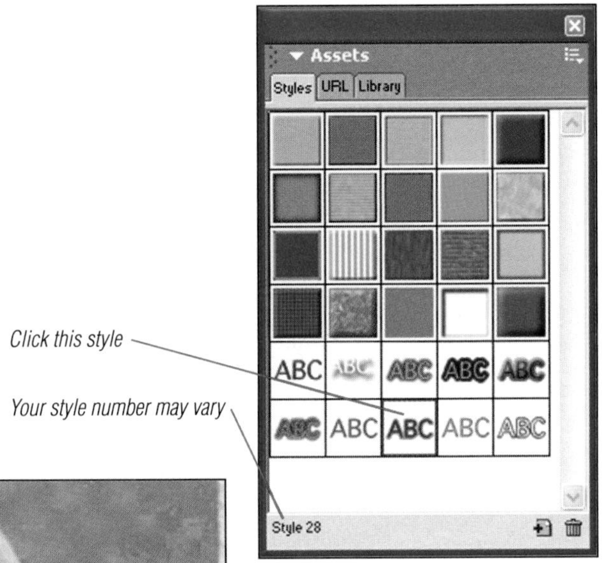

Click this style

Your style number may vary

FIGURE B-35
Style applied to text

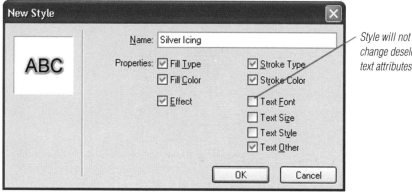

Style will not change deselected text attributes

Create a custom style and align objects

1. Double-click the Font Size text box on the Property inspector, type **24**, click the Color box █, then click the top left black color swatch.

2. Double-click the Outer Bevel effect in the Effects list, click the Color box █, type **#DFDFDF** in the hexadecimal text box, press [Enter] (Win) or [return] (Mac), then click a blank part of the Fireworks window.

3. Click the Options menu icon on the Styles panel, then click New Style to open the New Style dialog box. ▣

4. Double-click the Name text box, type **Silver Icing**, deselect the Text Font, Text Size, and Text Style check boxes, compare your dialog box to Figure B-36, then click OK.

   A new style, Silver Icing, is added to the bottom of the Styles panel.

5. Click the Pointer tool on the Tools panel, press and hold [Shift], then beginning at the top of the canvas, click each object to select it. ▸

6. Click Modify on the menu bar, point to Align, then click Center Vertical.

7. Click Select on the menu bar, then click Deselect.

8. Compare your image to Figure B-37, save your work, then close the file.

You created a new style and added it to the Styles panel, and then you aligned objects.

Create a vector object and modify its path.

1. Open fwb_2.png, then save it as **confection.png**.
2. Select the Pen tool, then set the following properties: Fill color: #66CC99.
3. Using the large white gumdrop as a guide, draw a triangle that approximates the gumdrop's height and width.
4. Convert the corner points to curve points, using Figure B-38 as a guide.
5. Use the Subselection tool to increase the height of the object, approximately half the distance to the document border.
6. Drag the object to the bottom left corner of the canvas.
7. Rename the object **Gumdrop**.
8. Save your work.

Align and group objects.

1. Use the Pointer tool to drag the purple circle in back of the multicolored circle.
2. Align the two objects so that they are centered vertically and horizontally.
3. Group the two circles.
4. Move the grouped circles to the top of the right stick, then group them with the stick.

5. Rename the grouped object **Lollipop**.
6. Save your work.

Combine objects' paths.

1. Click the right green wing, then use the arrow keys to move it up and left to merge it with the left green wing.
2. Select both the left and right wings.
3. Combine the paths of the two objects, using the Union command.
4. Rename the combined object **Insignia**.
5. Save your work.

Apply a gradient to an object and modify the gradient.

1. Select the Gumdrop object and apply a Ripples gradient to it.
2. Edit the gradient, and change the left color swatch to **#006600**.
3. Modify the right gradient by dragging the right fill handle to the bottom right corner of the gumdrop. (*Hint*: The fill handle should resemble the hands of a clock set to 5 o'clock.)
4. Add the following fill properties: Edge: Anti-Alias, Texture: Grain, 25.
5. Save your work.

Apply effects to objects.

1. Select the Insignia object.
2. Apply an Inner Bevel effect with the default settings.
3. Add a stroke with the following settings: Stroke Color: Black, Category: 1-Pixel Soft, Type: Pencil, Tip Size: 1.
4. Drag the Insignia object to the middle of the Gumdrop object. (*Hint*: Move the Insignia object on the Layers panel, if desired.)
5. Apply an Inset Emboss effect to the Gumdrop object with the default settings.
6. Save your work.

Apply an effect to text.

1. Select the Text tool with the following properties: Font: Times New Roman, Font Size: 22, Color: Red, Bold, and Italic.
2. Position the pointer in the top left corner of the canvas, then type **Sugarless Tastes Great**.
3. Apply a white Glow effect to the text. (*Hint*: Click the Shadow and Glow command on the Effects pop-up window to access the Glow option, then change the color to White, and the Halo effect to 1.)
4. Save your work.

Apply a style to text.

1. Open the Styles panel.
2. Select the text.
3. Apply Style 1 to the text. (*Hint*: Substitute a different style, if desired.)
4. Save your work.

FIGURE B-38
Completed Skills Review

Add a new style.

1. Change the Font Color to White and the Font Size to 28.
2. Edit the Inner Bevel effect in the Effects section to the following settings: Bevel edge shape: Smooth, Width: 6.
3. Add a new style to the Styles panel, name it **Snow**, and do not have the style affect Text Font, Size, or Style.
4. Compare your document to Figure B-38.
5. Save your work.

modify free-transform

You're in charge of office security at your business. In the last four months, several employees, including the owner, have neglected to engage their screen savers when they've left their desks for lunch, meetings, and so on. So far, friendly reminders and rewards haven't done the trick, so you're going to e-mail the same obnoxious attachment to everyone. You'll develop a simple, but effective, message using Fireworks vector tools and effects.

1. Create a new document that is 504 × 246 pixels with a white background, then save it as **remember_me**.
2. Create a rectangle that fills the background, and apply the following properties to it: Fill: Pattern: Light Panel, Edge: Anti-Alias, Texture: none; Stroke: Color #666666, 4 px Basic Hard Line, Edge, Texture, and Rectangle Roundness: 0; Opacity: 72%; Inner Glow effect with default settings.
3. Move the short right gradient handle to the right edge of the canvas, so that the handles appear to be at 3 o'clock, then lock the Background layer.
4. Create and name a new layer **Ruler**, then using Figure B-39 as a guide, draw a rectangle that has a Linear gradient, then adjust the swatches on the color ramp as follows: Left and Right: #CCCCCC, Middle: #FFFFFF. (*Hint*: Click beneath the color ramp to add a color swatch.)

5. Add a black 1 px 1-Pixel-Hard stroke, and Drop Shadow and Inner Bevel effects with default settings.
6. Use the Line tool to create evenly spaced hash marks that resemble those on a ruler, then group the rectangle and the lines.
7. Create the following text in the font and effects of your choice: **don't rule out computer security**. (*Hint*: The text in the sample is bold Eras Medium ITC and has a Raised Emboss effect applied to it.)

FIGURE B-39
Completed Project Builder 1

8. Create a new layer named **Message**, create a polygon with a Folds gradient using the colors of your choice, then apply an Outer Bevel effect with the following properties: a matching color; Bevel edge shape: Ring; Width: 6; Softness: 3; Angle: 149; Button preset: Raised.
9. Create white **Clean up your act** text in the same font you chose for the ruler and apply a Drop Shadow effect to it with default settings.
10. Save your work, then compare your document to Figure B-39.

Impact Potions, a new energy drink aimed at the teen market, is sponsoring a design contest. They want you to introduce the drink by using the design in a pop-up window on other teen Web sites. They haven't decided on the container yet, so you can create the bottle or can of your choice.

1. If desired, obtain images that will reinforce your message delivery and enhance the vector shapes you will create. You can obtain an image from your computer, from the Internet, from a digital camera, or from scanned media. You can use clipart from the Web that is free for both personal and commercial use (check the copyright information for any such clipart before downloading it).

2. Create a new document and save it as **impact_potion**.

3. Create a beverage container using the vector tools of your choice, apply a fill, style, or stroke, and combine paths as necessary. (*Hint*: The can in the sample is an oval and a rectangle combined with the Union command.)

4. Create a label for the container, applying fills, strokes styles, transparency, and effects as necessary.

5. Create text for the pop-up window, applying fills, strokes, styles, transparency, and effects as necessary. (*Hint*: The Impact text in the sample has a style and the Drop

Shadow effect applied to it; the text objects on the can are attached to paths.)

6. Rename objects or layers on the Layers panel as appropriate.

7. Experiment with changing the order of effects in the Effects list.

8. Examine the sample shown in Figure B-40, then save your work.

FIGURE B-40
Completed Project Builder 2

One of the many advantages to using Fireworks for your images is the ability to combine vector and bitmap images into one document. For a performance artist, such as the country musician Dwight Yoakam, an official Web site can reinforce both the artistic message and mood. Photographs and Fireworks-generated images combine to convey the feel of an old-time café and street scene. Many images also link the viewer to other pages within the site. Because dynamic Web sites are updated frequently to reflect current trends, this page may be different from Figure B-41 when you open it online.

1. Connect to the Internet and go to *www.course.com*. Navigate to the page for this book, click the Student Online Companion, then click the link for this unit.
2. Open a document in a word processor, or open a new Fireworks document, then save the file as **yoakam**. (*Hint*: Use the Text tool in Fireworks to answer the questions.)
3. Explore the site and answer the following questions:
   - When they were created in Fireworks, which objects could have been grouped?
   - Do objects appear to have been combined? If so, which Combine Paths commands could have been used and why?
   - Identify gradients, textures, styles, or other effects applied to objects.
   - Are there objects that appear to be a combination of vector shapes, that include photographic images objects, or that appear to have an effect applied to them? (*Hint*: Visit the site during the day and during the night and note the differences.)
4. Save your work.

FIGURE B-41
Design Project

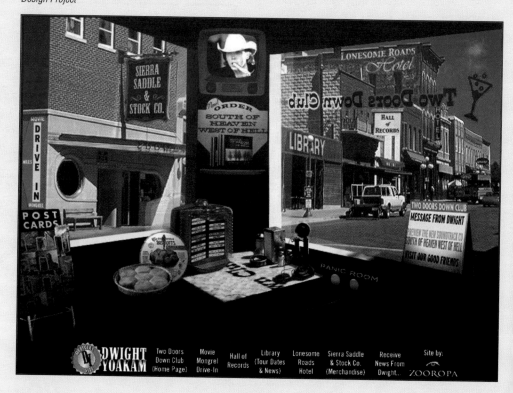

Your group can assign elements of the project to individual members, or work collectively to create the finished product.

Vintage Wheels, a classic car club, is known for the unusual prizes the club awards to winners of their road rallies. To promote the rallies, the prizes are shown on the group's Web page. Your group has been selected to design and promote this year's grand prizewinner: a custom belt buckle. The only requirement is that the buckle honor a classic car and be large enough to be seen from a distance. You can select the classic auto of your choice.

1. If desired, obtain an image for the buckle. You can obtain an image from your computer, from the Internet, from a digital camera, or from scanned media. You can use clipart from the Web that is free for both personal and commercial use (check the copyright information for any such clipart before downloading it).
2. Create a new document and save it as **classic_buckle**.
3. Create two or more vector objects for the buckle and add fills, styles, strokes, or transparency to them. (*Hint*: The ovals in the sample have a combination of Inner Shadow, Inner Bevel, Inset Emboss, and Outer Bevel effects applied to them.)

4. Apply at least one Combine Paths command to the objects.
5. Create text as desired and apply fills, styles, and effects to them.

FIGURE B-42
Completed Group Project

6. Examine the sample shown in Figure B-42, then save your work.

lu lu

IMPORTING, SELECTING
AND MODIFYING GRAPHICS

1. Work with imported files.

2. Work with bitmap selection tools.

3. Learn about selection areas.

4. Select areas based on color.

UNIT C
IMPORTING SELECTING
AND MODIFYING GRAPHICS

Understanding Importing

Whether you want to create a simple image or a complex Web site, having the right graphic is crucial to the success of your project. Many times, the graphic you need may have been created in another application. Fireworks makes it easy to access such a graphic—regardless of whether it was created within the Macromedia application suite in a program such as FreeHand, created in another progam, such as Adobe Illustrator, or downloaded from a digital camera.

Fireworks allows you to import several types of files, including vector and bitmap files, as well as HTML tables. Being able to work with many different file types in the same document has obvious advantages. Fireworks lets you control file size by merging and flattening objects in your document, which combine pixels of different bitmap images or convert vector objects into bitmap images.

Once you import a bitmap image, you can use an assortment of tools to select the pixels on that image. You can select pixels based on an area or on color. Once you select pixels, you can manipulate them independently. For example, you can select and edit a defined set of pixels or blend a selection into surrounding pixels.

Tools You'll Use

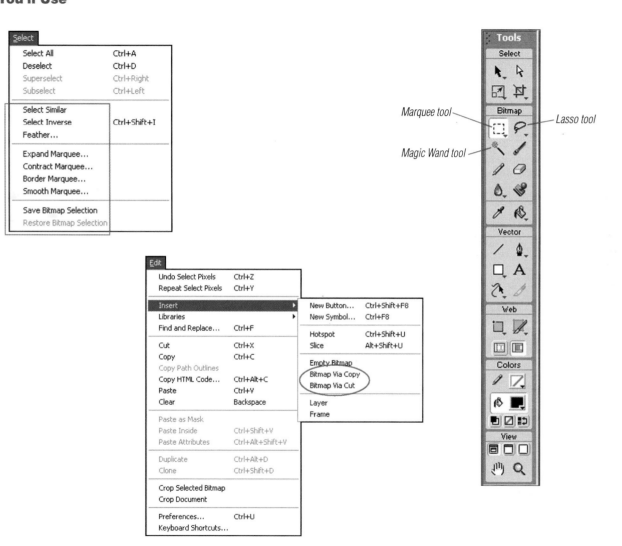

Marquee tool

Lasso tool

Magic Wand tool

Select menu:

Select All	Ctrl+A
Deselect	Ctrl+D
Superselect	Ctrl+Right
Subselect	Ctrl+Left
Select Similar	
Select Inverse	Ctrl+Shift+I
Feather...	
Expand Marquee...	
Contract Marquee...	
Border Marquee...	
Smooth Marquee...	
Save Bitmap Selection	
Restore Bitmap Selection	

Edit menu:

Undo Select Pixels	Ctrl+Z
Repeat Select Pixels	Ctrl+Y
Insert	▶
Libraries	▶
Find and Replace...	Ctrl+F
Cut	Ctrl+X
Copy	Ctrl+C
Copy Path Outlines	
Copy HTML Code...	Ctrl+Alt+C
Paste	Ctrl+V
Clear	Backspace
Paste as Mask	
Paste Inside	Ctrl+Shift+V
Paste Attributes	Ctrl+Alt+Shift+V
Duplicate	Ctrl+Alt+D
Clone	Ctrl+Shift+D
Crop Selected Bitmap	
Crop Document	
Preferences...	Ctrl+U
Keyboard Shortcuts...	

Insert submenu:

New Button...	Ctrl+Shift+F8
New Symbol...	Ctrl+F8
Hotspot	Ctrl+Shift+U
Slice	Alt+Shift+U
Empty Bitmap	
Bitmap Via Copy	
Bitmap Via Cut	
Layer	
Frame	

WORK WITH IMPORTED FILES

What You'll Do

In this lesson, you will import graphics with different file formats into a Fireworks document.

Considerations for Importing Files

If you use mostly vector objects in your documents, you can change their dimensions and appearance without affecting the quality of the graphic. When you import a bitmapped image or a vector or text object created in another program into your document, you may need to weigh the advantages of using the new images against the disadvantage of increasing your file size. In addition to other factors, such as color depth, the number of bitmap images in a document affects file size.

Many times, the format Fireworks supports when importing is version-specific. For example, you can import a CorelDRAW file, but only if it is version 7 or higher with bitmap compression turned off. Table C-1 shows the file formats that Fireworks supports for importing and exporting and shows you how you can use different file formats in Fireworks.

Using Different File Formats in Fireworks

Fireworks offers several ways to acquire an image for use in your document. For example, you have already seen that you can copy and paste or drag and drop images from one native Fireworks .png file to another. Fireworks also has many features that maximize your ability to work with different file formats created in different programs, such as being able to copy and paste a graphic open in a different application into your Fireworks document. In this example, because the copied graphic is placed on the Clipboard, you can paste it into your document as you would any other copied object. Dragging and dropping a selection from within Fireworks or between applications offers an additional advantage. Whenever you copy a selection, the selection is placed on the Clipboard, which consumes resources from your computer in order to store it. In contrast, using the drag and drop method saves memory.

Another easy way to acquire an image is to import a file with a compatible file format. Because individual elements in bitmap images are not editable, importing bitmap files is a relatively straightforward process. However, importing vector files offers the distinct advantage of being able to edit the individual paths that make up the graphic. Depending on the complexity of the original graphic, as well as its native format, Fireworks may import the graphic as a single grouped object or as an ungrouped collection of individual editable objects. You can import vector objects into Fireworks from many vector programs, including FreeHand, Adobe Illustrator, and CorelDRAW. Figure C-1 shows the import file types available in the Import dialog box. You can determine how Fireworks imports an Adobe Photoshop document by selecting different options in the Preferences dialog box shown in Figure C-2. For a vector-based file, you can select options in the Vector File Options dialog box, also shown in Figure C-2. For example, in the File Conversion section of the Vector File Options dialog box, you can determine whether to flatten layers or retain them. You can change settings in the Render as Images section to determine the number of individual objects Fireworks will import. In some cases, you may not need to edit the vector file, or may simply prefer to import the file as a single bitmap image.

QUICKTIP

You can select Photoshop conversion options, such as layers and text, by opening the Preferences dialog box from the Edit menu, and then clicking the Import tab. For vector-based files, you can select a wide range of options in the Vector File Options dialog box that opens when you import the file.

When you open a file that was created in another program, the original file is not affected by changes you make in Fireworks. The file that you open, however, becomes a native Fireworks .png document when you save it in Fireworks.

FIGURE C-1
Import dialog box

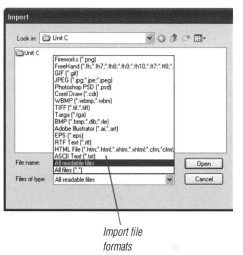

Import file
formats

FIGURE C-2
Import options

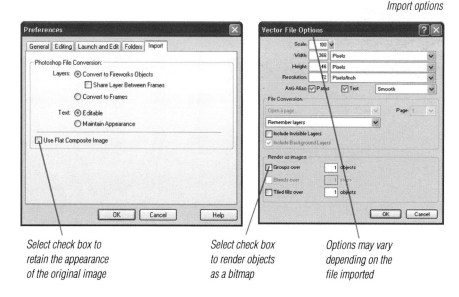

Select check box to
retain the appearance
of the original image

Select check box
to render objects
as a bitmap

Options may vary
depending on the
file imported

TABLE C-1: File Formats and Functions Supported in Fireworks MX

import & open	copy/paste	drag & drop	export
Adobe Illustrator (.ai, .art)	ASCII text	CorelDRAW 7 or later	Animated GIF
Adobe Photoshop PSD (.psd)	BMP	FreeHand 7 or later	Adobe Photoshop PSD
Animated GIF (.gif)	DIB	Illustrator 7 or later	Director
ASCII text (.txt)	EPS	Internet Explorer 3 or later	Dreamweaver Library
BMP (.bmp)	FreeHand 7 or later	Macromedia Flash 3 or later	Frames to Layers
CorelDRAW (uncompressed) (.cdr)	Illustrator 7 or later	Microsoft Office 97 or later	HTML & Images
EPS (.eps)	PICT (Mac)	Netscape Navigator 3 or later	Illustrator 7 or later
Fireworks PNG (.png)	PNG	Photoshop 4 or later	Images Only
FreeHand 7 or higher (.fh)	RTF		Layers to Frames
GIF (.gif)	TXT		Lotus Domino Designer
HTML (.htm, .html, .xhtm)	WBMP		Macromedia Flash SWF
JPEG (.jpg, .jpe, .jpeg)			
PICT (Macintosh only) (.pict)			
RTF (.rtf)			
Targa (.tga)			
TIFF (.tif, .tiff)			
WBMP (.wbmp)			

FIGURE C-3
Imported GIF

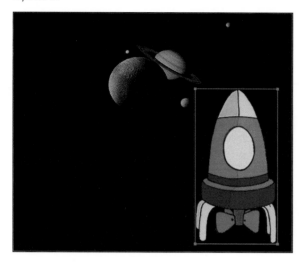

FIGURE C-4
Imported Fireworks file

Import a .gif file

1. Open fwc_1.png, save it as **horizons.png**, then verify that the Info panel is open.

2. Change the name of Layer 1 on the Layers panel to **Spaceships**.

3. Click File on the menu bar, click Import, then navigate to the drive and folder where your data files are stored.

4. Click the Files of type list arrow, then click GIF (*.gif) (Win).

   TIP You may need to scroll down the list to view the file type.

5. Click rocket.gif, then click Open.

6. Position the Insertion pointer on the canvas at approximately 353 X/143 Y, then click the mouse to import the file.

   TIP Enter the precise coordinates in the X and Y text boxes on the Property inspector after you click the mouse.

7. Compare your image to Figure C-3.

You imported a GIF file into a Fireworks document.

Import a Fireworks PNG file

1. Click File on the menu bar, then click Import.

2. Click the Files of type list arrow, click Fireworks (*.png) (Win), click saucer.png, then click Open.

3. Position the Insertion pointer on the canvas at approximately 65 X/290 Y, then click the mouse.

4. Compare your image to Figure C-4.

You imported a Fireworks file.

Import a vector file as editable paths

1. Click the Background layer, click the New/Duplicate Layer button on the bottom of the Layers panel, then change the name of the new layer to **Book**.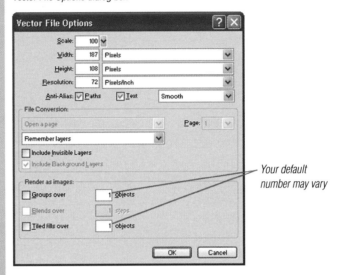

2. Click File on the menu bar, click Import, click the Files of type list arrow, click EPS (*.eps) (Win), then double-click book.eps to import it.

   The Vector File Options dialog box opens.

   > TIP   If the imported file was created in a program that is also designed for print media, such as Macromedia FreeHand or Adobe Photoshop, Fireworks will convert the original color mode from print colors, such as CMYK, to RGB mode, which uses colors designed for the Web.

3. Compare your dialog box to Figure C-5, then click OK.

4. Position the Insertion pointer in the upper left corner of the canvas, click the mouse, then compare your image to Figure C-6.

   The book appears on the canvas and the object appears on the Layers panel as a grouped object.

   You imported a vector file into a Fireworks document.

FIGURE C-5
Vector File Options dialog box

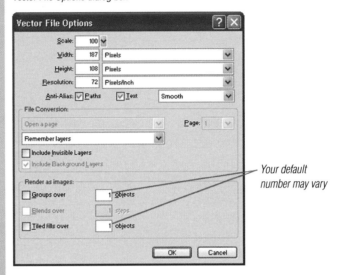

Your default number may vary

FIGURE C-6
Vector file imported as group

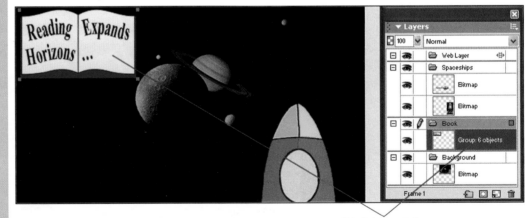

Objects in imported vector file are grouped

FIGURE C-7

Imported vector objects ungrouped

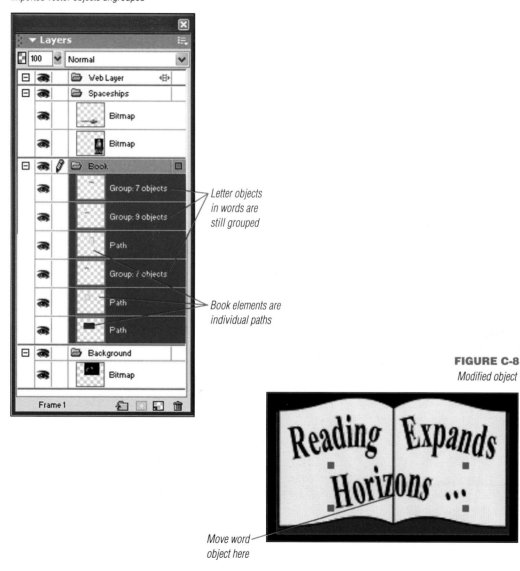

Letter objects
in words are
still grouped

Book elements are
individual paths

FIGURE C-8

Modified object

Move word
object here

Edit an imported vector object

1. Verify that the vector object is selected, click Modify on the menu bar, then click Ungroup.

   TIP You can also ungroup objects by pressing [Ctrl][Shift][G] (Win) or [command][Shift][G] (Mac).

2. If necessary, drag the bottom border of the Layers panel until all the layers are visible, then compare your Layers panel to Figure C-7.

   Some individual paths are ungrouped, while other objects remain grouped (the individual letters). You can ungroup all the objects if you want to edit them (for a total of 26 objects).

3. Click a blank part of the canvas to deselect the objects, click the Group: 9 objects object on the Layers panel, then drag the Horizons object to the location shown in Figure C-8.

4. Click the Book layer on the Layers panel to select all the objects on the layer, click Modify on the menu bar, then click Group.

   The numerous book objects are regrouped into one object.

5. Save your work.

You ungrouped and modified an object, and then regrouped the paths.

WORK WITH BITMAP SELECTION TOOLS

What You'll Do

In this lesson, you will use the marquee tools to select and change pixels on images.

Understanding Pixel Selection Tools

Being able to select the precise pixels in an image is the crucial first step to altering or editing them. Fireworks offers several ways to select and manipulate pixels in an image. This unit covers some of those ways. When you select pixels on an image, Fireworks creates a flashing perimeter, known as a **marquee selection**, around the pixels. (This perimeter is also referred to as "marching ants" because of the way it looks.) Marquee selections are temporary areas of selected pixels that exist until you modify the pixels themselves, for example, by cutting, copying, or recoloring them.

You can save and recall a bitmap selection, but only one selection at a time. You cannot save bitmap selections in your document when you close it. In this unit, we'll use the Marquee, Lasso, and Magic Wand tools to select and manipulate pixels in different ways. You can also use the selection tools in combination to select a complex area.

Once you create a marquee selection, you can transfer it to another bitmap by clicking another bitmap object on the same or on a different layer. You can copy or cut a pixel selection into the layer of a document by using the Bitmap via Copy or Bitmap via Cut Insert command options on the Edit

Moving marquee selections

To move a marquee selection after you have created it, click any of the bitmap selection tools and drag the marquee on the canvas. To move a marquee selection while you are creating it, create an initial marquee, press and hold the [Spacebar], move the selection to another area of the canvas, then release the [Spacebar] and continue drawing the marquee.

menu. For example, if you select pixels and then click the Bitmap via Cut command, Fireworks cuts the selected pixels from the original bitmap and then pastes them as a new object on the active layer. Similarly, when you create a bitmap using the Bitmap via Copy command, Fireworks copies the selected pixels and pastes them as a new object on the active layer.

Using the Marquee Tools

Marquee tools select pixels on an image in a specific shape. The properties available for the marquee tools are shown in Figure C-9.

You can press and hold [Shift] to constrain your rectangle or oval marquee to a square or circle. Use the Fixed Ratio style to constrain the height and width to a precise ratio and the Fixed Size style to set the marquee to an exact dimension.

Using the Transformation Tools

The transformation tool group consists of the Scale tool, Skew tool, and Distort tool. The Scale tool resizes an object; the Skew tool slants an object along the horizontal or vertical axes; and the Distort tool alters the size and proportion of an object and is useful for creating perspective in an object. When you select an object with any of the transformation tools, sizing handles surround the object. You can use these handles to transform the object. You can also use any transformation tool to rotate an object. The transformation tool pointer appears when you position the pointer over a sizing handle; the rotation pointer appears when you position the pointer in between the sizing handles or outside the object.

FIGURE C-9
Properties for the marquee tools

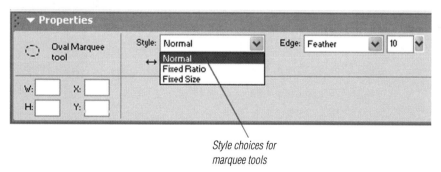

*Style choices for
marquee tools*

Select pixels using the Marquee tool

1. Click the Background layer on the Layers panel, click the New/Duplicate Layer button, then change the name of the layer to **Galaxy**. ⊞

2. Open galaxy.jpg.

3. Click the Marquee tool on the Tools panel, then verify that the Info panel is open. ⬚

4. Verify that Normal is the selected style in the Style list on the Property inspector and that Anti-alias is the Edge setting.

5. Place the pointer on the canvas at approximately 40 X/6 Y, then drag a rectangle that surrounds the galaxy, as shown in Figure C-10.

6. Click Edit on the menu bar, click Copy, click Edit on the menu bar, then click Paste.

   The copied pixels are not noticeable because they are pasted on top of the original image on the canvas. The selection appears as the top object on the Layers panel.

7. Click the Show/Hide Layer icon next to the original bitmap on the Layers panel, then compare your image to Figure C-11. 👁

You set properties for the Marquee tool and created a rectangular marquee selection.

FIGURE C-10
Using the Marquee tool

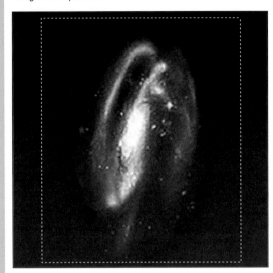

FIGURE C-11
Rectangular marquee selection

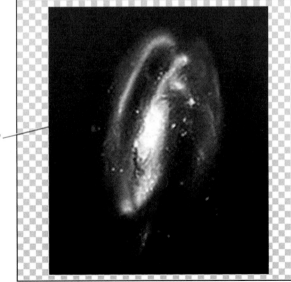

Anti-alias edge appears sharp

Importing, Selecting, and Modifying Graphics   Unit C

FIGURE C-12

Using the Oval Marquee tool

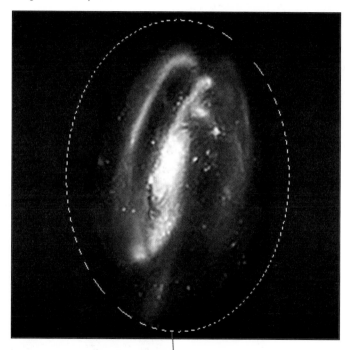

Move marquee by
dragging it or by
using the arrow keys

Select pixels using the Oval Marquee tool

1. Click the Show/Hide icons next to both galaxy bitmaps on the Layers panel to hide the rectangular selection and show the original image, respectively. 👁

2. Press and hold the Marquee tool 🔲 on the Tools panel, then click the Oval Marquee tool. ◯

3. Verify that Normal is the selected style in the Style list on the Property inspector, click the Edge of selection list arrow, click Feather, double-click the Amount of feather text box, then type **20**.

4. Place the pointer in the middle of the canvas, press and hold [Alt] (Win) or [option] (Mac), then drag an oval marquee around the galaxy, as shown in Figure C-12.

   Pressing and holding [Alt] (Win) or [option] (Mac) allows you to draw a marquee from the center point outward.

5. Drag the marquee or use the arrow keys to reposition the oval around the galaxy, if necessary.

   TIP You can reselect the marquee as many times as necessary. Notice that the marquee appears to be cropped when you release the mouse button if you extend it beyond the canvas.

   (continued)

6. Click Edit on the menu bar, point to Insert, then click Bitmap Via Copy to copy the selection.

7. Click the Show/Hide Layer icon next to the original bitmap on the Layers panel to hide it, then compare your image to Figure C-13.

You set properties for the Oval Marquee tool, created an oval marquee selection, and then created a new bitmap from the original.

Transform a selection

1. Drag a corner of the galaxy.jpg document window to make it smaller, then drag it to another part of the Fireworks window so that the horizons.png document window and the Info panel are visible.

2. Verify that the oval bitmap is selected, click the Pointer tool on the Tools panel, then drag the selection from galaxy.jpg to the location shown in Figure C-14. ↖

3. Close galaxy.jpg without saving changes.

4. Click the Scale tool on the Tools panel. ⊡

(continued)

FIGURE C-13
Oval marquee selection

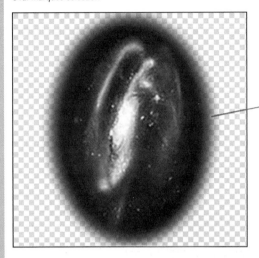

— Feathered edge

FIGURE C-14
Dropped selection

Reading Expands Horizons ...

My alien is an honor student

FIGURE C-15
Rotating a selection

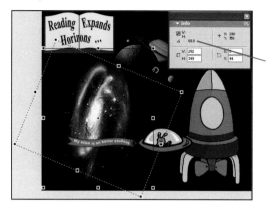

Degree of rotation

5. Place the pointer outside the object until the rotation pointer appears, drag the selection counterclockwise 68 degrees, as shown in the Info panel, then compare your image to Figure C-15.

6. Click the Opacity list arrow on the Property inspector, drag the slider to **60**, then press [Enter] (Win) or [return] (Mac).

7. Click the Pointer tool on the Tools panel, then drag the Book object and the Saucer object to the locations shown in Figure C-16.

8. Save your work.

You dragged and dropped an object, rotated it, and changed its opacity.

FIGURE C-16
Moved and rotated objects

Understanding different print resolution

If the bitmap selection you are copying has a print resolution that differs from the document into which you want to paste, a Resampling dialog box appears, asking if you want to resample the bitmap. Choose Resample if you want to preserve the selection's original dimensions, which will adjust the number of pixels as needed to maintain the bitmap's appearance. Choose Don't Resample to retain the number of original pixels, which may affect the size of the graphic when pasted.

LEARN ABOUT SELECTION AREAS

What You'll Do

▶ In this lesson, you will select pixels on an image using the lasso tools.

Using the Lasso Tools

As you have seen, the marquee tools select an area of pixels in a preset shape. Using the lasso tools, you can define an exact pixel selection with precision. The Lasso tool works well on images that appear to have curves, while the Polygon Lasso tool works well on images that have straight lines or asymmetrical outlines. With the Lasso tool, you create the marquee as you draw it on the canvas—its accuracy is linked to your tracing ability. The result is similar to the result obtained with tools such as the Pencil tool—what you draw is what you get, which may or may not be a good thing. Using the Polygon Lasso tool is similar to using the Pen tool—you create your marquee by clicking the mouse as you go along, although the final marquee does not contain points and is just like the other marquees you create.

Adding and Subtracting Pixels

To add pixels to an existing lasso selection, press and hold [Shift], then drag a new marquee. The pixels you select will be addded to the previously selected marquee. To subtract pixels from a marquee, press and hold [Alt] (Win) or [option] (Mac). Fireworks will delete the areas where the marquees overlap. To select just the intersection of marquees, create the first marquee, press and hold [Shift] [Alt] (Win) or [Shift] [option] (Mac), then create the second marquee. You can add or subtract pixels using other bitmap selection tools in much the same manner. Note that pressing [Shift] as you use the Polygon Lasso tool will constrain the lines that you can draw to 45-degree angle increments.

Using Select Menu Commands

Using commands on the Select menu, you can adjust a pixel selection after you create it, as shown in Figure C-17. You can edit the set of selected pixels, or add pixels to or subtract pixels from the selection marquee. The Select Inverse command selects all of the pixels except the ones enclosed by the marquee. Other commands, such as Expand Marquee or Contract Marquee, allow you to enter the number of pixels that add to or subtract from the selection's border. Creating a marquee can be a grueling process. Fortunately, once you are satisfied with a selection, you can use the Save Bitmap Selection and Restore Bitmap Selection commands to save it and recall it at any time during the current editing session or after the file has been saved, closed, and re-opened.

FIGURE C-17
Applying Select menu commands to a selection

Original selection —

Use Select Inverse to
delete nonselected pixels

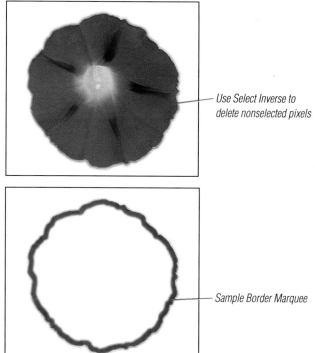

Sample Border Marquee

Select pixels using the Lasso tool

1. Open astrocat.jpg.

2. Click the Zoom tool on the Tools panel, click the canvas until you can view the image in detail, then drag the borders of the document window until the entire image is visible. $\mathcal{Q}$

   You may need to adjust the magnification settings a number of times before you are satisfied.

   > TIP You can also increase magnification by clicking the Set magnification icon on the bottom of the document window and then clicking a magnification setting from the Set magnification pop-up menu. 100% ▾

3. Click the Lasso tool on the Tools panel, click the Edge of selection list arrow on the Property inspector, click Feather, double-click the Amount of feather text box, then type 1. $\mathcal{P}$

4. Drag the pointer along the perimeter of the cat, as shown in Figure C-18, then notice the areas where the marquee is off the mark. $\mathcal{P}$

   Because the Lasso tool is sensitive to even the slightest deviations from the path you are drawing, the accuracy of your marquee will vary.

   > TIP You can change the pointer of most tools to a cross hair by pressing [Caps Lock], which may make it easier to see the pixels you want to select.

   (continued)

FIGURE C-18
Creating a marquee with the Lasso tool

Drag pointer along perimeter of image

Understanding Magnification and the Zoom Tool

You can increase the magnification of any area on the canvas. To change the magnification in preset increments, click the Zoom tool on the canvas or click a magnification setting in the Set Magnification pop-up menu on the bottom of the document window. To set a magnification between 6% and 6400%, use the Zoom tool to drag a zoom selection box on the canvas. The amount of magnification is based on the size of the zoom selection box. To zoom out of a selection, press and hold [Alt] (Win) or [option] (Mac), then click the canvas.

5. Click Select on the menu bar, then click Deselect.

> TIP You can also remove a marquee by drawing another one, by clicking an area outside the selection with a marquee or lasso tool, or by pressing [Esc].

You selected pixels on an image using the Lasso tool.

Create a marquee using the Polygon Lasso tool and save the selection

1. Press and hold the Lasso tool  on the Tools panel, then click the Polygon Lasso tool.

2. Click the pointer along the perimeter of the image, make sure you connect the start and end points, then compare your image to Figure C-19.

> TIP You can readjust your wrist or reposition the mouse on a flat surface in between clicks, which may assure a more accurate selection.

3. Click Select on the menu bar, then click Save Bitmap Selection to temporarily store the selection.

You selected pixels on an image using the Polygon Lasso tool, and then saved the selection.

FIGURE C-19
Marquee created with the Polygon Lasso tool

Marquee is less erratic

Transform a selection

1. Click Select on the menu bar, click Expand Marquee, type **10** in the Expand By pixels text box (if necessary), then click OK.

   The marquee expands 10 pixels in each direction.

2. Click Select on the menu bar, click Contract Marquee, type **20** in the Contract By pixels text box, then click OK.

3. Click Select on the menu bar, then click Restore Bitmap Selection.

   The original marquee selection is restored.

4. Click Select on the menu bar, click Smooth Marquee, then type **10** in the Sample Radius pixels text box (if necessary), click OK, then compare your image to Figure C-20.

   TIP Fireworks removes pixels to smooth out the jagged points on the marquee.

5. Click Select on the menu bar, then click Restore Bitmap Selection.

   TIP You can hide the marquee display by clicking the Hide Edges command on the View menu.

6. Click Select on the menu bar, click Select Inverse, then press [Delete].

7. Click Select on the menu bar, then click Restore Bitmap Selection.

8. Click Edit on the menu bar, then click Copy.

9. Close astrocat.jpg without saving changes.

You applied different marquee commands and restored the marquee.

FIGURE C-20
Result of Smooth Marquee command

Smoothing removes pixels

FIGURE C-21
Results of numeric transform

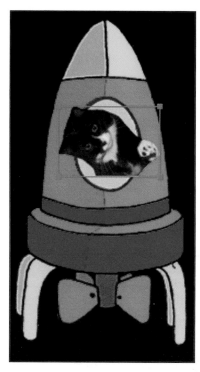

FIGURE C-22
Repositioned and rotated selection

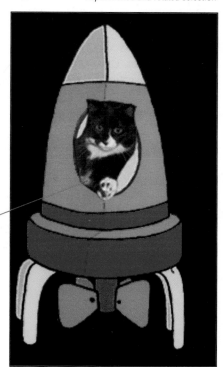

Position cat image
in window frame

Transform a copied selection

1. Click the Pointer tool on the Tools panel, then click the large rocket on the canvas. ▶

2. Click Edit on the menu bar, then click Paste.

3. Click Modify on the menu bar, point to Transform, then click Numeric Transform.

    The Numeric Transform dialog box opens, where you can scale an object by a percentage, resize it by pixels, or rotate an object.

4. Verify that Scale is selected from the drop-down list and that the Scale Attributes and Constrain Proportions check boxes are selected.

    The padlock indicates that the object will be resized proportionately.

5. Double-click the width percentage text box, type **50**, then click OK.

6. Drag the cat image on top of the rocket window, then compare your image to Figure C-21.

7. Click the Scale tool 🔄 on the Tools panel, position the rotation pointer outside the object, then drag the pointer clockwise to –73 degrees, as shown on the Info panel. ↻

8. Click the Pointer tool on the Tools panel, then drag the image to the location shown in Figure C-22. ▶

9. Save your work.

You transformed the copied selection.

SELECT AREAS BASED ON COLOR

What You'll Do

In this lesson, you will add select areas of color using the Magic Wand tool, merge layers, and then flatten the image.

Using the Magic Wand Tool

The marquee and lasso tools select pixels by enclosing them. The Magic Wand tool allows you to select similarly colored areas of a bitmap image. The Magic Wand tool includes Edge and Tolerance settings. **Tolerance** refers to the range of colors the tool will select. The higher the setting, the larger the selection range. The Magic Wand tool works well on areas of strongly defined color, such as photographic images.

QUICKTIP

Depending on your graphic, you may find it more efficient to add pixels to a Magic Wand selection by pressing and holding [Shift], rather than increasing the tolerance setting and reclicking the bitmap.

The Tolerance setting also affects the pixels selected when you click the Select Similar command on the Select menu. The Magic Wand tool selects pixels of contiguous color tone, not contiguous pixels on the image. When you use the Select Similar command, any matching pixels on the image are selected. Figure C-23 shows the areas selected using different Tolerance settings.

Merging and Flattening Objects and Layers

Once you start creating, copying, or importing vector and bitmap objects in a document, your Layers panel can quickly fill up and appear unruly. While creating and collapsing layers can help manage the large number of objects, you can also flatten or merge the objects you create into a single image, just as grouping objects assembles them into a single arrangement. Flattening and merging objects and layers helps to manage objects, layers, and file size. However, you can no longer edit individual objects after you flatten or merge them.

The Merge Down command on the Modify menu merges selected objects with the bitmap object that lies beneath the bottommost selected object. The Flatten Selection command on the Modify menu flattens two or more objects, even if they are on different layers (the top object moves to the bottommost object), converting them to bitmap objects. If you want to move all your objects to a single layer and remove all other layers, you can use the Flatten Layers command.

FIGURE C-23
Sample Magic Wand and Select Similar selections

Red pixels selected at Tolerance 16

Pixels selected with Select Similar command

Both red and orange pixels selected at Tolerance 64

Pixels selected with Select Similar command

Select and copy pixels using the Magic Wand tool

1. Click the bitmap object (with the planets) on the Background layer to select it.

2. Click the Magic Wand tool on the Tools panel, double-click the Tolerance text box on the Property inspector, type **64**, then verify that Anti-alias appears in the Edge text box.

3. Click the center of the small green moon, click Edit on the menu bar, point to Insert, then click Bitmap Via Copy to copy the selection on the Layers panel.

4. Click Select on the menu bar, click Deselect, click the Pointer tool on the Tools panel, click the copied bitmap, then drag it to the location shown in Figure C-24.

5. Click the Add effects button on the Property inspector, point to Adjust Color, click Hue/Saturation, enter the values shown in Figure C-25, then click OK.

    The colors change in the copied selection.

You selected pixels using the Magic Wand tool, and then copied, moved, and changed the color of the selection.

Select and alter pixels

1. Click the rocketship bitmap object to select it, click the Magic Wand tool on the Tools panel, then click the right yellow half of the nose cone.

(continued)

FIGURE C-24
Pixels selected and moved with the Magic Wand tool

Move copied selection here

FIGURE C-25
Hue/Saturation dialog box

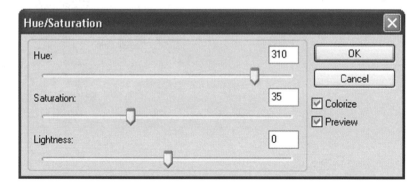

FIGURE C-26
Selected pixels

Your selected
pixels may
vary slightly

FIGURE C-27
Modified bitmap selections

Pixels modified
after being copied

Pixels modified after
being selected

FIGURE C-28
Flattened layers

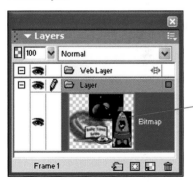

Bitmap and vector
objects flattened
onto one layer

2. Click Select on the menu bar, click Select Similar, then compare your image to Figure C-26.

The yellow areas in the rocketship are selected.

3. Click Filters on the menu bar, point to Eye Candy 4000 LE, then click Marble.

4. Click the Bedrock Color color box, click Name (Mac), click the first yellow color swatch, click OK, then click OK to close the Marble dialog box.

5. Click Select on the menu bar, click Deselect, then compare your image to Figure C-27.

You added similar pixels to a selection, and applied an effect to it.

Merge and flatten objects and layers

1. Click the Pointer tool on the Tools panel, then click the copied purple planet bitmap object on the Background layer. ↖

2. Click Modify on the menu bar, then click Merge Down.

The two planet bitmap objects on the layer merge into one.

3. Click Modify on the menu bar, then click Flatten Layers to move all the objects to a single layer.

4. Click the Layer layer to select all its objects, click Modify on the menu bar, click Flatten Selection, compare your Layers panel to Figure C-28, then save your work.

You merged and flattened objects and layers.

Import files.

1. Open fwc_2.png, then save it as **sweet_essence.png**. (*Hint*: Because the canvas is narrow, readjust the size of the document window if desired.)
2. Verify that the Info panel is open.
3. Change the name of Layer 1 to **Small Bottle**.
4. Import smbottle.jpg, placing the import cursor on the top left corner of the canvas.
5. Center the small bottle on the blue bottle so that it appears to be floating inside it.
6. Import sweet.png, placing the import cursor on the top left corner of the canvas.
7. Move the text to the bottom of the canvas.
8. Save your work.

Edit an imported vector object.

1. Create a new layer and change the name to **Jellies**.
2. Import jelly beans.eps, accepting the default import settings, and placing the import cursor on the top left corner of the canvas.
3. Regroup the objects, and resize them so they fit across the top of the canvas.
4. Save your work.

Use the marquee tools.

1. Hide the Background layer, then select the text bitmap object.
2. Select the Marquee tool, verify that the Style is Normal and the Edge is Anti-alias, then draw a rectangular marquee around the text object.

3. Copy the selection using the Bitmap Via Copy command. (*Hint*: Use the Insert command on the Edit menu.)
4. Hide the original bitmap on the Layers panel, then note the selected area.
5. Delete the rectangular marquee selection.
6. Save your work.

Transform a selection.

1. Show the original text bitmap, then select the Oval Marquee tool.
2. Set the Edge to Feather 10 pixels on the Property inspector, then draw an oval marquee around the text object.
3. Select the inverse of the selection and then delete it.
4. Deselect all objects, select the Scale tool, select the oval bitmap object, then rotate the oval bitmap object –90 degrees (clockwise).
5. Center the text bitmap selection on top of the small blue bottle.
6. Select the Background layer on the Layers panel.
7. Save your work.

Use the lasso tools.

1. Open rings.png, then select the Lasso tool.
2. Set the Edge to Feather 1 pixel on the Property inspector, adjust the magnification setting as desired, then create a marquee around the center ring.
3. Deselect the marquee.

4. Select the Polygon Lasso tool, then create a marquee around the two adjoining green rings to the left of the orange ring.
5. Save the bitmap selection.
6. Save your work.

Transform a selection and a copied selection.

1. Expand the marquee 5 pixels.
2. Contract the marquee 15 pixels.
3. Smooth the marquee 10 pixels.
4. Restore the bitmap selection.
5. Select the inverse of the bitmap selection, then deselect it.
6. Restore the bitmap selection.
7. Copy and paste the object to the sweet_essence.png document.
8. Close rings.png without saving changes.
9. Position the green rings selection so it appears to be floating near the bottom of the bottle on the left.
10. Save your work.

Use the Magic Wand tool.

1. Open gumballs.tif, then select the Magic Wand tool.
2. Adjust the tolerance to 32 and the Edge to Feather 1 pixel.
3. Click the middle of the orange gumball, then click Select Similar.
4. Add pixels as necessary to the selection. (*Hint*: Press and hold [Shift].)

5. Drag and the drop the selection in the first bottle in the sweet_essence.png document. (*Hint*: If prompted to sample the selection, click Resample.)

6. Repeat for the yellow, white, and pink gumballs. (*Hint*: Work with each gumball separately.)

7. Close gumballs.tif without saving changes.

Select and alter pixels.

1. Using Figure C-29 as a guide, resize and change the layer position of the gumballs.

2. Select the white gumball object, then apply a Hue/Saturation effect to it with the following settings: Colorize check box selected; Hue: 300; Saturation: 40; Lightness: –6.

3. Save your work.

Merge objects and flatten layers.

1. Click the Jellies layer on the Layers panel, then merge down the layer. (*Hint*: Use the Modify menu.)

2. Click the Small Bottle layer on the Layers panel, then flatten the layers.

3. Select all the objects, then flatten the selection.

4. Save your work, then compare your image to Figure C-29.

FIGURE C-29
Completed Skills Review

You and your friends are going to partici-pate in a charity auction by creating a one-of-a-kind jacket. You are going to collect hundreds of different buttons and sew, staple, and glue them in solid cover-age over a jean jacket. The auction has a Web site, so you will use your Fireworks skills to create the background for a Web page announcing this item.

1. Obtain images of buttons and/or jean jackets in different file formats that will convey something unique about your jacket. You can obtain images from your computer, from the Internet, from a digital camera, or from scanned media. You can use clipart from the Web that is free for both personal and commercial use (check the copyright information for any such clipart before downloading it).

2. Create a new document and save it as **mybuttons.png**.

3. Create a background image using any of the images you've obtained or create one using vector tools, and applying a fill, stroke, style, or effect to it. You can also adjust its transparency. (*Hint*: The background in the sample is a rectangle filled with the Blue Jean pattern.)

4. Import the following files and the files you obtained in Step 1 into your document or open and select them using the bitmap selection tools.
   - button1.ai
   - button2.gif

5. Create visual elements using the images in your document, changing their size, color,

and other properties as needed. (*Hint*: Various buttons have been skewed or distorted.)

6. Flatten the layers and selections in your document, if desired.

7. Save your work, then examine the sample shown in Figure C-30.

FIGURE C-30
Completed Project Builder 1

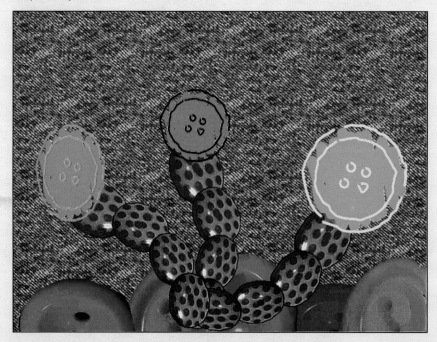

You're driving a moving truck across the country with a friend, and to occupy the time when you're not driving, you will use your new digital camera to take photographs. To memorialize this road trip, you will create a Web page dedicated to your adventure.

1. Obtain images that will fit your theme. You can obtain images from your computer, from the Internet, from a digital camera, or from scanned media. You can use clipart from the Web that is free for both personal and commercial use (check the copyright information for any such clipart before downloading it).

2. Create a new document and save it as **roadtrip.png**.

3. Import the files into your document or open and select them using the bitmap selection tools.

4. Create an interesting arrangement of your images, changing their size, color and other properties as needed. (*Hint*: The lights of the long building in the example were selected using the Select Inverse command.)

5. Flatten the layers and selections in your document as necessary.

6. Save your work, then examine the sample shown in Figure C-31.

FIGURE C-31
Completed Project Builder 2

Before you can build a visual element of a Web page, you need the visuals. As a designer, you'll want to be able to access as many images as possible in order to create a meaningful visual experience. Because dynamic Web sites are updated frequently to reflect current trends, this page may be different from Figure C-32 when you open it online.

1. Connect to the Internet and go to *www.course.com*. Navigate to the page for this book, click the Student Online Companion, then click the link for this unit.
2. Open a document in a word processor, or open a new Fireworks document, then save the file as **homecinema**. (*Hint*: Use the Text tool in Fireworks to answer the questions.)
3. Explore the site and answer the following questions:
   - Identify the images that could have been imported or copied from another file into the following:
     • the site as a whole
     • the source image
   - Is a cropping technique evident? If so, identify.
   - How do the images affect the site design?
   - How are photographic images and illustrations used in the site?
   - Who is the target audience for this site, and how does the design reinforce that goal?
4. Save your work.

FIGURE C-32
Design Project

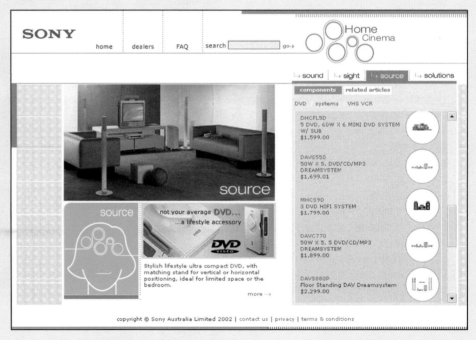

GROUP PROJECT

Your group can assign elements of the project to individual members, or work collectively to create the finished product.

Students from the entomology department at a local college are preparing an educational Web site for the reluctant public. The group, Give a Bug a Break, wants to show how beneficial insects are to the ecosystem and our lives. Your group is in charge of developing a sample template the group can show to potential sponsors.

1. Obtain images of insects, and choose an insect to feature in the document. You can obtain images from your computer, from the Internet, from a digital camera, or from scanned media. You can use clipart from the Web that is free for both personal and commercial use (check the copyright information for any such clipart before downloading it).
2. Create a new document and save it as **mybug.png**.
3. Import the files into your document or open and select them using the bitmap selection tools.

4. Create an interesting arrangement of your images, changing their size, color, and other properties as needed. (*Hint*: The praying mantis has a feathered edge on an oval marquee and is placed on an oval vector object with inner bevel and emboss effects.)

5. Flatten the layers and selection in your document as necessary.
6. Save your work, then examine the sample shown in Figure C-33.

FIGURE C-33
Sample Group Project

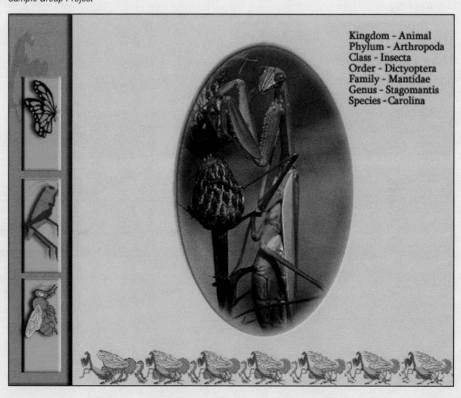

Kingdom - Animal
Phylum - Arthropoda
Class - Insecta
Order - Dictyoptera
Family - Mantidae
Genus - Stagomantis
Species - Carolina

MODIFYING PIXELS AND MANIPULATING IMAGES

1. Alter pixels on a bitmap.

2. Work with masks.

3. Sample and store color.

4. Use the Creative commands to change images.

UNIT D
MODIFYING PIXELS AND MANIPULATING IMAGES

Altering Pixels

As you work with bitmap images in Fireworks, you will often want to edit them so that they have the impact you want them to have. The look and feel of your design dictates what you may need to do to the pixels on a bitmap graphic; for example, you might want to lighten, darken, blur, smudge, erase, or mask parts of an image. Fireworks has several bitmap tools designed specifically for editing an image pixel by pixel, if necessary.

Being able to mask an image offers many possibilities. Using a **mask**, you can modify the shape and transparency, including

gradients, of an underlying image. You can use either a vector object or bitmap image as the masking object.

In addition, you can sample colors in a bitmap using the Eyedropper tool. You can pick out an exact pixel to use to match colors throughout your document.

Fireworks also includes built-in Creative commands on the Commands menu that enhance your ability to modify an image, from adding objects such as arrowheads, to manipulating pixels in new ways using commands like Twist and Fade.

Tools You'll Use

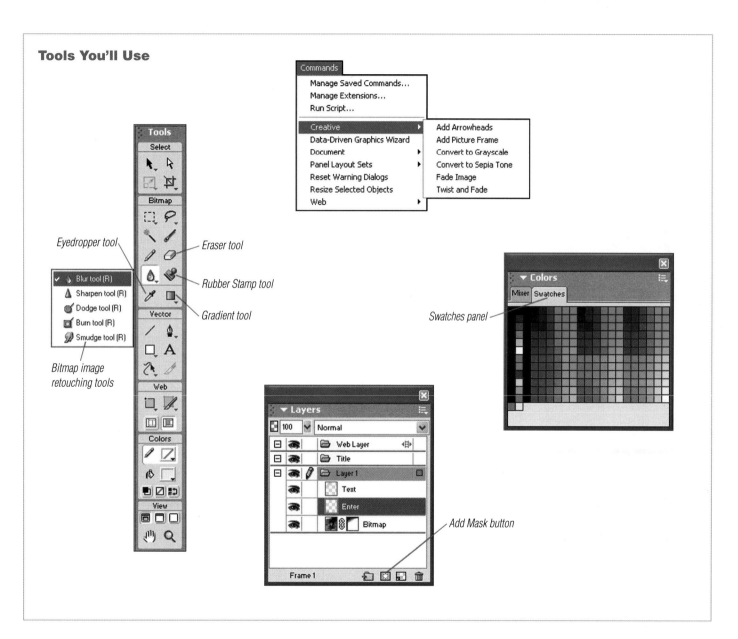

Eyedropper tool

Eraser tool

Rubber Stamp tool

Gradient tool

Bitmap image
retouching tools

Blur tool (R)
Sharpen tool (R)
Dodge tool (R)
Burn tool (R)
Smudge tool (R)

Commands

Manage Saved Commands...
Manage Extensions...
Run Script...

Creative
Data-Driven Graphics Wizard
Document
Panel Layout Sets
Reset Warning Dialogs
Resize Selected Objects
Web

Add Arrowheads
Add Picture Frame
Convert to Grayscale
Convert to Sepia Tone
Fade Image
Twist and Fade

Swatches panel

Add Mask button

ALTER PIXELS ON A BITMAP

What You'll Do

In this lesson, you will use various bitmap tools to lighten, darken, rubber stamp, erase, and blur pixels in your document.

Understanding the Image-Retouching Tools

The bitmap image-retouching tools in Fireworks consist of the Rubber Stamp, Blur, Smudge, Sharpen, Dodge, and Burn tools. They are referred to as retouching tools because the tools change the appearance of the bitmap pixels with which they come in contact.

The Blur tool and the Sharpen tool change the focus of the pixels you touch in opposite ways. The overall effect is similar to commands on the Filters menu or in the Effects section of the Property inspector. However, with those commands, you apply the effect to large areas of an image or the entire image. The Blur and Sharpen tools allow you to have precise control over which pixels in a bitmap are affected and to what extent. You can also set the intensity with which you blur or sharpen each area of an image, as shown in Figure D-1.

Another set of companion tools are the Dodge and Burn tools, which lighten or darken areas of an image, respectively. The Range setting that is available on the Property inspector when you use these tools has three options that allow you to target specific color areas: Shadows has an impact on the dark regions; Highlights has an impact on the lighter regions; and Midtones has an impact on the shades in between the two. The Exposure setting works much like the exposure setting on a camera: it determines how much light is applied to the selected area.

> **QUICKTIP**
> You can switch between the Dodge and Burn tools by pressing and holding [Alt] (Win) or [option] (Mac) as you drag the pointer.

Using the Smudge tool has much the same effect as blending colors on an artist's canvas. The colors are blended in whatever direction the pointer is moving. In addition to adjusting the tip size, shape, edge, and pressure of the Smudge tool, you can select two other options to enhance the effect. You can select a smudge color from the color pop-up window that initiates each new smudge, and you can select the Use Entire Document check box to smudge using colors from every object on every layer. Figure D-1 shows sample applications of the Blur tool and Smudge tool.

QUICKTIP

The Blur, Sharpen, Dodge, Burn, and Smudge tools are all part of the same bitmap image tool group on the Tools panel, which you can select by pressing [R]. You can adjust the tip size, shape, and edge for each of these tools.

Using the Rubber Stamp Tool and the Eraser Tool

The Rubber Stamp tool and the Eraser tool also work with pixels in opposite ways. The Rubber Stamp tool allows you to replicate pixels from one area on the bitmap and stamp them onto another. You can use the Edge setting to blend the area selected by the tool and the image area together. Unlike the other image-retouching tools that you simply drag on the canvas, using the Rubber Stamp tool is a two-step process. First, you select the area you want to replicate, and then you stamp the desti-nation area with the selected pixels. The Eraser tool erases pixels on the selected image and reveals the pixels of an underly-ing image based on the properties you set

in the Property inspector. For example, you can adjust the brush size and shape, edge softness, and opacity of the eraser. You can think of the Eraser tool as changing the opacity of the erased pixels to zero or what-ever opacity setting you choose, which has the net effect of making them transparent, but not physically separating them from the image. For example, if you bisect an image by erasing pixels across the breadth of the image and then move the object, it moves as a whole, just with a transparent line in the middle. Figure D-2 shows sam-ple applications of the Eraser tool and Rubber Stamp tool.

FIGURE D-1
Blur tool and Smudge tool examples

Blur tool

Smudge tool

FIGURE D-2
Eraser tool and Rubber Stamp tool examples

Eraser tool

Rubber Stamp tool

Use the Burn tool to darken pixels

1. Open fwd_1.png, then save it as **se_asia.png**.

2. Press and hold the Blur tool 🔘 on the Tools panel, then click the Burn tool. 🔘

3. Enter the properties shown in Figure D-3.

4. Position the pointer on the ground by the plants, then drag the pointer to burn all of the ground, as shown in Figure D-4.

   The pixels of the dirt appear darker.

   > TIP As long as you press and hold the mouse button, the Dodge and Burn tools will not continue to lighten or darken pixels, regardless of how many times you sweep over the same area with the pointer. If you release the mouse button and then press it again, sweeping over the area again will lighten or darken the area with the selected exposure setting.

You darkened the pixels in the image using the Burn tool.

FIGURE D-3
Properties for the Burn tool

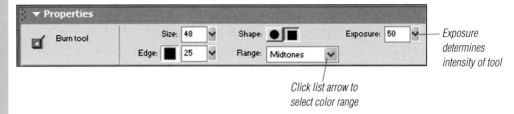

Exposure determines intensity of tool

Click list arrow to select color range

FIGURE D-4
Burning pixels

Burned pixels

Drag pointer to burn dirt a darker color

Pixels to be burned

Understanding the origin of Burn and Dodge

The terms "burn" and "dodge" are not unique to computer graphics—their source is traditional photography. While this makes for an interesting etymological note, the words and their namesake tools are not exactly intuitive when you see them on the Tools panel. Burning makes a print darker (in photographic printing after the main exposure, you would give extra exposure of light to the area you wanted to darken, often by using a piece of cardboard that has a hole in it). Dodging lightens an area (you shade the area from light, often with a solid piece of cardboard). The Dodge and Burn tool icons illustrate this concept.

FIGURE D-5
Positioning the Dodge tool

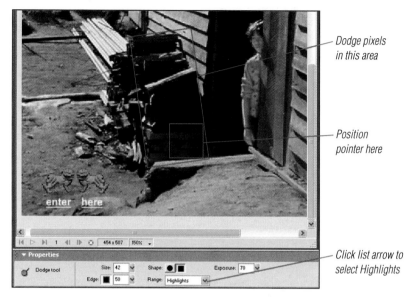

Dodge pixels
in this area

Position
pointer here

Click list arrow to
select Highlights

FIGURE D-6
Results of the Dodge tool

Dodged pixels

Lesson 1 Alter Pixels on a Bitmap

111

Use the Rubber Stamp tool

1. Click the Zoom tool on the Tools panel, then click the red wrapper on the ground until you can see it in detail. 🔍

   TIP To return to 100% magnification at any time, press [Ctrl][1] (Win) or [command][1] (Mac).

2. Click the Rubber Stamp tool on the Tools panel. 🖋

3. Enter the properties and position the pointer in the location shown in Figure D-7.

   TIP To repeatedly stamp with the initially selected area, select the Source Aligned check box.

4. Press and hold [Alt] (Win) or [option] (Mac), then click the mouse button to select pixels.

   The cross hair remains over the selected area.

5. Position the pointer over the red wrapper, then click the mouse to stamp over the red pixels, as shown in Figure D-8.

   The red pixels are covered by the selected area.

   TIP You can stamp the area as many times as necessary until the red pixels have been covered.

You replicated the pixels in one area and stamped them onto another.

FIGURE D-7
Properties for the Rubber Stamp tool

Place pointer over area to be sampled

Your magnification may vary

Click Source Aligned check box to stamp with the same area

FIGURE D-8
Results of stamping

Stamped pixels cover pixels of the red wrapper

FIGURE D-9

Properties for the Eraser tool

FIGURE D-10

Results of the Eraser tool

Erased pixels

FIGURE D-11

Properties for the Blur tool

Click list arrow
to set amount
of blurring

FIGURE D-12

Results of blurring

Blurred area

Use the Eraser tool to remove pixels

1. Drag the scroll bars so that the Enter object is centered in the document window.

2. Click the Pointer tool, then click the Enter object on the Layers panel to select it. 🖈

3. Click the Eraser tool on the Tools panel, then enter the properties shown in Figure D-9. ⌀

4. Drag the pointer over the right foo-dog and "here" text to erase them.

   The pixels of the dog and text are erased, revealing the pixels of the underlying ground.

5. Click the Set magnification pop-up menu on the bottom of the document window, then click 100%. 100% ▾

6. Compare your image to Figure D-10.

You erased pixels on the Enter object using the Eraser tool.

Use the Blur tool

1. Click the Pointer tool on the Tools panel, then click the Bitmap object to select it. 🖈

2. Press and hold the Dodge tool 🔍, click the Blur tool on the Tools panel, then enter the properties shown in Figure D-11. 💧

3. Drag the pointer over the plants in the background, then compare your image to Figure D-12.

4. Save your work.

You blurred pixels in the image.

WORK WITH MASKS

What You'll Do

In this lesson, you will create bitmap and vector masks, and disable, enable, and apply a mask.

Understanding Masks

In the real world, a mask can hide any object, or control what areas it does reveal, but your masking flexibility is limited by the materials at your disposal. Because Fireworks is both a vector and a bitmap application, you have more masking options. By applying different masking techniques and adjusting properties, you can make your masks quite creative and artistic. Fireworks offers several methods for applying a mask, and you may want to experiment with techniques and combinations before settling on the right one for your purposes. One efficient use of a mask is to cover the parts of an image you do not want to appear while preserving the bitmap as a whole.

One of the many advantages of using masks in Fireworks is that you make all your changes on the mask, not on the source image. That way, you can modify the mask as you wish—the source image is undisturbed. Fireworks masks are always editable, all the time. Regardless of the technique you use to create a mask, you can edit, replace, disable, apply, or delete any mask you create. When you add a mask to an object, a **mask thumbnail** appears next to the object thumbnail on the Layers panel. When the mask is selected, it is surrounded by a yellow box. You can select just the mask or just the object, or both, depending on your editing needs.

Working with Bitmap and Vector Masks

You can use a bitmap or a vector object as either the **mask object** or the object being masked. For example, you might use a **bitmap mask** to create a mist or fog effect as the mask, setting the transparency of the mask object to determine the visibility and appearance of the object(s) beneath it. You can also use the outline of a bitmap object to mask the objects beneath it.

QUICKTIP

To use the outline of a bitmap object as the mask object, select the objects, point to Mask on the Modify menu, click Group as Mask, select the mask thumbnail, then select Alpha Channel as the Mask to option on the Property inspector. The alpha channel is the opaque area of the object.

When you use a vector object as the mask object, a different set of masking opportunities presents itself. The **vector mask** is the shape through which the underlying object is viewed, and you can include the fill and stroke of the vector object. You use the shape of the vector object to cut or crop the underlying image, just as a metal form can be used to cut a shape in concrete or cookie dough. The underlying object can be a bitmap or vector object. You can also paste an image inside a vector object, such as text. Figure D-13 shows sample bitmap and vector masks and their properties on the Property inspector.

Deleting a mask

You can delete a mask using commands from the Layers panel or by using the Mask command on the Modify menu. Fireworks gives you three options when you choose to delete a mask: You can apply the mask, which eliminates the editability of the mask by creating a solitary bitmap that has the mask incorporated in it. You can discard the mask to remove the mask and any changes you've made to it. Finally, you can cancel the delete operation and return to the state of the mask before you clicked the Delete Mask command. When you disable a mask, you can view or modify the pixels in the unmasked full image.

QUICKTIP

You can convert a vector mask to a bitmap mask by flattening it.

FIGURE D-13
Sample vector and bitmap masks

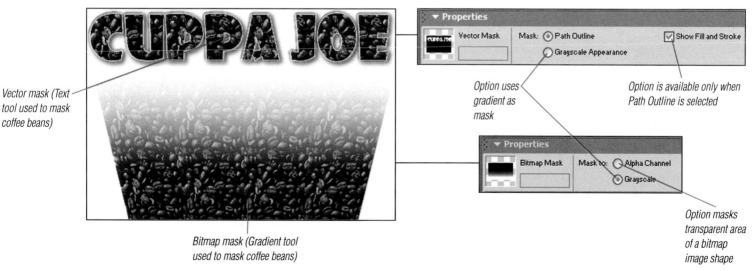

Vector mask (Text tool used to mask coffee beans)

Option uses gradient as mask

Option is available only when Path Outline is selected

Bitmap mask (Gradient tool used to mask coffee beans)

Option masks transparent area of a bitmap image shape

Create a bitmap mask

1. Click the Bitmap object on the Layers panel (if necessary), then click the Add Mask button on the bottom of the Layers panel. ▦

2. Press and hold the Paint Bucket tool 🪣 on the Tools panel, then click the Gradient tool. ▢

3. Click the Fill Color box 🪣▢ on the Property inspector, click the Preset list arrow, click White, Black, then click a blank part of the Fireworks window.

4. Using Figure D-14 as a guide, drag the pointer in the location shown. 🪣

   > TIP You can redraw a gradient as many times as necessary.

5. Compare your image to Figure D-15.

6. Save your work, then close se_asia.png.

You created and applied a bitmap mask.

FIGURE D-14
Applying a bitmap mask

Stop dragging here

Begin dragging here

FIGURE D-15
Applied mask

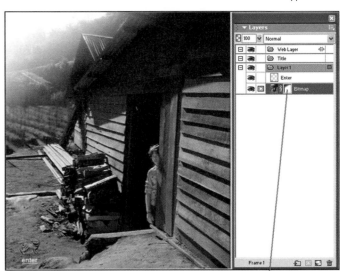

Selected mask has yellow border

Using other mask commands

You can quickly add a mask using reveal and hide commands. To apply a bitmap mask to an entire object, point to Mask on the Modify menu, and then click Reveal All to apply a transparent mask, or click Hide All to apply an opaque mask. Similarly, you can apply a mask to selected pixels, such as a marquee selection: point to Mask on the Modify menu and then click Reveal Selection or Hide Selection.

FIGURE D-16

Results of Paste Inside command

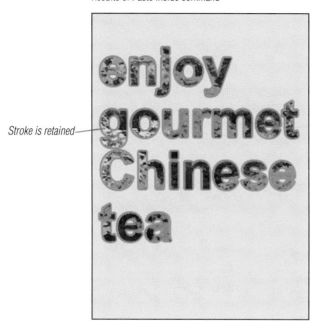

Stroke is retained

Create a vector mask using the Paste Inside command

1. Open fwd_2.png, then save it as **tea.png**.

   TIP Notice that the text has a stroke applied to it.

2. Click the Pointer tool on the Tools panel, click the Bitmap object to select it, click Edit on the menu bar, then click Cut.

3. Click the text object to select it, click Edit on the menu bar, then click Paste Inside.

   The leaves bitmap appears inside the text, which retains the stroke. The two objects are also now grouped as one on the Layers panel.

   TIP You can also press [Ctrl][Shift] V (Win) or [command][Shift] V (Mac) to paste inside.

4. Compare your image to Figure D-16.

You created a vector mask using the Paste Inside command.

Learning about advanced masks

Power users of Fireworks have created tutorials on its most powerful features, including creating masks. For an intensive examination of masks, visit the Macromedia Application Development Center at*www.macromedia.com/desdev* and search on Fireworks masks.

Create a vector mask using the Paste as Mask command

1. Verify that the Bitmap and its mask are selected, click Modify on the menu bar, click Ungroup, then click a blank area outside the canvas to deselect both objects.

   The text and bitmap objects reappear unmasked.

2. Click the text object to select it, click Edit on the menu bar, then click Cut.

3. Click the bitmap object to select it.

4. Click Edit on the menu bar, click Paste as Mask.

   The text masks the bitmap and loses the stroke.

   > TIP   You can also access the Paste as Mask command by pointing to the Mask command on the Modify menu.

5. Click the Add effects button in the Effects section on the Property inspector, point to Shadow and Glow, click Drop Shadow, drag the Softness slider to **5**, then press [Enter] (Win) or [return] (Mac). +.

6. Compare your image to Figure D-17.

You created a vector mask using the Paste as Mask command. You also used a Drop Shadow effect to add impact to your image.

FIGURE D-17
Drop Shadow effect added to results of Paste as Mask command

Stroke no longer appears on text

FIGURE D-18
Disabled mask

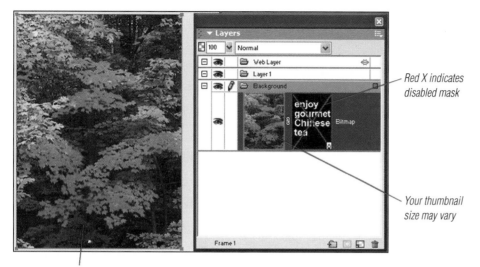

Red X indicates
disabled mask

Your thumbnail
size may vary

Bitmap object
appears without text

FIGURE D-19
Applied mask

Single bitmap with
mask applied to it

1. Verify that the Bitmap and its mask are
selected, click Modify on the menu bar, point
to Mask, then click Disable Mask.

The image is no longer masked and a red X
appears over the mask thumbnail on the
Layers panel.

> TIP   You can disable a mask as long as
> either the mask or the object is selected.

2. Compare your image to Figure D-18.

> TIP   Depending on the thumbnail size
> selected for the Layers panel, the red X may
> not be noticeable.

3. Click the mask thumbnail to select it, which
also enables the mask.

4. Click Modify on the menu bar, point to Mask,
then click Delete Mask.

5. Click Apply when the Apply mask to bitmap
before removing? prompt appears.

The object on the Layers panel appears as a
single bitmap thumbnail without a mask.

6. Compare your image to Figure D-19.

7. Save your work, then close tea.png.

*You disabled, enabled, and applied a mask to an
object. You also converted an object and its mask
into a single bitmap object.*

SAMPLE AND STORE COLOR

What You'll Do

rediscover
south
east
asia

enter

▶ In this lesson, you will select a pixel color from a bitmap image and apply it to a vector object, and then add the color to the Swatches panel.

Using the Eyedropper Tool

Being able to match the colors in your document exactly is very useful. Like its glass and rubber counterpart, the Eyedropper tool can pick up or **sample** a drop of color, which in Web graphics is a pixel. The Eyedropper tool can sample a single pixel, the average of a 3x3 pixel area, or the average of a 5x5 pixel area. You can use the Eyedropper tool to sample color in any object or image in your document, and designate it as the current stroke, fill, or text color. You can even sample colors throughout the Fireworks program environment, or in any program displayed on your computer screen—including Web pages. Figure D-20 shows a color being sampled in a document.

QUICKTIP

To sample a color outside the Fireworks program environment in another program, in an open window, or on your desktop, press and hold the mouse button, position the pointer over the color you want to sample, then release the mouse button (Win). Macintosh users can use the same sampling technique they use within Fireworks.

Understanding how color works on the Web

The colors in your image correspond to the colors in a color palette—in other words, only the colors defined in the color palette appear in your graphic. However, not all the colors in your images or the colors that you choose from a color pop-up window will appear the way you expect them to when displayed on the Web.

Adding Sampled Colors to the Swatches Panel

The Swatches panel contains colors from the active Fireworks color palette. Once you sample a color, you can add it to the Swatches panel so that you can access it at any time. You can also edit and delete swatches in the Swatches panel. Because the Swatches panel is not document-specific, once you add a color swatch, you can use it in all your documents.

QUICKTIP

To increase the size of the color swatches in the Swatches panel, drag any of the corner handles to increase the size of the panel.

The prevailing assumption is that computer monitors can display 256 colors; however, the vast majority of monitors can display many more, up to approximately 16,777,000 colors. Depending on your browser and computer platform, the appearance of a color may vary considerably. You can ensure that your colors will display correctly and consistently without dithering by selecting websafe colors. There are 216 websafe colors. You can apply the Web 216 color palette to ensure that your colors will be approximately the same on Windows, Macintosh, and Unix platforms. You can also apply a WebSnap Adaptive palette, which converts colors to a close equivalent on the Web 216 palette.

FIGURE D-20
Sampling a color

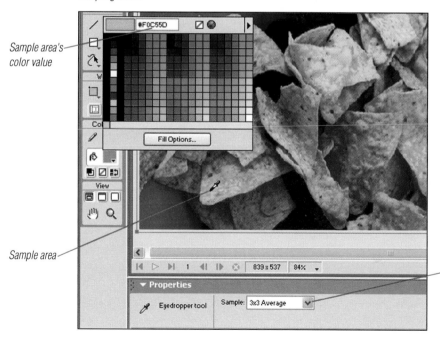

Sample area's color value

Sample area

Click list arrow to select number of pixels to be averaged

Sample a color using the Eyedropper tool

1. Open se_asia.png, then verify that the Info panel is displayed.

   TIP   You can use the Open Recent command on the File menu to see a short list of recently opened files.

2. Click the Text tool on the Tools panel, then enter the properties shown in Figure D-21. **A**

3. Click the upper left corner of the canvas at approximately 20 X/52 Y, then type the following words, each on a separate line: **rediscover south east asia**.

4. Click the Eyedropper tool on the Tools panel, click the Sample pop-up on the Property inspector, then click 5x5 Average.

5. Click the shirtsleeve on the canvas at approximately 290 X/346 Y.

   The text changes to the shade of red representing the average of all of the shades of red displayed in the 5x5 pixel area.

6. Click the Pointer tool on the Tools panel, click the Add effects button on the Property inspector, point to Shadow and Glow, then click Glow.

(continued)

FIGURE D-21

Properties for the Text tool

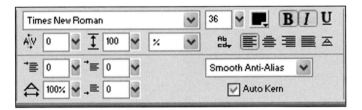

— Text color changes
to sampled color

7. Click the Halo (Win) or Glow (Mac) offset list arrow, drag the slider to **1**, click the Color box 🖐 🔲, double-click the hexadecimal text box, type **#FFCCFF**, then press [Enter] (Win) or [return] (Mac).

8. Click Select on the menu bar, click Deselect, then compare your image to Figure D-22.

You sampled a color and applied it to text. You also used a Glow effect to add impact to your text.

Add a swatch to the Swatches panel

1. Click Window on the menu bar, then click Swatches to display the Swatches panel.

   TIP You can also open the Swatches panel by pressing [Ctrl][F9] (Win) or [command][F9] (Mac).

2. Position the pointer in the blank bottom portion of the panel, then click the mouse to add the swatch. 🖐

   The red swatch is added to the bottom of the Swatches panel.

   TIP To delete a swatch, press and hold [Ctrl] (Win) or [command] (Mac), position the pointer over the swatch, then click the mouse. ✂

3. Compare your Swatches panel to Figure D-23.

4. Save your work, then close se_asia.png.

You added the sampled swatch to the Swatches panel.

Your swatches
may vary

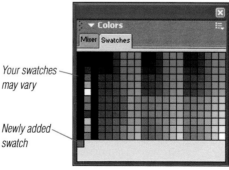

Newly added
swatch

USE THE CREATIVE COMMANDS TO CHANGE IMAGES

What You'll Do

In this lesson, you will apply the Add Picture Frame and Twist and Fade Creative commands.

Using the Creative Commands

Fireworks contains built-in programs designed by third parties that work seamlessly in the application. For example you may have already experimented with Alien Skin effects and filters. The Creative commands add even more variety to your Fireworks projects. Sample applications of two of the Creative commands are shown in Figure D-24.

The Add Arrowheads command allows you to add an arrowhead to any open path you've drawn. For example, you can draw a line with the Line tool or plot a path with the Pen tool, and then apply any of 17 different shapes to the start or end of the arrow.

The Add Picture Frame command combines document information with fill and effect settings from the Property inspector You can select a pattern for the picture frame from any of the patterns available on the Property inspector as a fill or texture.

Using the Twist and Fade command

The Twist and Fade command taxes your computer's memory and processing resources considerably. The more objects and steps you add, the greater the demand. You may find it useful to close other open programs or restart your computer before you experiment with this feature. For additional information and updates to the Twist and Fade extension, visit the creators' Web site: www.phireworx.com.

You can convert the colors of any object in your document to grayscale or sepia. The Convert to Grayscale and Convert to Sepia commands only affect the selected objects so that you can have color and monochromatic images in the same document.

The Fade Image command applies one of eight available vector masks to your selected object or objects. Each mask is already designed to fade your selected object in a different distance and direction. Styles choices include fade-ins from different sides in rectangular or elliptical shape. You can apply the command to any selected object(s) in your document.

The Twist and Fade command is an easy way to radically change an object. This command duplicates the selected object, and then resizes, spaces, rotates, and changes the opacity of the duplicates. The results, as shown in the sample in Figure D-24, can be remarkable.

QUICKTIP

To make it appear that the objects fade out as they are duplicated and twisted, click Options in the Twist and Fade dialog box, then click the fade opacity option.

FIGURE D-24
Sample Creative commands

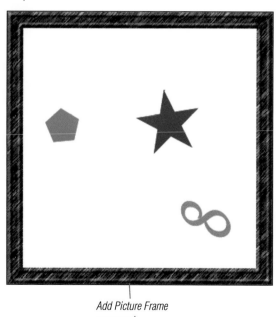

Add Picture Frame
command

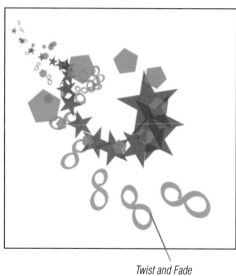

Twist and Fade
command

Apply the Twist and Fade command

1. Open tea.png.

2. Import leaves.png, then position the leaves in the location shown in Figure D-25.

3. Click Commands on the menu bar, point to Creative, then click Twist and Fade.

   The Twist and Fade dialog box opens. You can preview the effects before you apply them.

4. Drag the sliders to the locations shown in Figure D-26, then click apply.

   The leaves appear to be falling and twisting.

5. Compare your image to Figure D-27.

You applied the Twist and Fade Creative command to an object.

FIGURE D-25
Positioning leaves on the canvas

Move leaves here

FIGURE D-26
Twist and Fade dialog box

Number of duplicate bitmap images

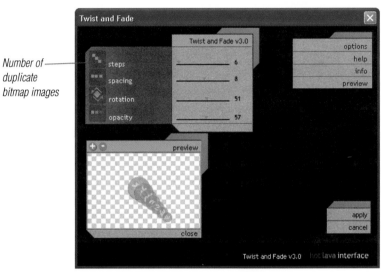

FIGURE D-27
Results of Twist and Fade command

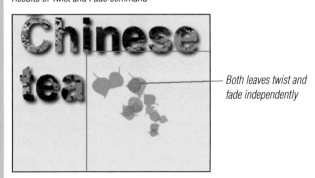

Both leaves twist and fade independently

FIGURE D-28

Results of Add Picture Frame command

Leaves pattern in
picture frame

1. Click Commands on the menu bar, point to Creative, then click Add Picture Frame.

   The Add Picture Frame dialog box opens.

2. Click the Select a pattern list arrow, scroll down the list, click Leaves, double-click the Frame Size text box, then type **12**.

3. Click OK, then compare your image to Figure D-28.

   The Add Picture Frame command automatically applies the frame to the entire document, regardless of the object selected. A new layer, Frame, is added to the Layers panel.

   | TIP   Maximize the document window, if necessary.

4. Save your work, then close tea.png.

You added a picture frame and chose its size and pattern.

Darken and lighten pixels.

1. Open fwd_3.png, then save it as **goats.png**.
2. Verify that the Info panel is open.
3. Select the Burn tool and set the following properties: Brush tip size: 70, Edge: 100, Square brush tip, Range: Highlights, Exposure: 35.
4. Verify that the habitat layer is selected, darken the pixels of the top rock ledge in one motion, from the trees to just before the standing goat at the top of the canvas.
5. Select the standing goat to the upper right of the picture, select the Dodge tool, and then set the following properties: Brush tip size: 20, Edge: 100, Round brush tip, Range: Midtones, Exposure: 50.
6. Lighten the pixels of the goat at the top of the canvas.
7. Save your work.

Replicate and stamp pixels.

1. Select the Rubber Stamp tool and set the following properties: Size: 100, Edge: 78, Source Aligned selected.

2. Make sure the Habitat object is selected, then select pixels in the rock face in between the large walking goat and the baby goats on the left side of the canvas.
3. Stamp the pixels over the large goat to the left so that it no longer appears. (*Hint*: You can drag the pointer or click repeatedly.)
4. Save your work.

Erase and blur pixels.

1. Select the Eraser tool and set the following properties: Size: 45, Edge: 100, Round eraser, Opacity: 60%.
2. Make sure that the Goat in the wild object is selected, then erase the blue sky to the left of the goat at the top of the canvas. (*Hint*: Use Figure D-29 as a guide.)
3. Select the Blur tool and set the following properties: Size: 48, Edge: 28, Round brush tip, Intensity: 30.
4. Blur the trees at the top of the canvas.
5. Save your work.

Create a bitmap mask.

1. Add a mask to the Habitat layer using the Add Mask button on the Layers panel.
2. Select the Gradient tool and a Linear gradient that is White, Black.
3. Place the pointer slightly below the ledge where the baby goats are standing, then drag the pointer to the bottom of the canvas.
4. Save your work.

Create vector masks.

1. Open fwd_4.png, then save it as **perCents.png**.
2. Create a mask that pastes the bitmap inside the text. (*Hint*: Cut the bitmap.)
3. Ungroup the object and mask.
4. Create a mask that pastes the text as a mask. (*Hint*: Cut the text.)
5. Save your work.

Disable, enable, and apply a mask.

1. Disable the mask.
2. Enable the mask.

3. Delete the mask and apply changes.

4. Save your work.

Sample and store color.

1. Make sure the goats.png document is active, then show and select the Text object.

2. Select the Eyedropper tool, then sample the baby goat with a 5x5 average at approximately 378 X/235 Y.

3. Display the Swatches panel and add the swatch to the panel.

4. Compare your image to Figure D-29.

5. Save your work, then close goats.png.

Use Create commands.

1. Make sure that the bitmap object is selected, then apply a twist and fade command and set the following properties: steps: 5, spacing: 14, rotation: 4, opacity: 79.

2. Apply a picture frame and set the following properties: pattern: Flames, Frame Size: 10.

3. Compare your image to Figure D-29.

4. Save your work, then close perCents.png.

FIGURE D-29
Completed Skills Review

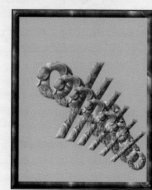

To boost morale, your company is going to hold a treasure hunt. Your division was assigned the lowest morale rating, so management has decided you should coordinate the event. Your first step is to announce the treasure hunt in an e-mail message.

1. Obtain images that pertain to a treasure hunt and use the one provided. You can obtain images from your computer, from the Internet, from a digital camera, or from scanned media. You can use clipart from the Web that is free for both personal and commercial use (check the copyright information for any such clipart before downloading it).

2. Create a new document and save it as **treasure_hunt.png**.

3. Import **ship.jpg**, and resize it as necessary to fit in your document.

4. Use the images you've obtained to create at least one vector or bitmap mask. (*Hint*: The sailing ship in the sample is a bitmap mask of the ship and a map with the Alpha Channel option selected.)

5. Apply at least one Creative command to the objects. (*Hint*: The arrows were created and twisted using Creative commands.)

6. Create other visual elements using the images you've downloaded, changing their size, color, and other properties as needed.

7. Save your work, then examine the sample shown in Figure D-30.

A local organic food coop is going to feature a produce item each month. They want to include the item in both in-store posters and on their Web page. You're going to develop the intro splash screen, featuring at least two uses of the fruit or veggie. You can choose the produce item of your choice.

1. Obtain images that will fit your theme. You can obtain images from your computer, from the Internet, from a digital camera, or from scanned media. You can use clipart from the Web that is free for both personal and commercial use (check the copyright information for any such clipart before downloading it).

2. Create a new document and save it as **myproduce.png**.

3. Import at least two files into your document or open and select them using the bitmap selection tools.

4. Apply bitmap or vector masks to at least two of the images. (*Hint*: The two coconut images in the sample each have bitmap masks applied to them.)

5. Apply a vector mask to text. (*Hint*: The text has another coconut image pasted inside it.)

6. Use the bitmap retouching tools or sample the colors in the document, as necessary. (*Hint*: Various coconuts have been erased or rubber stamped.)

7. Apply one of the Creative commands to the object of your choice. (*Hint*: The image has the Add Picture Frame command applied to it.)

8. Save your work, then examine the sample shown in Figure D-31.

FIGURE D-31
Completed Project Builder 2

Finding the right images for your project is one of the first steps in creating a good design. Using those images in your design often requires that you change them so that they best convey your intent or message. Because dynamic Web sites are updated frequently to reflect current trends, this page may be different from Figure D-32 when you open it online.

1. Connect to the Internet and go to *www.course.com*. Navigate to the page for this book, click the Student Online Companion, then click the link for this unit.

2. Open a document in a word processor, or open a new Fireworks document, then save the file as **earthtrends**. (*Hint*: You can use the Text tool in Fireworks to answer the questions.)

3. Explore the site and answer the following:
   - Identify the possible order of the images above and below the navigation bar on the Layers panel.
   - Is a masking technique evident? If so, identify.
   - Which images could have been erased, rubber stamped, or sampled?
   - Who is the target audience for this site, and how does the design reinforce that goal?
   - How are photographic images and illustrations used in the site?

   - What changes would you make to this site?

4. Save your work.

FIGURE D-32
Design Project

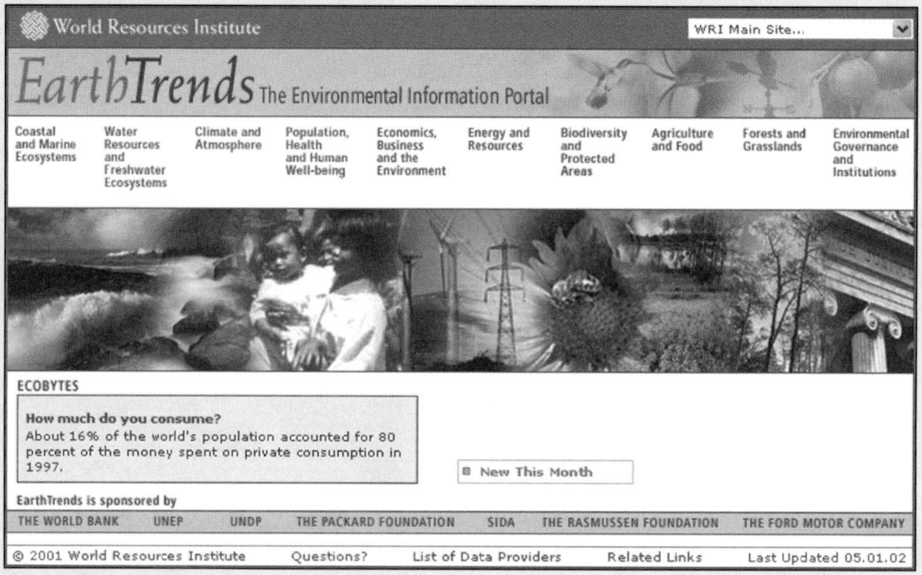

Your group can assign elements of the project to individual members, or work collectively to create the finished product.

Your class on international trading requires your group to create a faux import company and design its Web page. Your group must decide on the country or region, and the wares you'll sell.

1. Obtain images of the country you've chosen or the products you'll sell. You can obtain images from your computer, from the Internet, from a digital camera, or from scanned media. You can use clipart from the Web that is free for both personal and commercial use (check the copyright information for any such clipart before downloading it).

2. Create a new document and save it as **imports.png**.

3. Import the files into your document or open and select them using the bitmap selection tools.

4. Apply a vector or bitmap mask to at least one image. (*Hint*: The lake and building image has a bitmap mask applied to it.)

5. Use the bitmap retouching tools, as necessary. (*Hint*: The trees have been rubber stamped, the building at the left has been blurred, and parts of the images have been erased.)

6. Sample the colors in the document, as necessary. (*Hint*: The title text was sampled using the color of the boat and has an Eye Candy 4000 LE Motion Trail effect applied to it.)

FIGURE D-33
Completed Group Project

7. Apply at least one Creative command to your document. (*Hint*: The lake and building image has been converted to a sepia tone.)

8. Save your work, then examine the sample shown in Figure D-33.

dal lake imports
enter

WORKING WITH INTERACTIVITY

1. Create slices and hotspots.

2. Create links.

3. Create rollovers.

4. Create buttons.

UNIT 7
WORKING WITH INTERACTIVITY

Understanding Web Functionality

One important goal of any Web site is to engage the viewer. Interactivity is one way to accomplish this. Your Web site can change appearance or perform specific tasks based on input from the user. For example, you can set up a graphic to display additional information when a user rolls the mouse over it, or you can design a button that sends the user to another page on your site when the user clicks it. Anyone who has surfed the Web has taken advantage of interactivity. Fireworks makes it easy to add these features to your own site.

You can split your document into manageable or functional pieces by defining individual slices in your document. Once defined, for example, you can optimize each slice separately based on the type of artwork it contains, and how important the image quality is in the exported file. You can also add interactivity that causes something to happen in response to a mouse action. For example, when the mouse pointer moves over a slice, the text can change color, or a drop-down menu or image can appear anywhere on the canvas. Fireworks offers several ways to add behaviors to a slice, depending on the complexity of the behavior or on your work preference. Best of all, you don't need to learn any programming language.

You can use hotspots to link users to Web pages within your Web site or anywhere on the Web. You can apply behaviors to hotspots or use hotspots to enable behaviors.

You can also easily create buttons in your document that aid your visitors in navigating your Web site.

Tools You'll Use

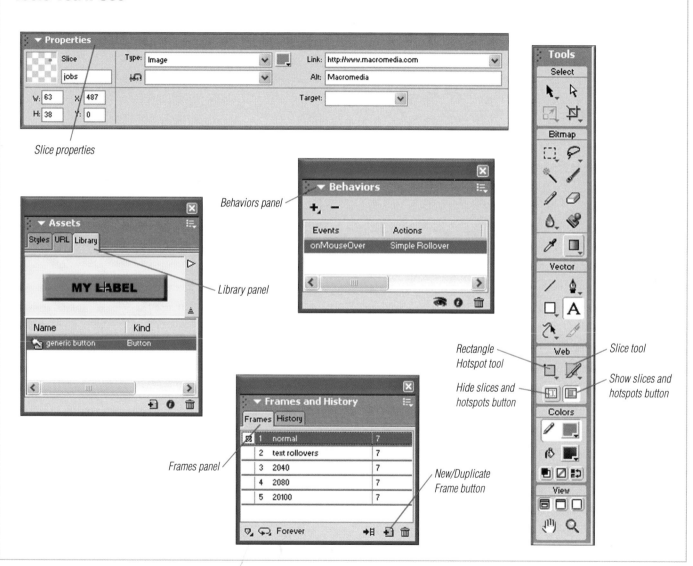

Slice properties

Behaviors panel

Library panel

Rectangle
Hotspot tool

Hide slices and
hotspots button

Frames panel

New/Duplicate
Frame button

Slice tool

Show slices and
hotspots button

CREATE SLICES AND HOTSPOTS

What You'll Do

In this lesson, you will add slices and hotspots to a document.

Understanding Interactivity

On a conceptual level, **interactivity** involves a dialog or an exchange between the user and the Web site. Interactivity can be as simple as a button changing appearance when the user clicks it, or as complex as an animation that is launched each time a user clicks a graphic. Interactivity allows visitors to your Web site to affect its content—input from the user via the mouse or the keyboard can cause something to happen onscreen.

Understanding Slices and Hotspots

You use slices and hotspots to add interactivity to your Web document. Think of a **slice** as containing the image (and any interactivity you've assigned) beneath it. Each slice exports as a separate image file, which offers distinct advantages. You can add individual functionality to each slice, which will help visitors navigate your site and will give the site its unique look and feel. You can also easily update the information associated with individual slices,

especially information that changes frequently, such as a featured product or person. Finally, you can export each slice in the file format that best matches its use in your Web page. For example, you may want to export photographs as JPEGs, or line art as GIFs. To create a slice, you can use the Slice tool or the Polygon Slice tool on the Tools panel and then draw the slice shape you want, or you can select an object and use the Slice command from the Insert command on the Edit menu.

A **hotspot** is an area in your document to which you can assign a Web address, known as a **uniform resource locator (URL)**, or other type of navigational interactivity, such as an e-mail message pop-up window. Hotspots initiate specific actions, such as linking to a new Web page, after being triggered by a mouse action. A hotspot can also initiate a behavior in a browser, such as a swap image pop-up menu. You can create a hotspot of just about any shape, using the Rectangle Hotspot tool, Circle Hotspot tool, or

Polygon Hotspot tool on the Tools panel. You can also create a single hotspot from multiple images. You can apply many of the same options, such as inserting URL links, to both slices and hotspots. The options on the Property inspector change slightly, depending on whether you select a slice or a hotspot. An **image map** is a graphic that has one or more hotspots associated with it. For example, let's assume that you have one large graphic, such as a map, and you'd like users to be able to click on a region of the map for specific information. You can create hotspots over each region, assign a different URL to each hotspot, and then export the graphic containing the hotspots as an HTML file that includes image map data.

QUICKTIP

Before you can use a slice or hotspot tool, first click the Show slices and hotspots button on the Tools panel or click the Show/Hide icon on the Web Layer of the Layers panel.

What precisely is in a slice or a hotspot? Until you export them, they don't actually "contain" anything. During export, Fireworks uses slices and hotspots to write HTML code. The code instructs your Web browser to execute certain commands, such as changing a button color, swapping an image, or linking to a URL.

When slicing, you should try to create neatly spaced slices that emulate a grid pattern, and remember to try to leave no region unsliced. Slicing allows you to optimize and export the areas in your document in pieces. In order to export efficiently, the pieces should fit together well. If you leave gaps in between slices, Fireworks will export additional files, which can increase the number of downloadable files. For optimal functioning, slices should be contiguous (adjacent to each other); if they do overlap, Fireworks will apply the attributes assigned to the topmost slice. The sample document shown in Figure E-1 depicts a document partially sliced, with slices and hotspots turned off and on in a document.

FIGURE E-1
Slices and hotspots in a document

Document as it appears to user

Hotspots have blue overlay

Slice guides

Slices have green overlay

Web Layer contains slices and hotspots

You can use the Pointer tool, the Subselection tool, or the transform tools (Scale, Skew, and Distort) to edit the shape of a hotspot.

Understanding the Web Layer on the Layers Panel

Because slices and hotspots are Web objects, Fireworks stores them on the **Web Layer** of the Layers panel. The Web Layer is always the topmost layer on the Layers panel and you cannot delete it. However, you can create, name, hide, show, and delete objects on the Web Layer just as you do with other objects on the Layers panel.

The names of the slices on the Web Layer determine the name of the image file when you export the slice. Slice names cannot have spaces, uppercase letters, forward slashes, and high ASCII characters. High

ASCII characters extend the basic ASCII set. They include characters and letters from foreign languages and drawing symbols for characters 128 to 156. You can change the default naming convention for all slices by selecting options in the Document Specific tab of the HTML Setup dialog box, available on the File menu. You should refer to Help for additional information before you make changes.

Customizing Slice Overlay and Guide Colors

By default, Fireworks uses a light blue overlay for hotspots, a lime green overlay for slices, and red slice guide lines. Depending on the colors in your document, you may want to change these colors so you can distinguish them more readily (the overlays won't be visible to the user). You can change the hotspot or slice overlay color by selecting a slice or hotspot, and

then clicking the color box on the Property inspector to open the color pop-up window. You can edit guides by opening the Guides dialog box from the Guides command on the View menu to change slice guide color or to hide or show the slice guides. You can change the color of an individual slice or a group of slices, which can help you organize them in your document. Figure E-2 shows how to change slice overlay and guide colors.

You can view slice guides and slice overlays in the Preview, 2-Up, or 4-Up tabs in the document window, although the slice overlay is always seen as a translucent white. Click the Slice Guides command or the Slice Overlay command on the View menu to add or remove the check mark and turn the guides and overlay on or off.

FIGURE E-2
Slice overlay and guide colors

Click color box to change slice guide color

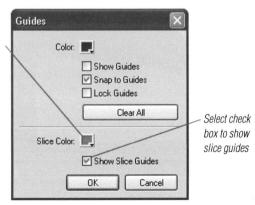

Select check box to show slice guides

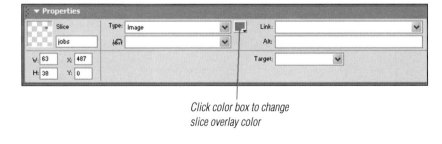

Click color box to change slice overlay color

FIGURE E-3
Newly added slice

Slice covers image

Fireworks autonames slice on Property inspector

Slice is assigned a default name in the Layers panel

Create a slice from an object

1. Open fwe_1.png, then save it as **offworld.png**.

2. Click View on the menu bar, then verify that Slice Guides and Slice Overlay are selected.

3. Verify that the Show slices and hotspots button is selected on the Tools panel.

   Slices and hotspots already inserted in the document are visible.

   | TIP   Objects on the Web Layer appear grayed out until the Show slices and hotspots button is active.

4. Click the Pointer tool on the Tools panel (if necessary), then click the head object on the canvas to select it.

5. Click Edit on the menu bar, point to Insert, click Slice, then compare your image to Figure E-3.

   A slice covers the head and a new Slice object appears at the top of the Web Layer on the Layers panel.

   | TIP   You can also insert a slice by pressing and holding [Alt][Shift][U] (Win) or [option][Shift][U] (Mac).

6. Name the Slice object **head** on the Web Layer.

   The slice name automatically changes in the Edit the object name text box on the Property inspector.

   | TIP   You can also name a slice on the Property inspector.

You inserted a slice on top of an object.

Use the Slice tool to create a slice

1. Click the CONTACT US text on the red navigation bar to select it.

2. Click Edit on the menu bar, point to Insert, click Slice, then compare your image to Figure E-4.

   The slice covers the text only, leaving the remaining part of the navigation bar unsliced.

3. Press [Backspace] (Win) or [delete] (Mac) to delete the slice.

4. Click the Slice tool on the Tools panel, then draw a slice over the CONTACT US navigation bar and text, as shown in Figure E-5.

   | TIP   Zoom in on the object if necessary.

5. Change the name of the Slice object to **contactus** in the Edit the object name text box on the Property inspector, then press [Enter] (Win) or [return] (Mac).

   The slice name automatically changes on the Web Layer on the Layers panel.

You created a slice using the Slice tool.

FIGURE E-4
Slice inserted over text

Slice covers text

FIGURE E-5
Drawing a slice with the Slice tool

Draw slice over text and navigation bar

Remaining blue   Text slice guide
area to be sliced

FIGURE E-7

Results of resizing slice

title: GIF

Slice covers   Drag slice to be
entire area   even with existing
                      slice guides

1. Click the Pointer tool on the Tools panel, then click the Off This World title text to select the slice, as shown in Figure E-6. ↖

   The slice guidelines created by the text slice are visible. You will extend the slice to cover the remaining blue area above the words Off This World.

2. Click View on the menu bar, point to Guides, then verify that Snap to Guides is not selected.

3. Drag the left sizing handles to the left side of the canvas.

   Resizing a slice or polygon is similar to resizing any object on the canvas.

   | TIP   You can drag the slice guides of any
   | slice to change its size or position.

4. Drag the other sizing handles until the slice covers the upper blue area, then compare your image to Figure E-7.

   | TIP   Slices should align with other slices.

You edited a slice to cover an area.

Create a hotspot with the Circle Hotspot tool

1. Click the Show/Hide Layer icon next to the planetback slice object on the Web Layer to hide it. 👁

2. Click the Pointer tool on the Tools panel (if necessary), then click the planet object on the canvas to select it. 🖰

3. Press and hold the Rectangle Hotspot tool 🔲 on the Tools panel, then click the Circle Hotspot tool. 🔵

4. Draw a circular hotspot around the WHO'S PLAYING text, as shown in Figure E-8.

   | TIP   Use the arrow keys to align the hotspot.

5. Change the name of the Hotspot object to **who**.

You created a circular hotspot.

FIGURE E-8

Results of the Circle Hotspot tool

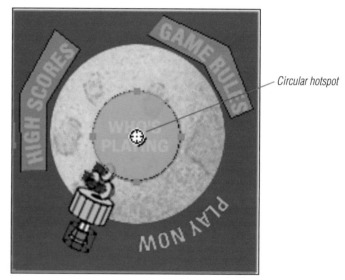

Circular hotspot

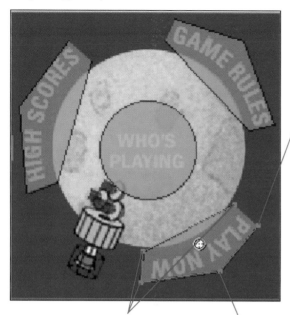

Begin clicking here

Click remaining
points in succession

Click next point
in this direction

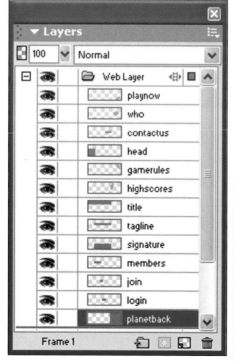

Use the Polygon Hotspot tool

1. Press and hold the Circle Hotspot tool ⬭ on the Tools panel, then click the Polygon Hotspot tool. ⬡

   TIP   You can use the Polygon Slice tool to create a polygon slice in the same manner. ✎

2. Click the canvas in the locations and direction shown in Figure E-9 to create a polygon hotspot.

   A polygon hotspot covers the text, but does not touch the other hotspots so that the links will be distinct.

3. Change the name of the hotspot to **playnow**.

4. Click the Show/Hide Layer icon next to the planetback slice object on the Web Layer to show it. ☐

5. Compare your Web Layer on the Layers panel to Figure E-10.

6. Save your work, then close offworld.png.

You created a polygon hotspot.

CREATE LINKS

What You'll Do

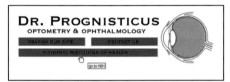

 In this lesson, you will add relative, absolute, and e-mail links to slices, add alternate text to the links, and preview the links in Fireworks and in a Web browser.

Assigning a URL to a Slice or a Hotspot

After you create a Web object, you can assign a URL to it and link it to a Web page. For example, you can select a hotspot in the document and enter a URL and other options in the Property inspector. You can insert a URL in the Link text box, or select a URL from a previously entered address or a selected URL library. When a user clicks the link in a Web browser, the browser will navigate to that Web page. If you enter **alternate text** in the Alt text box on the Property inspector, it will appear when you position the mouse pointer over a slice or hotspot. Alternate text resembles a tool tip in Fireworks—the text that appears when you hold the mouse over a tool on the Tools panel. Note, however, that alternate text behaves differently (or not at all) depending on your browser and computer platform. In some Web browsers, this text may appear as the linked URL is loading in the browser. Alternate text also appears if

graphics are not turned on in a Web browser and can be crucial for visually impaired Web surfers. For example, if the user has a screen reader to interpret pages, the reader will read the alternate text out loud. Without the alternate text, the screen reader has nothing to read and the user does not know that the image exists.

You can determine how the linked Web page will be displayed in the browser by selecting an option in the Target text box. For example, the Web page can open in a separate window, or replace the current Web page. Target options are shown in Figure E-11 and described in detail below.

- **_blank** opens the link in a new browser window (unnamed)
- **_parent** opens the link in the parent frameset (the Web page that joins the frame pages together) of the current frame
- **_self** replaces the link in either the current frame or browser window
- **_top** opens the link in the full browser window, replacing all frames

146

You can assign different types of URLs as links. An **absolute URL** is fixed and is the full and exact address of a Web page. Use absolute URLs when linking to a Web page outside of your Web site. A **relative URL** is a link based on its location as it relates to the current page in the Web site's folder. You can use a relative URL to link to a page within your Web site. You can also create a **mailto URL** to open an e-mail address window.

Accessing URLs

You may want to add the same URL to several slices or hotspots in different documents, such as a Home button. Fireworks stores each URL you enter in the Current URL list in the URL panel and displays it on the Property inspector. You can use the URL panel to store often-used URLs, or delete and edit URLs. Once you open a document that contains a URL list, you can access these addresses for every document you open during the *current* editing session. If you add a URL to a library, you can access it at any time and in any document. You can add individual URLs to the main URLs.htm library, create your own **libraries** (such as related groups of URLs), and import URLs from a Netscape Navigator Bookmarks file or from an Internet Explorer Favorites file.

Understanding Preview Options

When you add interactivity such as a URL link to a slice, you can preview the mouse action change on the Preview tab of the document window. The Preview tab displays the document as it would appear in a Web browser, using the current optimization settings. To actually link to the URL and view alternate text, you will need to preview your document in a Web browser. Fireworks allows you to preview a document in up to two different browsers. Depending on the computer and the browser, your Web document may appear and function differently. It's a good idea to preview your Web page using different settings on different systems.

FIGURE E-11

Link properties on the Property inspector

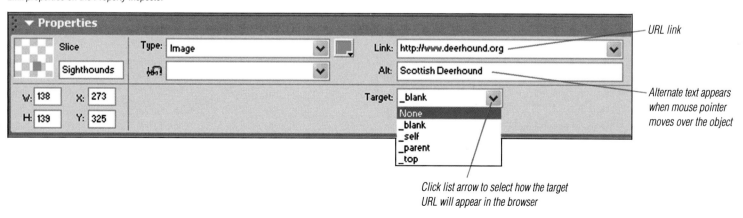

URL link

Alternate text appears when mouse pointer moves over the object

Click list arrow to select how the target URL will appear in the browser

Assign a relative and absolute link to slices

1. Open fwe_2.png, then save it as **eyedoc.png**.

2. Click the Show slices and hotspots button on the Tools panel (if necessary). 🔲

3. Click the Pointer tool on the Tools panel, then click the SEARCH OUR SITE slice to select it. ↖

4. Click the Link text box on the Property inspector, type **searchpage.htm**, then press [Enter] (Win) or [return] (Mac).

   TIP When published, the html file referenced by a relative link is in the same folder as the current html file.

5. Click the Alt text box, type **search our site**, press [Enter] (Win) or [return] (Mac), then compare your Property inspector to Figure E-12.

6. Click the NATIONAL INSTITUTES OF HEALTH slice to select it.

7. Click the Link text box on the Property inspector, type **http://www.nih.gov/**, then press [Enter] (Win) or [return] (Mac).

   TIP Once you add a link, you can assign it to another slice or hotspot by selecting a Web object, clicking the Link list arrow, and then clicking the link you want.

8. Click the Alt text box, type **go to NIH**, then press [Enter] (Win) or [return] (Mac).

9. Click the Target list arrow, then click _blank.

   The URL will open in a new browser window.

You assigned links to slices and set alternate text and a target.

FIGURE E-12
Entering alternate text

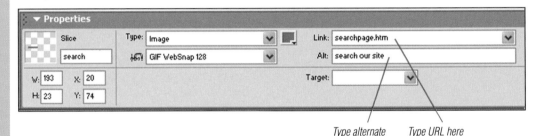

Type alternate text here   Type URL here

1. Click the Preview tab on the document window.

   The current slice appears without a white translucent slice over it.

2. Click the Hide slices and hotspots button on the Tools panel. 🔲

3. Move the mouse pointer over the SEARCH OUR SITE and NATIONAL INSTITUTES OF HEALTH objects, then compare your image to Figure E-13.

   | TIP   Alternate text is not visible on the Preview tab.

4. Click File on the menu bar, point to Preview in Browser, then click the first browser in the list to open the primary browser.

   | TIP   You can press [F12] to open the primary browser. Press [Ctrl][F12] (Win) or [command][F12] (Mac) to open the secondary browser.

(continued)

FIGURE E-13
Preview in Fireworks

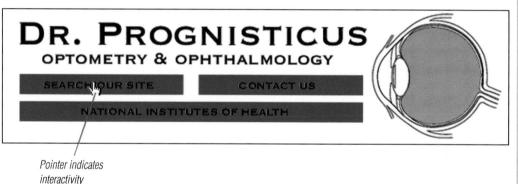

Pointer indicates interactivity

5. Move the mouse pointer over the SEARCH OUR SITE and NATIONAL INSTITUTES OF HEALTH objects, then compare your image to Figure E-14.

The alternate text is visible when the mouse pointer moves over the objects.

| TIP Depending on your browser, alternate text may not be visible.

6. Click the NATIONAL INSTITUTES OF HEALTH object.

If you are online, the browser opens the home page of the National Institutes of Health in a new browser window.

7. Close your browser windows.

You previewed the document in Fireworks and in your primary browser.

FIGURE E-14
Preview in a Web browser

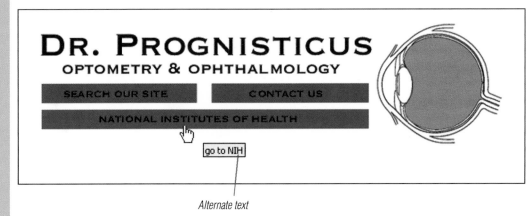

Alternate text

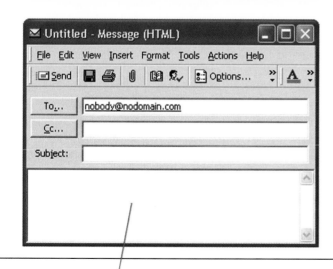

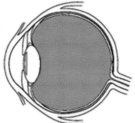

E-mail message window

1. Click the Original tab on the document window
2. Click the Show slices and hotspots button on the Tools panel.
3. Click the contact slice on the Layers panel to select it.
4. Click the Link text box on the Property inspector, type **mailto:nobody@nodomain.com**, then press [Enter] (Win) or [return] (Mac).
5. Click the Alt text box, type **contact us**, then press [Enter] (Win) or [return] (Mac).
6. Preview your image in your browser, move the mouse pointer over the CONTACT US link, then click the object.

    A new Untitled e-mail message window opens addressed to nobody@nodomain.com.
7. Compare your image to Figure E-15, close the e-mail window without saving, then close your browser.

    | TIP   If prompted to save changes, click No.
8. Save your work, then close eyedoc.png.

You assigned an e-mail message window link to a slice.

CREATE ROLLOVERS

What You'll Do

 In this lesson, you will create rollovers for different slice objects.

Understanding Rollovers

In a basic Web page, graphics often change appearance in response to a mouse action—more specifically, one graphic is often swapped for another graphic when you click it or roll over it with the mouse. In Fireworks, a rollover contains a behavior. A **rollover** is a graphic element in a Web page that changes appearance when you trigger it with the mouse. The trigger can be a roll or a click and the result can occur anywhere on the Web page. A **disjoint rollover** is a rollover that swaps an image in a different part of the screen than where you triggered it. In order to create a rollover, you need to coordinate a few items: first, you need to create at least two images and at least one new frame, then create a slice over the image to be swapped. Finally, add an action that results in a change in appearance.

You create a rollover action by adding a behavior to a slice, button, or hotspot. A **behavior** is a preset piece of JavaScript code that consists of an **event trigger** (such as a mouse click on an object) that causes an **action** (such as text changing color or a photograph appearing). **JavaScript** is a Web-scripting language that interacts with HTML code to create interactive content. You can think of behaviors as the means by which Fireworks encapsulates JavaScript so you can easily add them to Web objects.

Fireworks provides different ways to add a behavior: You can add a behavior from the Behaviors panel, drag and drop a behavior onto a slice, or write your own JavaScript. The Behaviors panel contains five main behavior groups, ranging from a simple rollover to a pop-up menu and navigation bar, as shown in Figure E-16. Dragging and dropping from a slice or hotspot onto another slice is the fastest way to add a behavior. When you add a behavior to a slice or a hotspot, a **behavior handle** appears at the center of the object. You can drag a behavior handle and drop a rollover behavior onto the same slice or onto a different slice. A blue behavior line extends from the behavior handle to the top left of the affected slice, indicating that you've applied a behavior to the slice. You can use the drag and drop behavior to attach a behavior to one or more slices, and to easily swap an image in a rollover.

Usually, you create two images for a rollover: one for the event trigger, or *before* version, and another copy of the object as the action, or *after* version.

Using the Frames Panel for Behaviors

The Frames panel contains the frames for your document. Fireworks uses **frames** to house various rollover and button state images and to play animation (which you'll learn about in the next unit). By default, each document has one frame, Frame 1, which contains the images that appear when a user first opens the Web page. In order to function, a rollover requires at least one additional frame. For example, in a simple rollover, the original image appears in Frame 1, and the "after" image appears in Frame 2. After you create a

behavior, you can modify or move the images in your document without affecting the behavior. You can edit the objects that lie beneath a slice or hotspot by hiding the slice or hotspot before you edit the object. Figure E-17 shows the progression of a simple rollover.

QUICKTIP

You can also edit an object while slices and hotspots are displayed by clicking and holding the Pointer tool on the Tools panel and then clicking the Select Behind tool.

FIGURE E-16
Behaviors panel

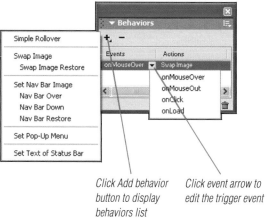

Click Add behavior button to display behaviors list

Click event arrow to edit the trigger event

FIGURE E-17
Progression of a simple rollover

Original (before) image in Frame 1

Trigger event in Behaviors panel

Mouse triggering an action in Frame 2

Add a swap image behavior to a slice

1. Open fwe_3.png, then save it as **eyetest.png**.

2. Click Window on the menu bar, click Frames, click Window on the menu bar, then click Behaviors.

   The Frames panel opens, showing four frames with the first frame, normal, selected, and the Behaviors panel opens.

3. Click the Preview tab on the document window, then move the mouse pointer over the vision measurements (20/20, 20/40, and 20/80 text objects), noticing how the text color changes as the mouse rolls over each number pair.

   The 20/100 text object does not have a behavior assigned and does not change.

4. Click the text rollovers frame (Frame 2) on the Frames panel, then compare your image to Figure E-18.

   Each of the text objects has been copied to Frame 2 in red. If you were working in a new document, you would need to add a frame at this step. You will use the text rollovers frame as the target for your rollover.

5. Click the Original tab on the document window, click the normal frame on the Frames panel, then click the Show slices and hotspots button on the Tools panel. 🔲

   The document has slices already inserted in it.

   (continued)

FIGURE E-18
Text rollovers frame

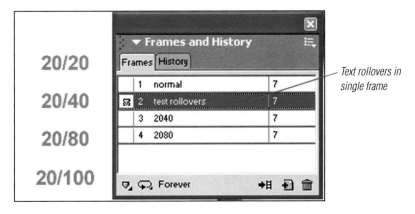

Text rollovers in single frame

FIGURE E-19
Swap Image dialog box

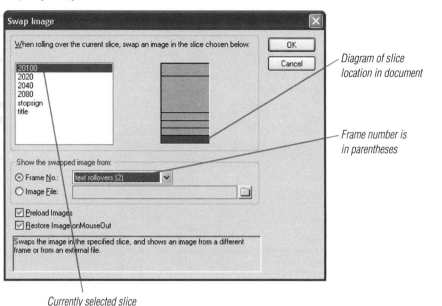

Diagram of slice location in document

Frame number is in parentheses

Currently selected slice

6. Click the 20100 slice on the Web Layer to select it, then click the Add behavior button on the Behaviors panel. ⊞

7. Click Swap Image from the behaviors list, then compare your dialog box to Figure E-19.

   The Swap Image dialog box opens, showing a list and diagram of existing slices.

8. Verify that 20100 is the currently selected slice and that text rollovers (2) appears as the Frame No., click OK, then compare your image to Figure E-20.

   The Swap Image behavior appears in the Behaviors panel, and a blue behavior line appears from the Behavior handle to the edge of the slice. The image will swap from Frame 2, text rollovers.

9. Click the Preview tab on the document window, then click the Hide slices and hotspots button on the Tools panel. ⊡

10. Roll the mouse pointer over the 20/100 text object, noticing that it changes color, just like the other text objects.

You applied a Swap Image rollover behavior to a slice.

FIGURE E-20
Swap Image behavior applied to slice

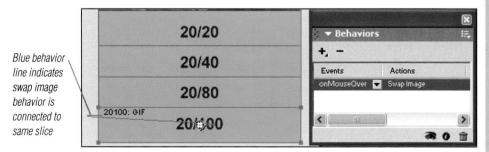

Blue behavior line indicates swap image behavior is connected to same slice

Create and duplicate a frame

1. Click the Original tab on the document window.

2. Click the 2080 frame (Frame 4) on the Frames panel, then click the New/Duplicate Frame button on the bottom of the Frames panel.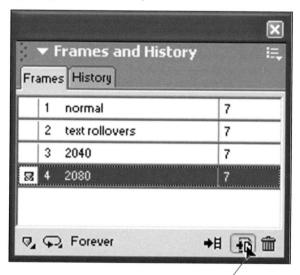

   A new blank frame, Frame 5, appears as the bottom frame. It would require several steps to copy the stop sign into the blank frame and prepare it for the rollover.

3. Click the Delete Frame button on the bottom of the Frames panel to delete Frame 5.

4. Click the 2080 frame on the Frames panel (if necessary), then drag it to the New/Duplicate Frame button on the bottom of the Frames panel, as shown in Figure E-21.

   A copy of the 2080 frame appears in Frame 5.

   TIP   You can also duplicate a frame by clicking the Options menu icon and then clicking Duplicate Frame.

5. Double-click 2080 in Frame 5, type **20100**, then press [Enter] (Win) or [return] (Mac).

You duplicated an existing frame in the Frames panel and renamed it.

FIGURE E-21
Duplicating a frame in the Frames panel

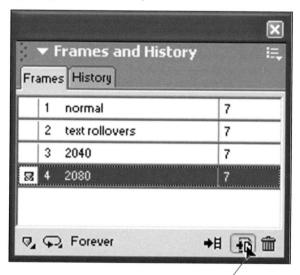

Drag selected frame on top of New/Duplicate Frame button to duplicate it

FIGURE E-22

Multiple rollovers from a single slice

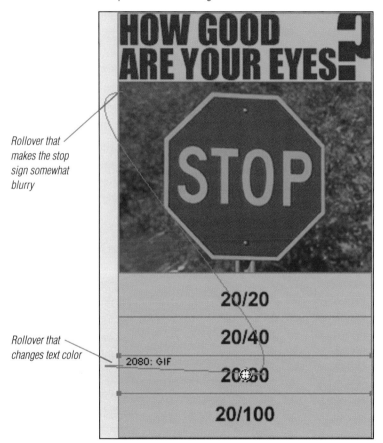

Rollover that makes the stop sign somewhat blurry

Rollover that changes text color

1. Click the 20100 frame on the Frames panel (if necessary), then click the stop sign image on the canvas to select it.

2. Double-click the Gaussian Blur effect in the Effects section on the Property inspector, drag the Blur Radius slider to 7, then click OK.

   The stop sign image is very blurry.

3. Click the Show slices and hotspots button on the Tools panel, then click the normal frame (Frame 1) on the Frames panel.

4. Click the 2080 slice on the canvas, then compare your image to Figure E-22.

   Two behavior lines are visible: the rollover behavior connected to the text and the rollover behavior that connects the text to the stop sign.

5. Click the 20100 slice on the canvas.

   The behavior line for the existing text rollover is visible.

(continued)

6. Position the pointer over the behavior handle, then drag a behavior line to the top left corner of the stop sign image, as shown in Figure E-23. 🖐

   The behavior line connects the slice to the image and a small Swap Image dialog box opens.

7. Click the Swap Image From list arrow, click 20100 (5), then click OK.

   A new behavior line connecting the 20100 slice to the stop sign appears on the canvas. When the mouse rolls over the 20/100 text object, the stop sign image will swap with the image in Frame 5, 20100 (5), and appear very blurry.

You added a disjoint rollover to a slice.

Adding a disjoint rollover

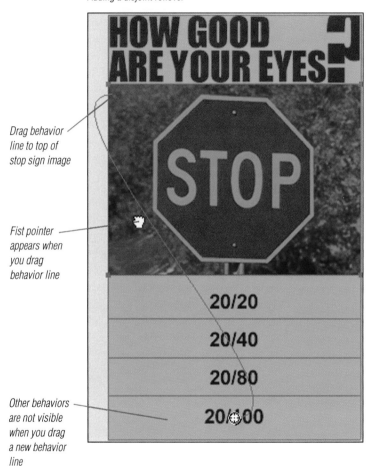

Drag behavior line to top of stop sign image

Fist pointer appears when you drag behavior line

Other behaviors are not visible when you drag a new behavior line

FIGURE E-24
Previewing rollovers

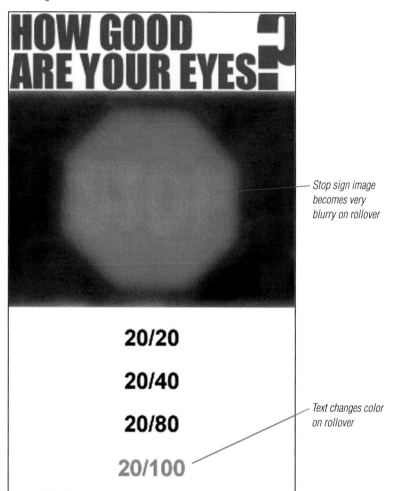

Stop sign image
becomes very
blurry on rollover

20/20

20/40

20/80

20/100

Text changes color
on rollover

1. Click the Preview tab on the document window, then click the Hide slices and hotspots button on the Tools panel. 🔲

2. Roll the mouse over each of the vision measurements starting with 20/20, as shown in Figure E-24, noticing the changes in the text and the stop sign image.

   When the mouse rolls over each text object, the text color changes to red and the stop sign becomes increasingly blurry.

3. Save your work, then close eyetest.png.

You previewed and tested the rollovers in Fireworks.

CREATE BUTTONS

What You'll Do

 In this lesson, you will convert an object to a symbol and use it to create buttons.

Understanding Symbols and Instances

As you work with Web graphics, you'll find that you want to reuse graphical elements in your documents. The easiest way to reuse a specific object is to convert it to a **symbol**. Fireworks uses three types of symbols: graphic, animation, and button. Graphic symbols can be a combination of objects. Animation symbols have different properties, such as frame count, distance, direction, and scale, each with a slightly different depiction of the image. Button symbols contain four frames that correspond to the button's appearance based on a mouse action.

Fireworks stores symbols in the **Library panel.** Symbols are document-specific, although you can drag a symbol from one document to another. As soon as you convert an object on the canvas to a symbol or drag, import, or copy a symbol from the Library panel onto the canvas, it is known as an **instance**. You can think of an instance as being a shortcut to its symbol—any edit you make to the symbol affects each instance in the document, which makes global modifi-

cations to a symbol extremely efficient. You also reduce file size considerably by using symbols instead of duplicating graphics in your document. Using the Symbol Properties dialog box, you can name a symbol and choose the type of symbol you need.

> **QUICKTIP**
>
> If you reuse a graphic element in a document, it's advisable to convert that object to a symbol and modify properties of its instances as needed.

Understanding Buttons and Button States

Adding buttons to your Web page can serve a dual purpose. Functionally, they provide your users with a well-configured way to navigate around the site. Visually, buttons can be a design element that distinguishes your site from others. Fireworks lets you create a button from nearly any graphic or text. As you've probably noticed in your own Web surfing, a button changes appearance based on the mouse action you've performed. A button can have up to four **states** associated with it, although most contain two: Up (or normal) and Over. For example, modifying a button in the Over state will cause the button's appearance to change when you roll the mouse over it. Figure E-25 shows common button states.

QUICKTIP
When you drag an instance of a button symbol to the canvas, the instance automatically has a slice added to it.

You can assign button states using the Button Editor. The button states are described below.

Up—Default state, not affected by mouse movement.

Over—State when mouse passes over button.

Down—State when user clicks button.

Over While Down—State when mouse passes over button after user clicks it (in Down state).

Active Area—The active area of the button is defined by a slice object linked to the button. Use the Property inspector to define the URL and other link properties when the button instance is selected on the canvas.

Using the Library Panel
You can create, duplicate, edit, and import symbols in your document using the Library panel. When you create a new document, the Library panel is empty. As you create symbols, Fireworks adds them to the Library panel. The Library panel is divided into a preview area and a list of symbols. You can sort symbols by name, type, and date and toggle their sort order. Each symbol type has a unique icon in the Library panel, but the instances of every symbol on the canvas share a common small arrow icon, indicating that the object is a symbol instance. Figure E-26 shows a sample Library panel.

QUICKTIP
You can duplicate a symbol in the Library panel by dragging it on top of the New symbol button.

FIGURE E-25
Button Editor and sample button states

Up   Over   Down

FIGURE E-26
Symbols in the Library panel

Symbol preview

Create a button symbol

1. Open fwe_4.png, then save it as **petpalace.png**.

   > TIP Verify that the Hide slices and hotspots button is selected. [□]

2. Click Window on the menu bar, then click Library.

   > TIP You can also open the Library panel by pressing [F11].

3. Click the Pointer tool on the Tools panel (if necessary), press and hold [Shift], click the red rectangle, then click the MY LABEL text on the canvas. [↖]

4. Click Modify on the menu bar, point to Symbol, then click Convert to Symbol.

   The Symbol Properties dialog box opens.

   > TIP You can also convert an object to a symbol by pressing [F8].

5. Type **generic button** in the Name text box, click the Button option, then click OK.

   A new button symbol, generic button, appears in the Library panel, and an arrow icon appears on the instance on the canvas.

6. Compare your image to Figure E-27.

You converted two objects to a single button symbol.

FIGURE E-27
Button added to Library panel

Arrow icon indicates
object is an instance

New button symbol

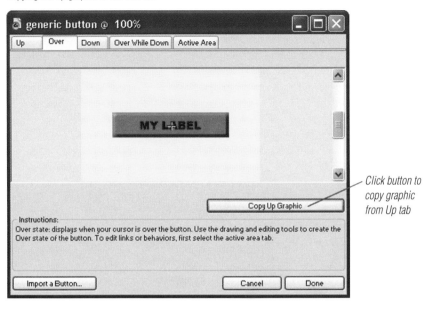

generic button @ 100%

| Up | Over | Down | Over While Down | Active Area |

MY LABEL

Click button to
copy graphic
from Up tab

Copy Up Graphic

Instructions:
Over state: displays when your cursor is over the button. Use the drawing and editing tools to create the
Over state of the button. To edit links or behaviors, first select the active area tab.

Import a Button...   Cancel   Done

Add a rollover state to a button

1. Double-click the generic button instance on the canvas.

    The Button Editor opens, with the title of the currently selected symbol in the title bar.

2. Click the Over tab, click the Copy Up Graphic button to copy the objects from the Up tab, then compare your Button Editor to Figure E-28.

3. Click the rectangle object, then double-click the Inner Bevel effect in the Effects section on the Property inspector.

4. Click the Button preset list arrow, click Highlighted, then click a blank part of the document window.

5. Click the MY LABEL text object, click the color box on the Property inspector, click the first white color swatch, then click the Done button on the Button Editor.

6. Click the Preview tab on the document window.

7. Roll the mouse pointer over the generic button to view it in the Over state, then compare your image to Figure E-29.

    The rectangle appears lighter and the text turns white.

You added a rollover state to a button.

FIGURE E-29
Previewing the button in the Over state

Button in
Over state

Duplicate button instances

1. Click the Original tab on the document window.

2. Verify that the generic button symbol is selected on the canvas.

3. Press and hold [Alt] (Win) or [option] (Mac), then drag a duplicate instance of the button instance directly below the original instance, as shown in Figure E-30.

4. Click Edit on the menu bar, then click Repeat Duplicate to duplicate and place another instance on the canvas.

   Three duplicate button instances are aligned on the canvas.

   > TIP You can also repeat the last action pressing [Ctrl][Y] (Win) or [command][Y] (Mac).

You duplicated two button instances.

Customize and preview instances

1. Click the top instance to select it, select the text in the Button Name text box on the left side of the Property inspector, type **dogs**, then press [Enter] (Win) or [return] (Mac).

   The button symbol on the Layers panel is renamed "dogs."

2. Select the text in the Text box on the Property inspector, type **DOGS**, press [Enter] (Win) or [return] (Mac), then compare your Property inspector to Figure E-31.

   The text on the dogs button instance is renamed "DOGS."

(continued)

Drag instance below original

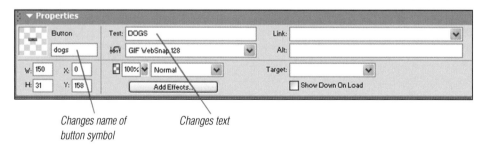

Changes name of button symbol

Changes text

Edited symbol
and text

FIGURE E-33
Previewing new buttons

Buttons contain —
simple rollovers

3. Repeat Steps 1 and 2 for the middle instance, changing the name of the button to **cats** and the text to **CATS**.

4. Repeat Steps 1 and 2 for the bottom instance, changing the name of the button to **birds** and the text to **BIRDS**.

5. Click the Show slices and hotspots button on the Tools panel, then notice that the buttons have slices added to them. 🖼

6. Click the Hide slices and hotspots button on the Tools panel, then click the Preview tab on the document window. 🖼

7. Test the buttons, then compare your image to Figure E-33.

  TIP   You would complete the document by adding a slice to the mouse area and adding links for the buttons.

8. Save your work, then close petpalace.png.

You edited the text for buttons and
previewed them.

Add slices to a document.

1. Open fwe_5.png, then save it as **zoo.png**.
2. Show slices and hotspots.
3. Select the Giraffe image and insert a slice over it.
4. Name the slice **giraffepic**.
5. Select the Slice tool, then draw a slice over the Feedback text.
6. Name the slice **feedback**.
7. Save your work.

Add hotspots to a document.

1. Select the Circle Hotspot tool, then draw a hotspot over the giraffe's face.
2. Name the hotspot **facepic**.
3. Select the Polygon Hotspot tool, then draw a hotspot that outlines the Zoo text and exclamation mark.
4. Name the hotspot **zoo**.
5. Compare your image to Figure E-34.
6. Save your work, then close zoo.png.

Create links in a document.

1. Open fwe_6.png, then save it as **tax4u.png**.
2. Show slices and hotspots.

3. Select the visit us slice and enter the following relative link: **visitorpage.htm**.
4. Enter the following Alt text: **Visit Us**.
5. Select the irs slice and enter the following absolute link: **http://www.irs.gov/**.
6. Enter the following Alt text: **Internal Revenue Service**.
7. Select the contact slice and enter the following e-mail link: **mailto:nobody@nodomain.com**.
8. Enter the following Alt text: **Contact Us**.
9. Hide slices and hotspots, then preview the document in Fireworks and in a browser.
10. Compare your image to Figure E-34.
11. Save your work, then close tax4u.png.

Add a swap image behavior to a slice.

1. Open fwe_7.png, then save it as **toyparade.png**.
2. Show slices and hotspots.
3. Select the dolls slice on the canvas.
4. Open the Behaviors panel.
5. Add a Swap Image behavior to the slice and select the buttons over (2) frame.

6. Hide slices and hotspots.
7. Preview the rollover in Fireworks.
8. Save your work.

Create a duplicate frame.

1. Return to Original view, then show slices and hotspots.
2. Open the Frames panel, then select the books over frame.
3. Add a new frame, then delete it.
4. Duplicate the books over frame.
5. Change the name of the duplicated frame to **dolls over**.
6. Select the Text tool with the following properties: Font: Arial Narrow, Font Size: 10, Color: White, Bold.
7. Change the text on the canvas to **COLLECTIBLE DOLLS & ACTION FIGURES**.
8. Save your work.

Add a disjoint rollover to a slice.

1. Select the dolls slice on the canvas. (*Hint:* You should still have the dolls over frame selected.)

FIGURE E-34
Completed Skills Review (1)

2. Drag the Behavior handle to the left side of the black rectangle where the text appears.

3. Select dolls over (6) as the Swap Image From frame.

4. Hide slices and hotspots.

5. Preview the rollover in Fireworks, then compare your image to Figure E-35.

6. Save your work, then close toyparade.png.

Convert objects to a button symbol.

1. Open fwe_8.png, then save it as **visitrome.png**.

2. Open the Library panel.

3. Select the green rectangle and the NAVIGATION text.

4. Convert the objects to a button symbol.

5. Change the name of the symbol to **navigation button**.

Create button states.

1. Open the Button Editor from the Symbol Properties dialog box.

2. Select the Over tab, then copy the Up graphic.

3. Change the color of the rectangle to **#999900**.

4. Change the text color to black (#00000).

5. Close the Button Editor, then preview the button in Fireworks.

6. Save your work.

Duplicate button instances.

1. Return to Original view.

2. Select the navigation button on the canvas.

3. Duplicate the navigation button on the canvas two times.

4. Save your work.

Customize and preview button symbols.

1. Change the name of the left button instance on the Property inspector to **airfares**.

2. Change the text on the button instance to **AIRFARES**.

FIGURE E-35
Completed Skills Review (2)

3. Change the middle button name to **hotels** and the text to **HOTELS**.

4. Change the right button name to **sights** and the text to **SIGHTS**.

5. Preview the buttons in Fireworks, then compare your image to Figure E-35.

6. Save your work, then close visitrome.png.

The people in your apartment building have decided to hold a massive yard sale and donate the proceeds to your local animal shelter. You've volunteered to add to the mass confusion by designing a Web site for the clothing section so that folks can catalog what they're bringing. You've seen these people, understand their fashion sense, and pretty much know what to expect to spring from their closets.

1. Obtain images that will reinforce your theme. You can obtain images from your computer, from the Internet, from a digital camera, or from scanned media. You can use clipart from the Web that is free for both personal and commercial use (check the copyright information for any such clipart before downloading it).

2. Create a new document and save it as **geekchic.png**.

3. Import the following file and the files you obtained in Step 1 into your document or open and select them using the bitmap selection tools.
   ■ picture.jpg

4. Create a title, tagline, and at least five objects for accessory- and clothing-related sections. (*Hint:* To keep with the geekchic visual style, try to avoid straight-line text.)

5. Draw hotspots over each of the accessory and clothing links and add appropriate absolute, relative, and e-mail links and alternate text.

FIGURE E-36
Completed Project Builder 1

6. Rename Web Layer objects and Layer objects.

7. Save your work, then examine the sample shown in Figure E-36.

You recently won a free art class about masks and mask making. After studying the universal fascination with masks, the class made their own masks. You have crafted what you'd hoped would be an elegant Venetian mask, but you've decided to express your mask appreciation using your Fireworks skills instead. An owner of a mask gallery has asked you to create a Web page for the gallery.

1. Obtain images of masks that will fit your theme. You can obtain images from your computer, from the Internet, from a digital camera, or from scanned media. You can use clipart from the Web that is free for both personal and commercial use (check the copyright information for any such clipart before downloading it).

2. Create a new document and save it as **maskgallery.png**.

3. Copy or import the files into your document or open and select them using the bitmap selection tools.

4. Create at least six additional objects or buttons as desired, then draw slices or hotspots over them as needed.

5. Apply multiple behaviors, including disjoint rollovers, to at least six slices, hotspots, or buttons. Add frames as necessary. (*Hint*: The objects at the bottom have a swap image applied to them.)

6. Add a relative, absolute, and e-mail link and alternate text to at least three slices. (*Hint*: The mask buttons and navigation buttons at the bottom have links and alternate text applied to them.)

7. Rename Web Layer objects and Layer objects and add slices as necessary.

8. Preview the document, save your work, then examine the sample shown in Figure E-37.

FIGURE E-37
Completed Project Builder 2

In general, creativity can be about bending or even breaking the rules. When it comes to interactivity in a Web site, however, you ultimately need to keep your users in mind. The discussion of form versus function in Web page design can be a lively one. Because dynamic Web sites are updated frequently to reflect current trends, this page may be different from Figure E-38 if you open it online.

1. Connect to the Internet and go to *www.course.com*. Navigate to the page for this book, click the Student Online Companion, then click the link for this unit.
2. Open a document in a word processor, or open a new Fireworks document, then save the file as **interactive**. (*Hint*: You can also use the Text tool in Fireworks to answer the questions.)
3. Explore several sites, then, when you find one or two that interest you, answer the following:
   - Discuss your ideas on real-world interactivity using the following examples. Include how motivation and expectation affect interactivity:
     - Opening the wrapper of your favorite candy bar.
     - Walking on an icy sidewalk.
     - Filling out a job or school application or completing a tax form.
   - Who is the target audience for this site, and how does the design reinforce that goal?
   - Describe the interactivity in this site.
   - Identify buttons and rollovers.
   - Identify hotspots and links.
   - Is the site form- or function-oriented? Explain.
   - How would you change the interactivity in this site?
4. Save your work.

FIGURE E-38
Design Project

Your group can assign elements of the project to individual members, or work collectively to create the finished product.

Your group is going to design an informative Web page that promotes learning through technology. Your group will choose the technology you want to promote and how to best convey your message.

1. Obtain images of the technology you've chosen. You can obtain images from your computer, from the Internet, from a digital camera, or from scanned media. You can use clipart from the Web that is free for both personal and commercial use (check the copyright information for any such clipart before downloading it).
2. Create a new document and save it as **mytech.png**.
3. Copy or import the files into your document or open and select them using the bitmap selection tools.
4. Create at least four objects or buttons as desired, then draw slices or hotspots over them as needed. (*Hint*: The circles have hotspots drawn on them.)
5. Apply multiple behaviors, including at least two disjoint rollovers, to the majority of your objects. Add frames as necessary. (*Hint*: The circles have an Over state that changes the color of the button and a disjoint rollover

behavior applied to them that displays explanatory text. The text slices have a swap image that changes the position of the text.)

6. Rename Web Layer objects and Layer objects and add slices as necessary.
7. Preview the document, save your work, then examine the sample shown in Figure E-39.

FIGURE E-39
Completed Group Project

UNIT F

CREATING ANIMATION

1. Prepare and plan animation.

2. Create basic animation.

3. Create frame animation.

4. Add tweening to animation.

5. Optimize and export files.

UNIT F
CREATING ANIMATION

Understanding Animation on the Web

Animation has become one of the most distinguishing and notorious features of the Web. While pop-up windows and messages may command your attention simply because they're in the way of what you really want to be looking at, animation entices you. The most sophisticated online animation shares a common feature with its 90-year-old ancestor—it tells a story, or shows change, however brief.

Fireworks features make it easy to add a lot of onscreen activity, so it may be tempting to animate everything you can. However, from a design perspective, you must keep your viewers in mind. Your visitors may very well leave a site that is over-the-top in animation and sound just as quickly as they would a static, dull site.

Creating basic animation in Fireworks is as easy as creating a symbol and then completing a dialog box. Depending on what you want to animate, you can change frames one-by-one, or you can create more extensive animation by selecting two or more instances of the same symbol, modifying one, and directing Fireworks to create the frames that show the transition between them.

Ultimately, you'll want to use your graphics or animation on the Web or perhaps in another application. The optimization and export features in Fireworks ensure that your graphics or animation are in the best format for the medium you've chosen, and fine-tuned for use.

Tools You'll Use

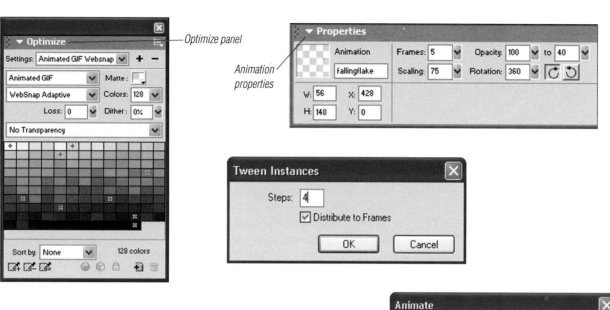

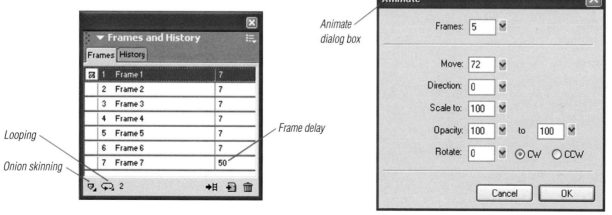

Optimize panel

Animation properties

Animate dialog box

Frame delay

Looping

Onion skinning

PREPARE AND PLAN ANIMATION

What You'll Do

 In this lesson, you will learn about planning. You will also learn how creating a storyboard before you create your Web site elements can lead to the best design for your site.

Planning—Keyboard—Action!

Following a plan, such as script, before speaking before a class or directing a $90M film is generally an asset that improves the final product. For multimedia projects, such as animations and Web sites, planning is the critical piece that can determine your success. When you integrate multimedia concepts into a Web page that includes interactive behaviors and animations, it's important to identify how these elements act together. You need to outline the structure of the Web page, such as its look and feel, as well as its content.

Understanding Storyboards

One of the most effective planning techniques is to create a storyboard. A

Storyboarding: from stick figure to action verb

Storyboards originated in the early days of animation filming. With only a text script to guide them, animation directors could not adequately explain or depict dialogue, camera angles, or camera effects. With a storyboard, each scene was sketched out, captioned, and thus made much easier to shoot. Animators made small rough storyboards, which they posted by their drawing tables. These small sketches were known as *thumbnails*. Today, storyboarding is essential to a complex animation or computer game proposal.

Storyboard styles can be quick sketches, four-color art pieces, or even 3D models, known as animatics. Storyboard panels, individual studies, and even a single cel panel from an animation all figure prominently in the collectibles market. For example, a cel and background from the 1934 Disney cartoon, Orphan's Benefit, starring Donald Duck, sold for $286,000 (limited edition reprints are $1,500). If your interests are more historically inclined, you could pick up a sketch of Leonardo Da Vinci's Horse and Rider for $12,600,000 (2001 auction price).

storyboard is a visual script you use to show the action. It consists of a series of panels that plot the key scenes and illustrate the flow of the animation. For some animations, it can resemble a comic strip. Usually, each panel in a storyboard correlates to a keyframe in the animation. Learning to "storyboard" can be the first translation of the images in your head into the language of animation. Figure F-1 shows a sample storyboard. Figure F-2 shows the animation based on that storyboard.

For some people, having a visual guide inspires their creativity and their animation. Others may not consider it useful or relevant to the animation process. One of the benefits of creating a storyboard is that you can clearly see the beginning, middle, and end of the animation, which can help

you identify and organize your ideas. Once you create a baseline storyboard, you can use it as a springboard for more ideas and enhancements.

First, you should visualize the overall concept and decide how it can work in Fireworks. Then you should construct the graphics for static images and animation, direct the movement of the animation, create the user interface, and present your product. You should begin by answering the following questions, adding any others that will further clarify your goals:

- What is the purpose of the animation or behavior? To introduce your logo? Solicit a mouse event? Just look cool?
- Where will this animation or interactive behavior appear?
- Who is the audience? Sale shoppers? Golfers? Online gamers?

- What resources do you have to work with? What is the source for your artwork? Who's paying for it?
- How many ideas do you need to express and how can you best convey them?
- Does your Web page have entertainment value, such as drama, humor, or shock?
- Who will review the storyboard? Clients? Friends?
- How will you receive and respond to feedback?

QUICKTIP

A quick way to determine if you need to remove or redo a scene on your storyboard is if you cannot determine what is going on in the scene without reading the storyboard panel's caption.

FIGURE F-1

Sample storyboard for restaurant animation

FIGURE F-2

Completed animation

Frame 1
heaping plate

Frame 6
rising steam
rolling meatball

Frame 15
small plate
rest. id

CREATE BASIC ANIMATION

What You'll Do

 In this lesson, you will insert instances of a symbol in the frames of a document, create an animation symbol, and store it in the Library panel.

Understanding Animation in Fireworks

Animation conveys action, and an action of some kind is often one of the goals of a Web site. Fireworks has several tools to use to add animation to your document. **Animation** is created by rapidly playing a series of still images in a sequence, which creates the illusion of movement.

You can use several techniques in Fireworks to animate objects. One easy way to create animation is to create an **animation symbol**.

You can create an animation symbol out of any object or instance on the canvas. Large Fireworks documents can include many symbols and their instances. Animation symbols are an efficient way to manage animation, and you can create instances of animation symbols in any document. Fireworks stores symbol information, such as color and shape, when you create the symbol. After that, you are free to create and modify instances of the symbol.

Understanding animation and persistence of vision

Translating light into sight involves a fancy, albeit instantaneous exchange between your eyes and your brain. Depending on the brightness of an image, you can retain its impression for approximately 1/30th of a second. Our capacity to retain an image even as a new image is "burned" on top of it is known as *persistence of vision*. It creates the illusion of movement. Because your eyes and brain cannot keep up with each new image, you're tricked into seeing smooth motion. Movies play at 24 frames per second, so our eyes never see that a film is dark approximately half the time. You can examine the concept of persistence of vision by watching a silent movie, which runs only 16 frames per second, and has noticeable flickering.

You can create an animation symbol by converting an object to a symbol and then selecting the Animation option in the Symbol Properties dialog box. You also create an animation symbol when you animate an object directly, using the Animate Selection command under the Animate command on the Modify menu. When you animate a selection, Fireworks automatically converts the object to an animation symbol and opens the Animate dialog box, shown in Figure F-3. You can select the number of frames for the animation, how far the animation will move and in which direction, how much it will change in size

or opacity, how much the symbol will rotate, and in which direction.

Click the Don't Show again check box to avoid seeing the prompt to add frames each time you animate a selection. To reset warnings, click Command on the menu bar, then click Reset Warning Dialogs.

You can adjust the animation trail in your document by dragging the **motion path**; each dot on the path corresponds to a frame in the animation. To extend the animation, drag the green or red **animation handles**. To move the animation (and the object), drag a blue animation handle.

QUICK**TIP**

Unlike Macromedia Flash or Director Studio, Fireworks does not use keyframes in animation.

Once you create a symbol, you can change the attributes of the graphic on which it is based, such as color or size, and affect each instance of the symbol in your document. If you change the attributes of individual instances, you can add to the illusion of sophisticated animation, such as numerous multi-colored lights blinking on and off. Using instances also helps you keep a manageable file size, since you're simply using several instances of a single symbol.

FIGURE F-3

Animate dialog box properties for sample animation

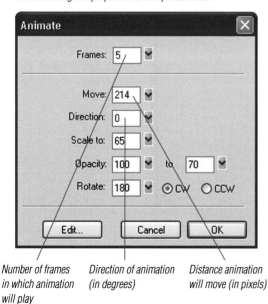

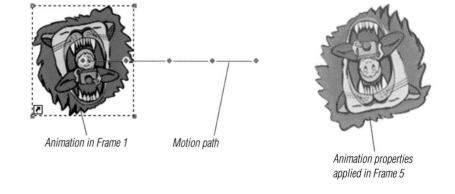

Animation in Frame 1   *Motion path*

Animation properties applied in Frame 5

Number of frames in which animation will play

Direction of animation (in degrees)

Distance animation will move (in pixels)

To edit the animation settings of an existing animation, select the animation instance on the canvas, and
then change properties on the Property inspector

Sharing Layers Across Frames

If you want non-animated objects on a
layer to appear in every frame, be sure to
set the layer to share across frames.
Otherwise, when you play an animation,
the static images will only be visible in the
first frame. If you share a layer across
frames, each frame will include all the

objects on that layer. You can edit an object
in a layer that is shared across all frames at
any time; Fireworks automatically updates
the changes in every frame, which helps
reduce file size.

QUICK**TIP**

To share a layer across frames, select a layer, then
select the Share This Layer option on the Options
menu in the Layers panel. To disable frame sharing,
deselect Share This Layer, then choose how you
want Fireworks to copy the object.

Previewing Animation

You can preview animation on the Original
and Preview tabs by using the **VCR controls**
on the bottom of the document window, as
shown in Figure F-4. You can play the animation as a whole or review it frame by
frame. Note that previewing an animation
from the Original tab may not convey an
accurate rendering of how your animation
will play on a Web page. You must first
select an Export file format in the Optimize
panel before you can accurately view and
assess how your animation will play.

FIGURE F-4
Playing an animation using VCR controls

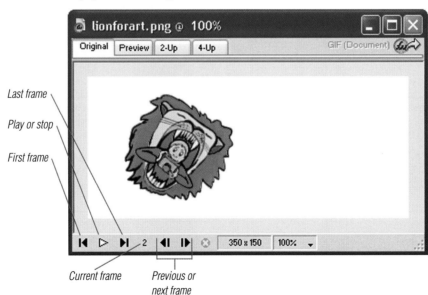

Last frame

Play or stop

First frame

Current frame

Previous or
next frame

1. Open fwf_1.png, then save it as **winterwonder.png**.

2. Open the Library, Info, and Frames panels.

   The document already contains instances of the snowflake symbol.

3. Click the New/Duplicate Layer button on the Layers panel, then change the name of the layer to **Falling**. 🗂

4. Drag an instance of the snowflake graphic symbol from the Library panel to the top right corner of the canvas.

5. Click Modify on the menu bar, point to Transform, click Numeric Transform, double-click the Width percentage text box, type **50**, then click OK.

6. On the Info panel, type **428** in the X text box, type **0** in the Y text box, then press [Enter] (Win) or [return] (Mac).

7. Compare your image to Figure F-5.

   The scale settings are applied only to the selected instance.

You added an instance to a document and modified it.

Create an animation symbol

1. Click Modify on the menu bar, point to Animation, then click Animate Selection.

   The Animate dialog box opens.

   > TIP You can also press [Alt][Shift][F8] (Win) or [option][Shift][F8] (Mac) to open the Animate dialog box.

   (continued)

FIGURE F-5
Rescaled instance

Instance positioned
and scaled

2. Enter the values shown in Figure F-6, click OK to close the dialog box, then click OK when prompted to automatically add new frames.

A motion path is attached to the new animation symbol on the canvas, a new animation symbol is added to the Library, and the snowflake instance on the Layers panel becomes an animation symbol.

3. Compare your image to Figure F-7.

4. Change the name of the Animation Symbol on the Property inspector to **fallingflake**.

You created an animation symbol and set animation properties.

Modify an animation

1. Drag the red animation handle to the bottom of the canvas, as shown in Figure F-8.

   TIP   Press and hold [Shift] to constrain the motion path to a straight line.

2. Click the Play button  on the bottom of the document window, then click the Stop button after the animation has played a couple of times. ■

The snowflake appears to fall, get smaller, and fade out, but none of the other images is visible except when the animation plays in Frame 1.

3. Click the First frame button on the document window to return to Frame 1 (if necessary), then click the fallingflake animation symbol to select it. |◀|

(continued)

FIGURE F-6
Animate dialog box

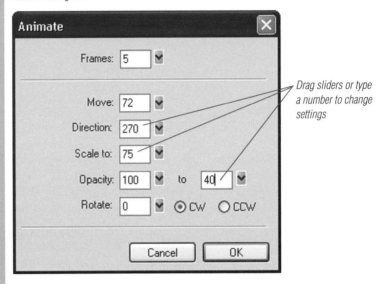

Drag sliders or type a number to change settings

FIGURE F-8
Modified motion path

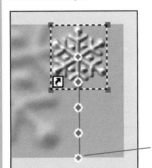

Drag red handle to bottom of canvas

FIGURE F-7
Newly created animation symbol

Green handle indicates start of animation

Blue handles indicate frames in animation

Red handle indicates end of animation

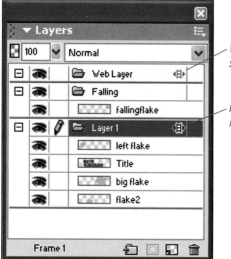

Web layer is always
shared across frames

Frame icon indicates layer
is shared across frames

4. Double-click the Rotation text box on the Property inspector, type **360**, then press [Enter] (Win) or [return] (Mac).

   The snowflake will rotate during the animation.

5. Click Layer 1 on the Layers panel to select all of its objects.

6. Click the Options menu icon on the Layers panel, click Share This Layer, click OK, then compare your Layers panel to Figure F-9.

   All the images will be visible when the animation plays.

You modified an animation and shared layers across frames.

Preview an animation

1. Click the Play button ▷ on the bottom of the document window, then click the Stop button after the animation has played a couple of times. ■

   The snowflake rotates and tumbles and the other images are visible in each frame.

2. Click the Preview tab on the document window, then repeat Step 1.

   The animation plays at a slower pace.

3. Click the Previous frame button until you reach Frame 3. ◀I

4. Compare your image to Figure F-10.

5. Save your work, then close winterwonder.png.

You previewed the animation on the Original and Preview tabs.

FIGURE F-10

Previewing animation

Static images from
Frame 1 appear in
each frame

Snowflake as it appears
in Frame 3

CREATE FRAME ANIMATION

What You'll Do

 In this lesson, you will create frame-by-frame animation, set the frame delay for different frames, and view several frames of the animation at once.

Understanding Frame-by-Frame Animation

You've seen how easy it is to animate an object and modify its properties. You can also copy objects into different frames and then modify the objects in each frame, a process known as **frame-by-frame animation**. When you create an animation symbol, Fireworks automatically copies the image to the selected number of frames. Frame-by-frame animation requires that you create individual frames for your animation manually.

Frame-by-frame animation lets you change the physical attributes of the objects in each frame, such as color and effects. Because you control the changes in each frame, you can create effects such as text blinking from one color to another, or create gradual shape changes or distortions. However, you must make the changes in every frame you create, which is not an easy task. On the other hand, you do realize a certain historical authenticity with traditional animators, who had to draw each frame of their animations by hand.

Managing Animation with the Frames Panel

You use the Frames panel to manage the frames in your animation. You can rename frames (by default, they are numbered sequentially), and add, delete, move, copy, or exclude frames as needed. You can also set the number of times your animation will play in the browser and set its direction: forward or reverse. You can add, copy, delete, and rename frames on the Frames panel just as you do the layers on the Layers panel.

In addition to previewing your animation one frame at a time, you can also view several or all of the frames simultaneously. **Onion skinning** allows you to view one or more additional frames while in the current frame. The term onion skinning refers to the super-thin sheets of transparent paper used in traditional animation as overlays to view an animation series. By seeing where and how the preceding and succeeding frames interact with the image in the current frame, you can precisely align your animation. The Onion Skinning pop-up menu offers several frame choices for viewing frames, or you can create a custom range of frames to view. When onion skinning is turned on, the frames that precede and succeed the current frame are displayed in a lower opacity. Figure F-11 shows sample onion skinning.

QUICKTIP

You can edit the objects that appear in the multiple frames when onion skinning is turned on. Click the Onion Skinning button on the bottom of the Frames panel, then click Multiple Frames.

Understanding Frame Delay

You can fine-tune your animation by adjusting the display time or **frame delay** for each frame. Frame delay is measured in hundredths of a second—the default frame delay is 7/100 of a second. Even a small change can affect your animation dramatically: the lower the number, the faster the frame animation will play. If the frame delay is too short, the image will appear indistinct; if it is too long, the image will appear jerky or erratic. The frame delay is displayed in the right column of the Frames panel. You can adjust the delay for one or more frames at any time by pressing and holding [Shift] as you click the frames whose frame delay you want to change. In addition to setting the frame delay, you can select the frames that will be included when you export the animation. When you deselect a frame, a large red X appears in place of the frame delay setting on the Frames panel, as shown in Figure F-12.

QUICKTIP

To exclude an animation frame from the exported file, double-click the frame delay column, then deselect the Include when Exporting check box.

FIGURE F-11
Sample onion skinning

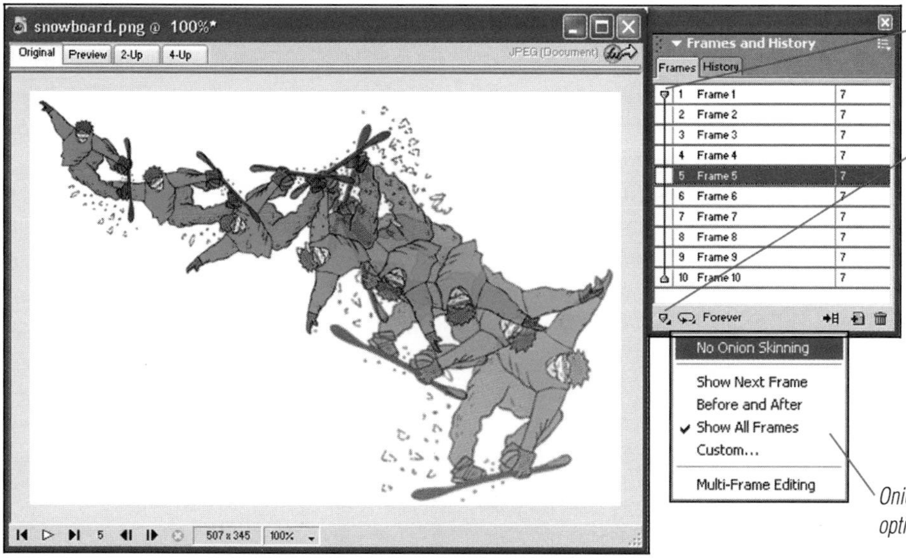

FIGURE F-12
Sample frame delay

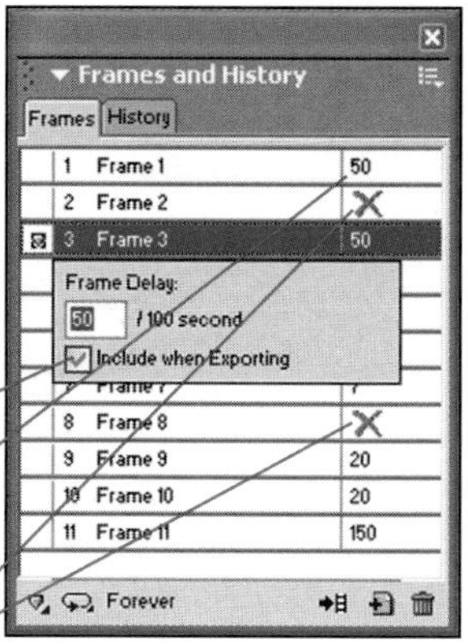

Range of frames included in onion skinning

Click Onion Skinning button to display options

Onion skinning options

Deselect check box to exclude a frame

Frames delay

Frames will be excluded during export

Create frame-by-frame animation

1. Open fwf_2.png, save it as **bearpaw.png**, make sure the Info panel is visible, then notice the instances visible in the document as you click Frame 2 on the Frames panel and then click Frame 3.

   The document has an instance of the left paw and right paw graphic symbols placed in Frames 2 and 3.

2. Drag Frame 3 on top of the New/Duplicate Frame button on the bottom of the Frames panel to duplicate it.

3. Drag an instance of the left paw graphic symbol from the Library panel above and in front of the right paw instance, as shown in Figure F-13.

4. Repeat Steps 2 and 3, creating three more frames, alternating between the left paw and right paw symbols, until your canvas resembles Figure F-14.

5. Drag Frame 7 on top of the New/Duplicate Frame button on the Frames panel, then drag an instance of the grizzlies graphic symbol from the Library panel to the center of the canvas.

(continued)

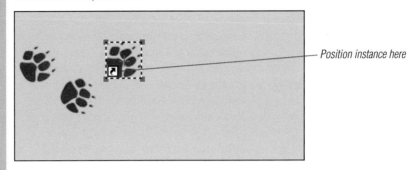

— Position instance here

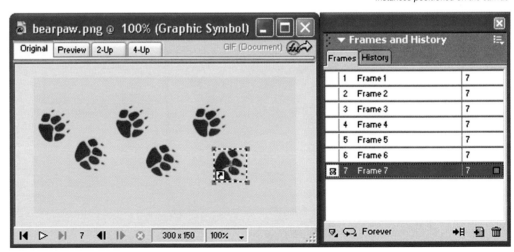

FIGURE F-15
Glow effect added to instance

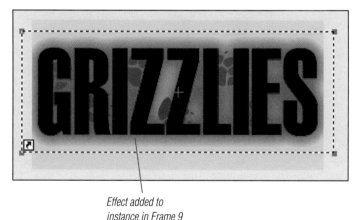

Effect added to
instance in Frame 9

6. Drag Frame 8 on top of the New/Duplicate Frame button on the Frames panel, click the Add effects button in the Effects section on the Property inspector, point to Shadow and Glow, then click Glow.

7. Click the Color box , click the first magenta color swatch, press [Enter] (Win) or [return] (Mac), then compare your image to Figure F-15.

You added instances to individual frames to create animation, and modified an instance, but not its symbol.

Adjust frame delay

1. Click the Play button on the bottom of the document window, then click the Stop button after the animation has played a couple of times.

   The animation plays quickly.

2. Click Frame 1 on the Frames panel, press and hold [Shift], then click Frame 7 to select Frames 1–7.

(continued)

3. Double-click the frame delay column, type **35** in the Frame Delay dialog box, verify that the Include when Exporting check box is selected, compare your Frames panel to Figure F-16, then press [Enter] (Win) or [return] (Mac).

The frame delay changes to 35 for the selected frames.

4. Double-click the Frame Delay column for Frame 9 on the Frames panel, type **100** in the Frame Delay dialog box, then press [Enter] (Win) or [return] (Mac).

5. Click the Play button ▷ on the bottom of the document window, then click the Stop button after the animation has played a couple of times. ■

The animation pauses at the end when the text is visible.

You set the frame delay for different frames and previewed the animation in Fireworks.

FIGURE F-16
Modifying frame delay

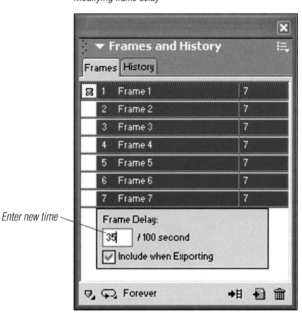

Enter new time

Creating animation by distributing objects to frames and importing files

You can distribute objects to frames by selecting them and then clicking the Distribute to Frames button on the bottom of the Frames panel, or by clicking the Distribute to Frames command on the Frames panel Options menu. Fireworks automatically adds a frame for each object. You can use this method to easily import a Photoshop image sequence or a FreeHand file that has a blend animation.

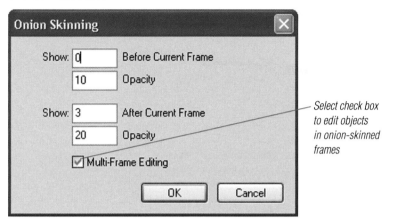

Select check box
to edit objects
in onion-skinned
frames

1. Click Frame 5 on the Frames panel.
2. Click the Onion Skinning button on the bottom of the Frames panel, then click Custom to open the Onion Skinning dialog box. 🏳️
3. Enter the values shown in Figure F-17, then click OK.

   Frame 5 is visible at 100% and the next three frames are visible at 20% opacity.
4. Compare your image to Figure F-18.
5. Click the Onion Skinning button on the bottom of the Frames panel, then click No Onion Skinning to turn off onion skinning. 🏳️
6. Save your work, then close bearpaw.png.

You viewed several frames of the animation simultaneously.

FIGURE F-18
Viewing onion skinning

Frames
following
current
frame are
visible at
lower
opacity

Vertical bar
indicates
frames being
onion-
skinned

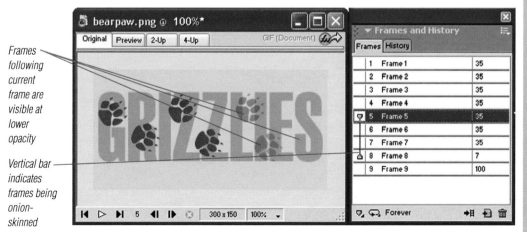

ADD TWEENING TO ANIMATION

What You'll Do

 In this lesson, you will add frames to blend the movement between two instances in an animation.

Understanding Tweening

Animation mimics motion, but the movement may not always seem to flow evenly from one action to the next. The solution is to ease the transition between motion frames—the more frames in an animation, the more smoothly it plays. Tweening modifies or blends two or more instances of the same symbol and distributes them to the number of frames you set. As a result, the movement appears more fluid and less erratic. In Fireworks, you can add as many tweened instances of a symbol as you need to create just the animation you want.

Tweening can be very effective when the instances you want to animate are significantly different from instance to instance. For example, you can animate a ball so that it zooms in and out, as shown in Figure F-17. When you tween instances, you can determine the number of steps you want to tween using the Tween Instances dialog box. The Tween Instances dialog box opens after you click Tween Instances from the Symbol command on the Modify menu. Fireworks creates new objects based on the number of steps you enter. The order in which the instances

History of tweening in animation

Successful commercial animation began in the early 20th century. In traditional film animation, a cadre of artists was needed to create just a few seconds of animated film. Senior artists would draw the animated objects' major action points, which were known as keyframes. Junior artists, known as tweeners, were responsible for completing the frames *in between*—from 8 to 24 frames were required for one second of film. In contrast, computer animation usually displays 10 to 20 frames per second. The largely unsung Disney animators of the 1930s and 1940s were among the most creative artists and innovative technology users of their time.

play is based on their stacking order on the Layers panel. The object lowest on the Layers panel will play first in the animation (in Frame 1).

In addition to determining the number of steps to tween in the Tween Instances dialog box, you can also choose whether to distribute the tweened objects to frames or display the tweening in a single frame. When you distribute objects to frames, each object appears in its own frame. For example, in Figure F-19, each tweened instance of the five beach balls plays in five frames, so the animation totals 25 frames. If you do not select the Distribute to

Frames check box, shown in Figure F-20, the tweened instances will appear in one frame. In fact, the image will look just like animation does when you turn on onion skinning to show all frames at 100%. Depending on the animation, precise alignment of the instances may be crucial. You can duplicate an instance by cloning it, which places an exact copy directly on top of the original. For example, if you move the clone with the arrow keys, you can ensure smooth flow in your animation.

You can break apart an instance and remove its link to the symbol. Breaking apart an instance creates a grouped object and

removes any animation or button symbol properties. To break the link between an instance and its symbol, click the Break Apart command from the Symbol command on the Modify menu.

When you've completed an animation or any graphic, you may want to modify the size of the canvas. You can trim the canvas to the edge of objects on the canvas by using the Trim Canvas command on the Modify menu. You can also use the Crop tool on the Tools panel to define the area that you want to crop, such as cropping the sides, but not the top, and so on.

FIGURE F-19
Sample tweening

FIGURE F-20
Tween Instances dialog box

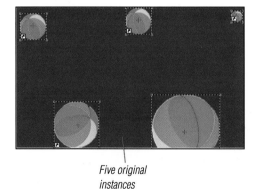

Five original instances

Original instances tweened five steps and distributed to frames

Add tweening to an animation

1. Open fwf_3.png, then save it as **snowcruncher.png**.

2. Drag an instance of the cruncher graphic symbol to the top of the canvas.

3. On the Info panel, type **12** in the X text box, type **0** in the Y text box, then press [Enter] (Win) or [return] (Mac).

4. Click Edit on the menu bar, then click Clone to duplicate the symbol and place it on top of the original.

   TIP You can also clone an instance by pressing [Ctrl][Shift][D] (Win) or [command][Shift][D] (Mac).

5. Press and hold [Shift], press ↓ 10 times to move the instance to the bottom of the canvas, then compare your image to Figure F-21.

6. Press and hold [Shift], then click the original instance to select both instances.

7. Click Modify on the menu bar, point to Symbol, then click Tween Instances to open the Tween Instances dialog box.

   TIP You can also press [Ctrl][Alt][Shift][T] (Win) or [command][option][Shift][T](Mac) to tween instances.

8. Type **4** in the Steps text box, make sure that the Distribute to Frames check box is selected, then click OK.

   The tweened instance appears at the top of the canvas.

   (continued)

Cloned instance

Importing animation files

You can open several files at once and set up a document for animation. First place the files you want to use in a folder, then, in Fireworks, click Open, select all of the files you want in the Open dialog box, then select the Open as Animation check box. Fireworks opens the files en masse, placing them on one layer on the Layers panel and each in its own frame on the Frames panel. Fireworks imports files in alphabetical order unless they are numbered.

Animation ends
with instance at
bottom of canvas

9. Click the Play button ▷ on the bottom of the document window, then click the Stop button after the animation has played a couple of times. ■

   The animation drops down from the top to the bottom of the canvas.

10. Click the Last frame button on the bottom of the document window, then compare your image to Figure F-22. ✦

You cloned an instance and applied tweening to two instances.

Enhance animation

1. Verify that Frame 6 is selected, then drag it on top of the New/Duplicate Frame button on the Frames panel. 🔁

2. Click the instance on the canvas to select it.

3. Select the value in the W text box on the Info panel, type **285**, select the value in the H text box, type **65**, then press [Enter] (Win) or [return] (Mac).

   The instance becomes wider and shorter and moves up on the canvas. The slight distortion of the instance will make it appear to crunch during animation.

4. Press and hold [Shift], press ↓ three times, release [Shift], press ← four times, then compare your image to Figure F-23.

(continued)

5. Double-click the frame delay column for Frame 7 on the Frames panel, type **50** in the Frame Delay dialog box, then press [Enter] (Win) or [return] (Mac).

6. Click the Play button  on the document window, then click the Stop button after the animation has played a couple of times. ■

The animation crunches slightly when it reaches the bottom of the canvas.

You copied a frame, modified an instance, and set frame delay.

Trim and crop the canvas

1. Click the First frame button on the document window. ⏮

2. Click Modify on the menu bar, point to Canvas, click Trim Canvas, then notice the canvas size on the bottom of the document window.

The width of the canvas becomes 285 pixels as excess space around the text is trimmed.

> TIP You can also press [Ctrl][Alt][T] (Win) or [command][option][T] (Mac) to trim the canvas.

3. Click the Crop tool on the Tools panel, then draw a bounding box that resembles the box shown in Figure F-24.

(continued)

FIGURE F-24
Using the Crop tool

Bounding box created
with Crop tool

FIGURE F-25

Trimmed and cropped canvas

4. Select the value in the W text box, type **285**, select the value in the H text box, type **112**, select the value in the Y text box on the Info panel, type **87**, then press [Enter] (Win) or [return] (Mac).

5. Position the Crop tool pointer above the bounding box on the canvas, press [Enter] (Win), then compare your image to Figure F-25.

   The height of the canvas becomes 112 pixels and only the bottom portion of the instance is visible on the canvas in Frame 1.

6. Click the Play button ▷ on the document window, then click the Stop button after the animation has played a couple of times. ■

   The animation appears to enter from the top of the canvas.

7. Save your work.

You trimmed and cropped the canvas.

OPTIMIZE AND EXPORT FILES

What You'll Do

 In this lesson, you will optimize a file, set how many times an animation will play in a browser, and export the file.

Understanding the Basics of Optimization

Exporting a file to the Web involves creating HTML and Javascript code—and often lots of it. The export process is two-fold: optimize the document (especially the slices that you've inserted over objects), and create the HTML code necessary to reconstitute the graphics properly. In Fireworks, this is an effortless process when you use the Optimize panel and the Export dialog boxes. You can also use the Export Wizard, which guides you through optimizing and exporting.

Fireworks has specific tools you can use to optimize your graphics. When you **optimize** a graphic, you match the format best suited for the type of graphic with the smallest file size that maintains image quality. The Optimize panel contains settings for the file type, compression, and properties specific to the selected file type. For example, if you choose GIF as the file type, you can adjust the number of colors in the exported graphic, known as **color depth**. If you choose JPEG as the file type, you can adjust the quality of the image using a slider control.

The Preview, 2-Up, and 4-Up tabs on the document window allow you to preview the results of the optimization controls you've set on the Optimize panel. The 2-Up and 4-Up tabs offer the advantage of being able to compare different settings side-by-side, so you can experiment with different settings to determine the point at which you finally sacrifice image quality for decreased file size. Figure F-26 shows different optimization settings for a GIF file.

The Optimize panel contains the following list of preset optimization choices:

- **GIF Web 216**—Makes all colors websafe.
- **GIF WebSnap 128** or **GIF WebSnap 256**—Converts non-websafe colors to their closest websafe equivalent, up to 128 or 256 colors, respectively.
- **GIF Adaptive 256**—Contains up to 256 actual colors used in the graphic.
- **JPEG – Better Quality** and **JPEG – Smaller File**—Sets the quality higher or lower: the lower the setting, the more quality you lose during compression, but the file size is smaller.

- Animated GIF WebSnap 128—Sets the file format to animated GIF and Websafe colors.

QUICK**TIP**

You can customize an optimization setting and add it to the list of presets using the Save current settings button on the Optimize panel.

When you choose GIF as the optimization setting, you can choose from several palettes, from black and white to palettes specific to your Windows or Macintosh system. You can also optimize each slice in your document individually. For example, you can optimize a slice that contains a photographic image as a JPEG, or even selectively optimize areas of the slice so that the background can be compressed with a lower quality setting. You can optimize other slices in your document, such

as text, as GIF files with only the colors necessary to display the text color.

QUICK**TIP**

You can lock one or more colors in a palette to maintain consistency by clicking the Lock button at the bottom of the Optimize panel.

You can further reduce file size by selecting the Remove Unused Colors option, and the Interlaced option (for GIF and PNG file types) on the Optimize panel. **Interlacing** allows the file to download gradually from low to high resolution. You can accomplish the same result for JPEG files by selecting Progressive JPEG from the Layers panel Options menu. If you lower the quality setting for JPEG images, you can increase the smoothing setting in small increments to help maintain appearance.

Understanding Transparency

Regardless of the shape of the image, JPEG files and other file formats are rectangular. The image appears against its own background color, and the graphic's boundary is the rectangle, not the individual features of the image. GIF file formats permit a transparent background—the image appears to blend with the background of your Web page, creating the appearance of an image boundary. Having a transparent background is particularly effective when you save an animation as an animated GIF. You can select three types of transparency: No Transparency, which includes the canvas color and appears similar to a JPEG; Index Transparency, which allows you to set a specific color or colors as the transparent color or colors and affects both the canvas and the graphic; and Alpha Transparency, which sets

FIGURE F-26
Comparing GIF optimization settings

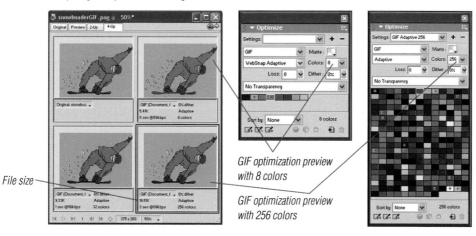

File size

GIF optimization preview with 8 colors

GIF optimization preview with 256 colors

the background color or any other selected color to be transparent. Once you select the transparency type, you can select the color in your document that you want to become transparent using the Select Transparency Color button on the Optimize panel.

QUICK**TIP**

The 8-bit and 32-bit PNG file formats also contain transparency.

Choosing the Number of Times a Movie Will Play

Web designers often assume that viewers will want or need to watch an animation repeatedly. For example, an e-mail image, such as an animated envelope or mailbox, may continuously open and close, in a process known as **looping**. You can choose how many times your animation will play by clicking the GIF animation looping button in the Frames panel, then clicking a number or an option in the list. For example, None means the movie will play once and then stop; 5 means it will play five additional times after the first time, and Forever means it will never stop.

Understanding Exporting

You can set HTML export options using tabs on the HTML Setup dialog box, which you can open from the File menu. The Export feature generates the files necessary to view a graphic on the Web, or in other applications, such as Macromedia Flash, Macromedia Dreamweaver, or Adobe Photoshop. You can access the Export dialog box from the File menu. You can export the entire document or just portions of it. For example, you can export a single image, the document as an HTML file with its related images, one or more slices, or frames and layers as separate image files.

Depending on whether your file contains slices or image maps, you need to control different aspects of the export. For example, a simple graphic is a simple export: you name the file, accept the default settings, and then select the folder in which you want to save it. Options in the Export dialog box are shown in Figure F-27.

QUICK**TIP**

You should review the specific exporting options for files in the Using Fireworks MX Help system.

The Export Preview dialog box provides all the optimization and export features from the Optimize panel and more in a consolidated location. The Export Preview dialog box consists of three tabs: Options, which contains optimization and view settings; File, where you can scale and crop the image; and Animation, where you can modify animated GIF settings, although usually the default settings are adequate. You can open the Export Preview dialog box from the File menu, from the Optimization panel Options menu, or from the Export Wizard. Figure F-28 shows the Export Preview dialog box.

QUICK**TIP**

You can export an image to another application using the Quick Export button at the top left of the document window.

FIGURE F-27
Save as type list in the Export dialog box

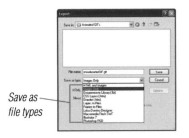

Save as
file types

FIGURE F-28
Export Preview dialog box

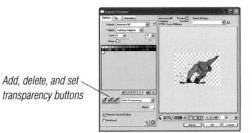

Add, delete, and set
transparency buttons

Set options on the Optimize panel and preview the animation in a browser

1. Click the GIF Animation Looping button on the bottom of the Frames panel, then click 2, as shown in Figure F-29. ↩

   The looping setting is not noticeable until the animation plays on the Web. To view the setting change, you'll view the animation in your browser.

2. Click Window on the menu bar, then click Optimize to open the Optimize panel.

   TIP You can also press [F6] to open the Optimize panel.

3. Click the Export file format list arrow, then click Animated GIF.

   (continued)

FIGURE F-29

Changing the looping setting

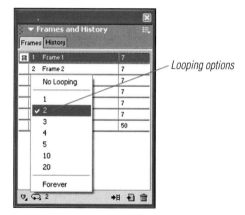

Looping options

4. Click the Indexed Palette list arrow, click WebSnap Adaptive (Win) or Web Adaptive (Mac), then compare your Optimize panel to Figure F-30.

5. Click the First frame button on the document window. ◄|

6. Click File on the menu bar, point to Preview in Browser, then click your browser.

The animation plays a total of three times, and then stops.

7. Close your browser.

You specified the number of times the animation should play, set the file format, and previewed the animation in a browser.

Change the color depth

1. Verify that 128 is the Colors setting on the Optimize panel and that a colors used number appears at the bottom right of the panel.

The number at the bottom of the panel is the actual number of colors used.

> TIP If a number is not visible on the Optimize panel, click the Rebuild button.

2. Click Frame 6 on the Frames panel.

3. Click the 4-Up tab on the document window, click the view in the top right corner to select it, then compare your image to Figure F-31.

(continued)

Settings on the Optimize panel

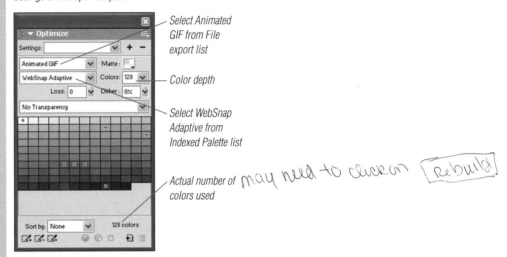

Select Animated GIF from File export list

Color depth

Select WebSnap Adaptive from Indexed Palette list

Actual number of *may need to click on* [Rebuild]
colors used

FIGURE F-31
Optimization viewed at 128 color depth

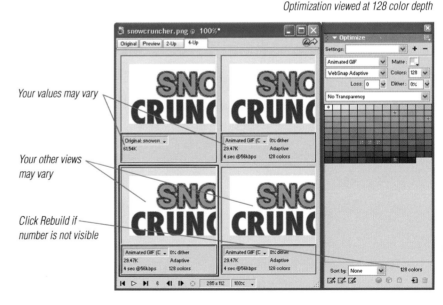

Your values may vary

Your other views may vary

Click Rebuild if number is not visible

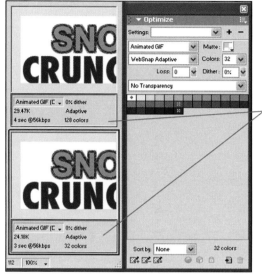

File size and time savings with 32 colors

4. Click the view in the lower right corner, click the Colors list arrow on the Optimize panel, click 32, then compare your image to Figure F-32.

   The file size is smaller and the download time is less, but the image quality is still acceptable.

   > TIP   If the file size and download times are not visible on the Optimize panel, click the Rebuild button or reselect the color depth.

You changed the color depth to reduce file size and download time.

Change the transparency of an animated GIF

1. Click the Choose type of transparency list arrow on the Optimize panel, then click Index Transparency, as shown in Figure F-33.

   Because the transparency setting is not visible until you preview the animation, the canvas still appears white in Original view, although a checkerboard pattern is visible in the selected view.

2. Click the Preview tab on the document window.

   The canvas color has a gray and white checkerboard pattern, indicating that it is transparent.

   (continued)

FIGURE F-33

Selecting a transparency option

Transparency list

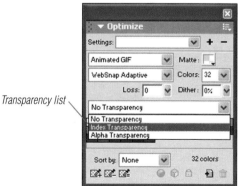

3. Compare your image to Figure F-34, then save your work.

4. Click File on the menu bar, point to Preview in Browser, then click your browser.

   The animation plays against the background color of your browser window.

5. Close your browser.

You changed the transparency of an animated GIF to index transparency.

Export an optimized file

1. Click the Original tab on the document window

2. Click File on the menu bar, then click Export to open the Export dialog box.

   TIP   You can also open the Export dialog box by clicking [Ctrl][Shift][R] (Win) or [command][Shift][R] (Mac).

   (continued)

Viewing modified transparency setting

Checkerboard pattern indicates transparency

FIGURE F-35
Export dialog box

Your drive and
folder may vary

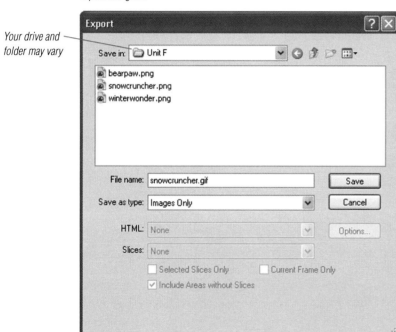

3. Navigate to the drive and folder where your solution files are stored, verify that Images Only appears as the Save as type, compare your dialog box to Figure F-35, then click Save.

4. Save your work.

5. Open the file management tool on your operating system, adjust the settings to display extensions, then navigate to the drive and folder where your solution files are stored.

6. Notice the newly exported file named snowcruncher.gif, then compare its file size to snowcruncher.png.

   TIP   Depending on the file association for GIF files on your computer, you may be able to view the animated GIF by opening it from your file manager or you may need to first open your browser and then play the animated GIF by opening it from the browser.

7. Close your file management tool, then close snowcruncher.png.

You exported the optimized file.

Create and modify an instance.

1. Open fwf_4.png, then save it as **birthdaymsg.png**.
2. Open the Library, Info, and Frames panels.
3. Create a new layer and change the name to **helium**.
4. Drag an instance of the balloon symbol to the lower right corner of the canvas at the following coordinates: X: **410**, Y: **95**. (*Hint*: The balloon will be partly off-canvas.)
5. Add an Adjust Color effect to the instance in the Effects section of the Property inspector, then select the Hue/Saturation effect with the following settings: Colorize option selected, Hue: **253**, Saturation: **100**, and Lightness: **30**.
6. Save your work.

Create an animation symbol.

1. Animate the instance with the following settings: Frames: **5**, Move: **157**, Direction: **77**, Scale to and Opacity: **100**, Rotate: **0**.
2. Change the name of the animation symbol to **heliumballoon**.
3. Play the animation in the document window.
4. Save your work.

Modify an animation.

1. Change the scale of the animation to **40** and add a rotation of **25 CCW**.
2. Select the objects on Layer 1 in the Layers panel and share them with layers.
3. Save your work.

Preview the animation.

1. Play the animation in the document window.
2. Play the animation in the Preview window.
3. Save your work, then compare your image to Figure F-36.
4. Close birthdaymsg.png.

Create frame-by-frame animation.

1. Open fwf_5.png, then save it as **gifts.png**. (*Hint*: Show guides, if they are not visible.)
2. Duplicate Frame 1, then drag the i symbol to the canvas. (*Hint*: Use the guide line to align the bottom of the instances.)
3. Repeat for the remaining letters until you have "Gifts" spelled out over five frames.
4. Duplicate Frame 5, then group the objects.
5. Add a Gaussian Blur effect of **2** and a Glow effect using the first yellow color swatch and default settings.
6. Save your work.

FIGURE F-36
Completed Skills Review (1)

Adjust frame delay.

1. Adjust the frame delay of Frames 1–5 to **20**.
2. Adjust the frame delay of Frame 6 to **50**.
3. Turn off guides.
4. Preview the animation in Fireworks.
5. Save your work.

Use onion skinning.

1. Select Frame 4.
2. Set a custom onion skinning that displays zero frames before the current at 20% and two frames after at 50%.
3. Preview the animation in Fireworks, then save your work.
4. Compare your image to Figure F-36, then close gifts.png.

Add tweening to an animation.

1. Open fwf_6.png, then save it as **birthdaysmile.png**.
2. Drag an instance of the big smile symbol to the middle of the canvas at the following coordinates: X: **108**, Y: **61**.
3. Clone the instance, scale it numerically to 25%, then move it to the top right corner of the canvas.
4. Move the scaled graphic symbol to the bottom of the Layers panel.
5. Tween the two instances with **5** steps and select the Distribute to Frames check box.
6. Select Frame 7, select the instance, and add an Adjust Color Invert effect to it.
7. Preview the animation in Fireworks.
8. Save your work.

Set Frame delay, trim, and crop the canvas.

1. Set the frame delay for Frames 1-6 to **15** and for Frame 7 to **75**.
2. Trim the canvas.
3. Select Frame 1.
4. Create a crop bounding box that measures 345 × 272 with a Y coordinate of **–27**. (*Hint*: The face will be partly off-canvas.)
5. Crop the canvas, then save your work.

Set optimize options.

1. Set the Looping to **5** on the Frames panel.
2. Open the Optimize panel.

3. Set the Export file format to Animated GIF.
4. Set the Indexed Palette to WebSnap Adaptive.
5. Preview the animation in a browser.
6. Save your work.

Change color depth.

1. Select Frame 7.
2. Set the color depth to 128.
3. Compare color depths of 128 and 32 in the 4-Up window.

FIGURE F-37
Completed Skills Review (2)

4. Select the 32 color depth in the 4-Up window.
5. Save your work.

Change transparency and export the file.

1. Set the transparency to Index Transparency.
2. Preview the animation in a browser.
3. Export the file to the drive and folder where your solution files are stored.
4. Save your work, then compare your image to Figure F-37.

Your friends insisted on putting all 21 candles and 1 for good luck on your birthday cake. After wiping up butter cream frosting for weeks, you've decided to create a reenactment of the event using your Fireworks skills. Your goal is to use animation to convince your friends never to try to light so many candles again.

1. Obtain images that will reinforce your birthday theme. You can obtain images from your computer, from the Internet, from a digital camera, or from scanned media. You can use clipart from the Web that is free for both personal and commercial use (check the copyright information for any such clipart before downloading it).
2. Create a new document and save it as **birthdaycake.png**.
3. Import the following files and the files you obtained in Step 1 into your document.
    - cake.gif
    - candle.gif
4. Convert objects to symbols as necessary.
5. Create frame-by-frame animation using at least one of the symbols, and modify instances as needed. (*Hint*: The candles were modified from one symbol and were created frame by frame.)

6. Build at least one animation that involves tweening. (*Hint*: The cake instance with glowing candles was created by adding tweening to two instances of the glowing cake and modifying the amount of glow.)

7. Trim, crop, or adjust frame delay, looping, and transparency as desired.
8. Optimize and export the file. (*Hint*: The sample is an animated GIF with 32 colors.)
9. Preview the animation, save your work, then examine the sample shown in Figure F-38.

FIGURE F-38
Completed Project Builder 1

One of your parents has donated to a fund that rewards elementary students who improve their reading skills. In addition to a monetary donation, they volunteered you to design a banner ad for the local library Web site.

1. Obtain images of books or other reading material that will fit your theme. You can obtain images from your computer, from the Internet, from a digital camera, or from scanned media. You can use clipart from the Web that is free for both personal and commercial use (check the copyright information for any such clipart before downloading it).

2. Create a new document and save it as **readbooks.png**.

3. Copy or import the files into your document and convert objects to symbols as necessary.

4. Build at least two animations using the techniques of your choice. (*Hint*: The sliding and tumbling book and the blur-to-sharp text are examples of tweening.)

5. Trim, crop, or adjust frame delay, looping, and transparency as desired.

6. Optimize and export the animation. (*Hint*: The sample is an animated GIF with 16 colors.)

7. Preview the animation, save your work, then examine the sample shown in Figure F-39.

FIGURE F-39
Completed Project Builder 2

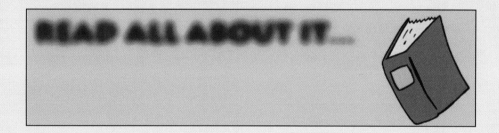

In general, creativity can be about bending or even breaking the rules. When it comes to interactivity in a Web site, however, you ultimately need to keep your users in mind. The discussion of form versus function in Web page design can be a lively one. Because dynamic Web sites are updated frequently to reflect current trends, this page may be different from Figure F-40 if you open it online.

1. Connect to the Internet and go to *www.course.com*. Navigate to the page for this book, click the Student Online Companion, then click the link for this unit.

2. Open a document in a word processor, or open a new Fireworks document, then save the file as **animation**. (*Hint*: You can also use the Text tool in Fireworks to answer the questions.)

3. Scroll down the page to find winners and nominees in several categories, or click the archived nominees link at the top of the page to view previous years.

4. Explore several sites, then, when you find one or two that interest you, answer the following questions:
   - What seems to be the purpose of this site?
   - Who is the target audience?
   - What animation is present? How does it serve the site?
   - How might an animation symbol, frame-by-frame animation, or tweened instances be used in this site?
   - Discuss how frame rate or looping might be used.
   - How would you change the animation in this site?

5. Save your work.

FIGURE F-40
Design Project

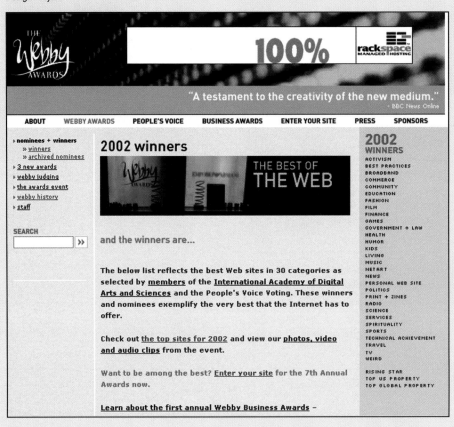

Your group can assign elements of the project to individual members, or work collectively to create the finished product.

Your class on popular culture just read an article about the staggering debt rate of people aged 18–30. Your group has been assigned to write a response and give a presentation on this topic. As an introduction to your online slide presentation, you first want to prove or dispel common myths about money. The sample shown in Figure F-41 demonstrates that yes, money does grow on trees. Your group can choose the financial myth or misconception of its choice and then prove it or dispel it.

1. Obtain images of the financial myth or misconception you've chosen. You can obtain images from your computer, from the Internet, from a digital camera, or from scanned media. You can use clipart from the Web that is free for both personal and commercial use (check the copyright information for any such clipart before downloading it).
2. Create a new document and save it as **mymoneymyth.png**.
3. Copy or import the files into your document.
4. Convert objects to symbols as necessary. (*Hint*: There are two dollar bills symbols and one tree symbol in the sample.)

5. Build animation using the techniques of your choice. (*Hint*: The dollar bill animation in the sample is frame-by-frame animation.)
6. Trim, crop, or adjust frame delay, looping, and transparency as desired.

FIGURE F-41
Completed Group Project

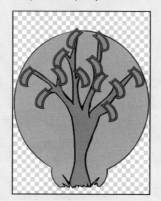

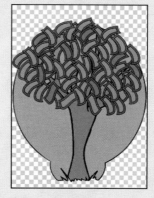

7. Optimize and export the animation. (*Hint*: The sample is an animated GIF with 64 colors.)
8. Preview the document, save your work, then examine the sample shown in Figure F-41.

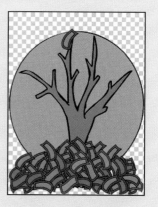

CREATING SOPHISTICATED
WEB PAGE NAVIGATION

1. Create a pop-up menu.

2. Create a navigation bar.

3. Integrate Fireworks HTML into an HTML editor.

UNIT G

CREATING SOPHISTICATED WEB PAGE NAVIGATION

Pop-up Menus and Navigation Bars

A successful Web site will help visitors find the information they want and then navigate to the relevant URL. You can design a Web site so that a pop-up menu and any submenus appear when triggered by a rolling mouse action. By filling out a series of dialog boxes, you can tailor the pop-up menu to look and function exactly the way you want.

Similarly, you can assemble button symbol instances to create a navigation bar with up to four states: Up, Over, and, if you want them, Down and Over while Down.

You can ensure that your graphic elements (such as vector or bitmap objects) remain consistent by embedding an existing button in another button.

Integrating HTML

Once you create a great-looking rollover, pop-up menu, or navigation, you may be challenged to export the document so that the HTML code integrates with your HTML editor. Fireworks makes it easy to export in the HTML style you need, or to copy HTML code into your HTML editor.

Tools You'll Use

Content tab

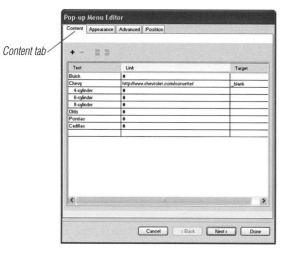

Appearance tab

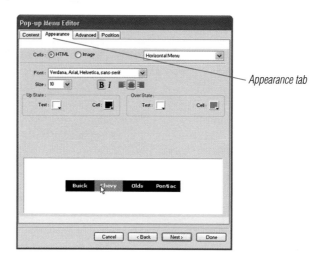

Advanced tab

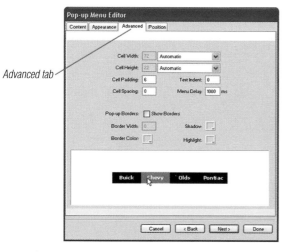

Position tab

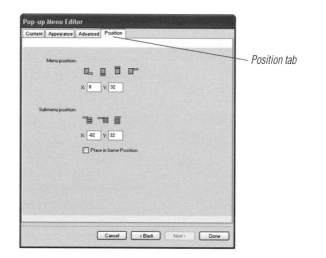

[HTML]
nyper text markup Language

CREATE A POP-UP MENU

What You'll Do

 In this lesson, you will add and edit a pop-up menu and submenu, and export the document.

Understanding Pop-up Menus

You've seen how rollovers can instantly infuse your site with change or information, or how you can link to another Web page. Many times, the information in your Web page consists of title topics and subtopics. You could create individual buttons for each entry, but that could easily clutter up your Web page and still not be easy for your users to understand or navigate. One solution is to create a pop-up menu that organizes and displays the topics hierarchically. A **pop-up menu** is a menu that appears when you move the mouse pointer over a trigger image in a browser. It contains a list of items that link to other Web pages. Pop-up menus are also known as pop-down or drop-down menus.

In addition to rollovers and swapped images, pop-up menus are one of the main categories of Fireworks behaviors. In fact, because it has Up and Over states, you create a pop-up menu by attaching it to a Web object: a slice or a hotspot. You can access the Pop-up Menu Editor by opening the Behaviors panel, clicking the Add behavior button, and then clicking Set Pop-Up Menu. The Pop-up Menu Editor consists of four tabs: Content, Appearance, Advanced, and Position. To create a pop-up menu, you just fill out the information in each

Using a custom style as the cell background

In addition to selecting the default styles on the Appearance tab, you can create a custom style and then select it from the Styles panel. Click the Options menu icon, click Export, then save the style in the Nav Menu folder on the drive where Fireworks MX is loaded. The Nav Menu folder contains the custom style files for pop-up menus. The location of the Nav Menu folder depends on your computer platform and operating system. To find out where it is on your system, search Using Fireworks Help for "configuration files."

tab. Depending on the look and function of your pop-up menu, you may not need to complete more than the Content tab.

The Content tab, shown in Figure G-1, is where you add the items in a menu or submenu, enter their URL links (the addresses), if any, and the URL targets (how they will appear in the browser). You can add menu or submenu items and then drag the entries to a new location in the list, similar to how you drag an object or layer in the Layers panel. By default, each item in the list is a menu item. To convert a menu item into a submenu item, select the item, and then click the Indent Menu button. You can turn a submenu item back to a menu item by clicking the Outdent Menu button. Figure G-2 shows a sample menu and submenu.

You can set and preview the style and overall look of the pop-up in its Up and Over states using settings on the Appearance tab. You can think of a pop-up menu as a small table—you can format the cell of the menu. For example, you can set the pop-up menu to appear vertically or horizontally, use HTML code or an image as the cell background in the menu, select font attributes, and choose a style for the pop-up menu in both states. Note that when you use an image as the cell background instead of HTML code, you increase the size of your file. Also keep in mind how a long menu or submenu will look on your Web page.

FIGURE G-1
Content tab in the Pop-up Menu Editor

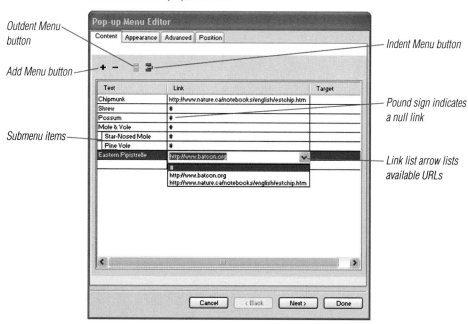

Outdent Menu button

Add Menu button

Submenu items

Indent Menu button

Pound sign indicates a null link

Link list arrow lists available URLs

The Advanced tab allows you to apply HTML table-specific values for the pop-up menu. For example, you can set cell dimension, padding, and spacing, as well as the width and color of the cell border, the length of time the menu remains visible after the mouse pointer moves away from it, and the indentation of the text. The Position tab enables you to set how the menu and submenu items appear onscreen, such as above, below, or offset from the menu. You can select a preset position button or enter X and Y coordinates.

QUICKTIP

For a menu, X and Y coordinate values of zero align the top left corner of the menu with that location on the slice. For a submenu, the X and Y values position the top left corner of the submenu with the top right corner of its parent menu item when the Place in Same Position check box is not selected.

Exporting Pop-up Menus

Although creating and positioning a pop-up menu in Fireworks is simple, ensuring that the pop-up menu will be read correctly by a Web browser is complex. Fortunately, when you export a document that contains a pop-up menu into HTML, Fireworks automatically generates the necessary JavaScript. When you complete the export process, you will notice that Fireworks exports a JavaScript file, mm_menu.js, to the same folder as the HTML file. Every time you add a behavior to your Fireworks document (anything from the Behaviors panel), Fireworks must generate JavaScript to create the interactivity. Fireworks behaviors are an easy interface for adding JavaScript functionality to your documents without having to write any code yourself.

FIGURE G-2
Sample menu and submenu

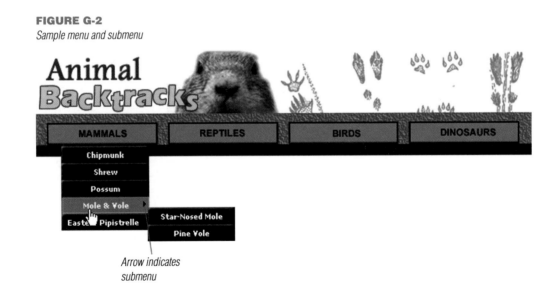

Arrow indicates submenu

FIGURE G-3

Selecting the Set Pop-Up Menu behavior

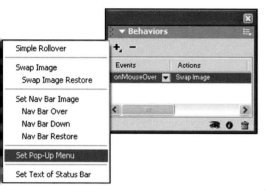

Create a pop-up menu

1. Open fwg_1.png, then save it as **gmparts.png**.

   TIP Click Maintain Appearance if Fireworks displays the Replace Fonts dialog box.

2. Click the Show slices and hotspots button on the Tools panel, then click the engines slice to select it. 🔲

3. Open the Behaviors panel.

   A Swap Image behavior already applied to the engine slice appears in the Behaviors panel.

4. Click the Add behavior button in the Behaviors panel, then click Set Pop-Up Menu, as shown in Figure G-3, to open the Pop-up Menu Editor. ➕

5. Double-click the empty menu item under Text (if necessary), type **Buick**, press [Tab], then type **#** to add a null value as the URL link.

   A new empty menu item appears when you tab to the Link column. In this instance, a null value indicates that the Link field is a dummy link, which serves as a placeholder for the actual link.

   TIP You can also click the Add Menu button to create a new empty menu item. ➕

6. Repeat Step 5, but type **Chevy**, **Olds**, **Pontiac**, and **Cadillac** as separate menu items with null links, then compare your Content tab to Figure G-4.

   TIP If you enter a URL link and leave the Target box blank, by default the URL link will replace the current page in the browser.

You created and added items to a pop-up menu.

FIGURE G-4

Menu items added to Content tab

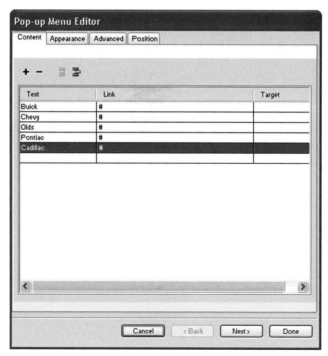

Add a pop-up submenu

1. Click the Chevy menu item, then click the Add Menu button to add an empty menu item beneath Chevy. ✚

2. Double-click the empty cell under Text, type **4-cylinder**, press [Tab], type #, press [Enter] (Win) or [return] (Mac), then click 4-cylinder to select the entire menu item, as shown in Figure G-5.

3. Click the Indent Menu button to make 4-cylinder a submenu item of Chevy. 🗗

4. Click the Add Menu button to add an empty menu item beneath 4-cylinder. ✚

5. Double-click the empty cell, type **6-cylinder**, press [Tab], type #, then click 6-cylinder to select the menu item.

   The new menu item is indented.

6. Repeat Steps 4 and 5, but type **8-cylinder**.

7. Compare your Content tab to Figure G-6.

You added items to a submenu.

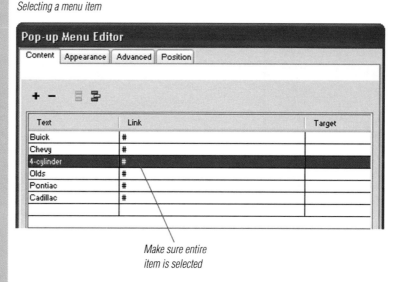

Make sure entire
item is selected

Submenu items
are indented

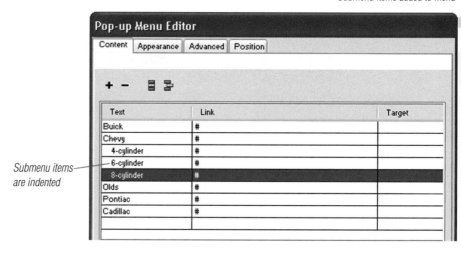

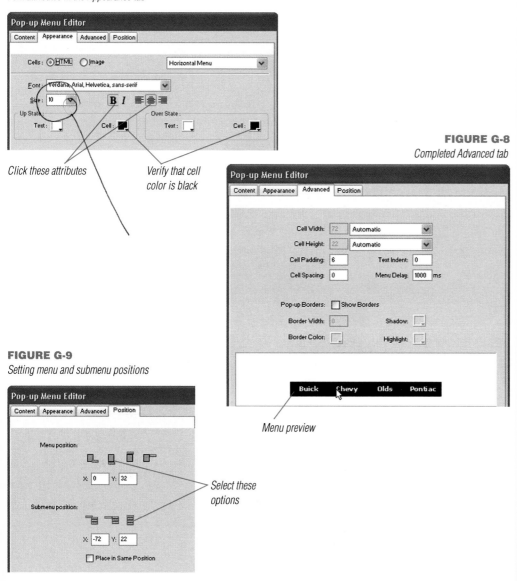

FIGURE G-7
Font attributes in the Appearance tab

Click these attributes

Verify that cell color is black

FIGURE G-8
Completed Advanced tab

FIGURE G-9
Setting menu and submenu positions

Menu preview

Select these options

Set menu appearance, table construction, and position

1. Click Next to display the Appearance tab.

   TIP   You can also click the tab name to open it.

2. Click the HTML option, click the Alignment of the pop-up menu list arrow, click Horizontal Menu, then enter the font attributes shown in Figure G-7.

3. Verify that white appears as the Text color box, and that black appears as the Cell color box in both the Up State and the Over State sections.

4. Click Next to open the Advanced tab.

5. Enter the values shown in Figure G-8.

6. Click Next to open the Position tab.

7. Click the bottom of slice button (2nd button) in the Menu position section.

8. Click the bottom of menu button (3rd button) in the Submenu position section, verify that the Place in Same Position check box is not selected, then compare your Position tab to Figure G-9.

9. Click Done to close the Pop-up Menu Editor.

You used the Pop-up Menu Editor to set options for the pop-up menu's appearance and the position of the pop-up menu.

Preview the pop-up menu

1. Notice that the slice behavior line is an outline of the pop-up menu.

   TIP   You can drag the menu outline to reposition the menu around the slice on the canvas.

2. Click the Hide slices and hotspots button on the Tools panel. [icon]

3. Click the Preview tab on the document window, then roll the mouse pointer over the engines button.

   The rollover is visible but the pop-up menu is not. Pop-up menus are not visible in Fireworks preview.

4. Click File on the menu bar, point to Preview in Browser, then click the first browser in the list to open the primary browser.

5. Roll the mouse pointer over the engines button, roll the mouse pointer over the Chevy button, then compare your image to Figure G-10.

   The menu and submenu are visible, but the submenu is not centered beneath the Chevy menu and there is no differentiation when you move the mouse pointer over the cylinder choices.

6. Close the browser.

You previewed the pop-up menu in Fireworks and in a browser.

FIGURE G-10
Previewing the pop-up menu in a browser

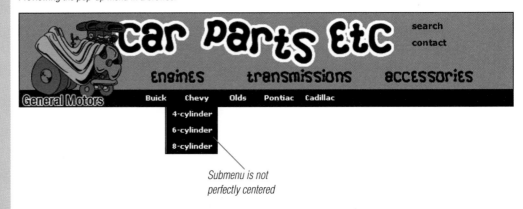

Submenu is not perfectly centered

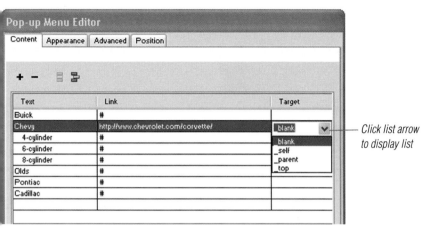

Pop-up Menu Editor

Content | Appearance | Advanced | Position

+   −   ▤   ▤

Text	Link	Target
Buick	#	
Chevy	http://www.chevrolet.com/corvette/	blank ▼
4-cylinder	#	blank
6-cylinder	#	_self
8-cylinder	#	_parent
Olds	#	_top
Pontiac	#	
Cadillac	#	

— *Click list arrow
to display list*

Edit the pop-up menu

1. Click the Show slices and hotspots button on the Tools panel, click the Original tab on the document window, then click the engines slice. 🔲

2. Double-click the Show Popup Menu behavior in the Behaviors panel to open the Pop-up Menu Editor.

   TIP   You can also double-click the menu behavior outline on the canvas to open the Pop-up Menu Editor.

3. Double-click the Link box for Chevy, then type **http://www.chevrolet.com/corvette**.

4. Click the Target box, click the Target list arrow, then click _blank to open the URL in a separate window, as shown in Figure G-11.

5. Click the Appearance tab, click the Over State Cell color box, type **#CC3300** in the hexadecimal text box, then press [Enter] (Win) or [return] (Mac).

6. Click the Position tab, select the value in the Submenu position X text box, type **–62**, then click Done.

7. Click File on the menu bar, point to Preview in Browser, then click the first browser in the list to open the primary browser.

8. Test the pop-up menu, then compare your image to Figure G-12.

   The submenu is centered beneath the menu, and the menu items are highlighted when the mouse pointer rolls over them.

   (continued)

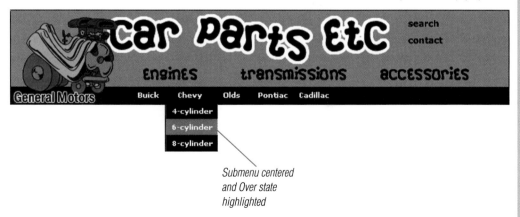

*Submenu centered
and Over state
highlighted*

TIP You can increase the amount of space between a menu item and the submenu arrow.gif by adding blank spaces after the last letter of the item in the Pop-up Menu Editor.

9. Click the Chevy button, then close both browser windows.

   The Chevy link opens a second browser window.

   TIP If you are not online, the Chevy link will not open.

You modified the pop-up menu and then previewed it in a browser.

Optimize and export the document

1. Click Select on the menu bar, then click Deselect to deselect all the slices.

2. Open the Optimize panel (if necessary).

3. Click the Settings list arrow in the Optimize panel, then click GIF WebSnap 128.

4. Click File on the menu bar, then click Export.

5. Create a new folder named **gmparts**, then open the folder.

6. Click the Save as type list arrow (Win) or the Save As list arrow (Mac), click HTML and Images, verify that your Export dialog box resembles Figure G-13, then click Save.

   Fireworks exports the images to the images subfolder in the gmparts folder and places the .htm file and the related mm_menu.js file in the gmparts folder.

   (continued)

FIGURE G-13
Options in the Export dialog box

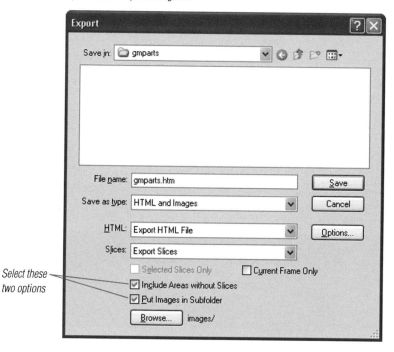

Select these two options

7. Open the file management tool that is on your operating system, adjust the settings to display extensions, then navigate to the drive and folder where you created the gmparts folder.

8. Compare your image to Figure G-14, then close your file management tool.

9. Save your work, then close gmparts.png.

You optimized and exported the document containing a pop-up menu and viewed the associated export files.

FIGURE G-14
Exported pop-up menu files

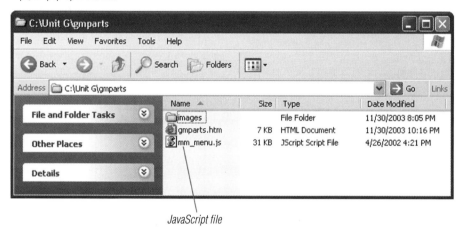

JavaScript file

CREATE A NAVIGATION BAR

What You'll Do

 In this lesson, you will create a navigation bar and optimize and export the document.

Understanding Navigation Bars

When you created buttons in previous units, you were building efficient navigation tools for your users. You can easily create buttons that are part of a navigation system known as a navigation bar, or nav bar. A **navigation bar** is a group of buttons that link to different areas inside or outside the Web site.

A nav bar can be positioned along any perimeter of the main Web page, usually along the top or left side, although many creative designers will incorporate the nav bar as part of the overall design, as shown in Figure G-15. A nav bar can be simple text, an image, or any combination thereof, depending on your design and file size requirements. Whatever its appearance, even if it appears to be melded into the overall design, the purpose of a nav bar remains constant: to maintain the same look from page to page, even though the functions may be page-specific. A well-functioning, uniform-looking nav bar is a good foundation for any successful site.

In Fireworks, you can create a nav bar by creating instances of button symbols that contain Down and Over While Down states in addition to an Up and Over state. When you create the Down and Over While Down states in the Button Editor, Fireworks adds a navigation bar image behavior to the Behaviors panel. Fireworks automatically inserts a slice when you drag a button instance to the canvas or when you convert an object to a button symbol.

You can also create a navigation bar by creating individual frames for each rollover state, and adding a Simple Rollover behavior to them. You can add slices to the rollover button, and then select the slices and use the Set Nav Bar Image behavior in the Behaviors panel. Figure G-16 shows the Set Nav Bar Image dialog box.

Building Navigation Bars Efficiently

Creating a nav bar for your users helps make your site efficient and easy to use. You can make the process of creating a nav bar in Fireworks equally easy and efficient. The buttons in a nav bar are interrelated in function and appearance; therefore, you want to minimize the opportunity for error if you need to edit the non-text portions of a button, and you want to maximize your speed in doing so.

You've seen how easy it is to create a button, then an instance, then add text, and then modify the button's appearance in different states. When you're creating buttons that will serve as a nav bar, you can also create different button states for the button object, duplicate button instances on the canvas, and then just edit the text label for each different button instance as desired.

Fireworks allows you to export the navigation bar for the Down state image of each button of the page that you are currently viewing. The Down state image is displayed when you select the Multiple Nav Bar HTML Pages check box in the Document Specific tab of the HTML Setup dialog box. To enable this feature, you must also ensure that the button object name is identical to the URL link prefix filename. For example, a Contact Us navigation button would have the following properties: text label: Contact Us (the text label can be any text or image), button object name: contact, and URL link: contact.htm. You can easily enter the button object name and URL link file name in text boxes on the Property inspector.

Navigation bar is an integral design element for the page

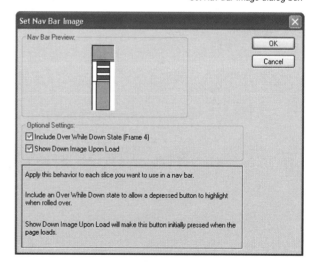

Create a generic button symbol with an Up state

1. Open fwg_2.png, save it as **recipes.png**, then make sure the Library and Behaviors panels are open.

2. Click the Pointer tool on the Tools panel, then click the small pale yellow rectangle on the canvas.

3. Click Modify on the menu bar, point to Symbol, then click Convert to Symbol to open the Symbol Properties dialog box.

4. Type **generic button** in the Name text box, click the Button option, then click OK.

5. Double-click the instance on the canvas to open the Button Editor.

6. Click the Text tool on the Tools panel, then enter the attributes shown in Figure G-17.

7. Center the pointer over the cross hair, then type **MY LABEL**.

8. Click the Pointer tool on the Tools panel, press and hold [Shift], click the rectangle to select both objects, click Modify on the menu bar, point to Align, then click Center Vertical.

9. Click Modify on the menu bar, point to Align, click Center Horizontal, then compare your Button Editor to Figure G-18.

You created a button symbol and added text to it in the Up state.

FIGURE G-17
Font attributes for the generic button

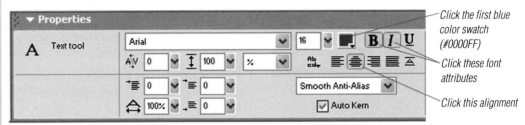

Click the first blue color swatch (#0000FF)

Click these font attributes

Click this alignment

FIGURE G-18
Text added to Up state

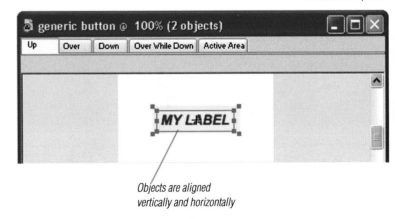

Objects are aligned vertically and horizontally

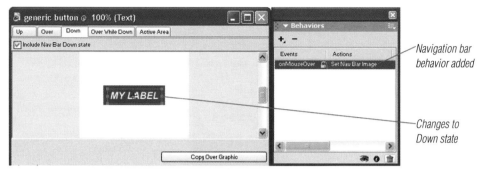

Navigation bar
behavior added

Changes to
Down state

Create other states for the button symbol

1. Click the Over tab, then click Copy Up Graphic.

2. Click the rectangle, click the Fill Color box on the Property inspector, type **#FFCC33** in the hexadecimal text box, then press [Enter] (Win) or [return] (Mac).

3. Click the Down tab, click Copy Over Graphic, click the rectangle, click the Fill Color box on the Property inspector, type **#9900CC** in the hexadecimal text box, then press [Enter] (Win) or [return] (Mac).

4. Click the text object, click the Color box on the Property inspector, click the first white color swatch in the color palette, then compare your Button Editor to Figure G-19.

5. Click the Over While Down tab, click Copy Down Graphic, click the rectangle, click the Fill Color box on the Property inspector, click the first blue color swatch in the color palette, then press [Enter] (Win) or [return] (Mac).

6. Click the text object, click the Color box on the Property inspector, then click the first white color swatch in the color palette.

7. Click the Active Area tab, then verify that the slices cover the buttons exactly.

8. Click Done, then compare your image to Figure G-20.

You created a button symbol.

FIGURE G-20
Newly created button symbol

Create instances of the generic button symbol

1. Click View on the menu bar, point to Grid, then verify that Snap to Grid is selected.

2. Press and hold [Alt] (Win) or [option] (Mac), then drag an instance of the button instance.

3. Click Edit on the menu bar, then click Repeat Duplicate to duplicate and place another instance on the canvas.

4. Verify on the Property inspector that the coordinates of the middle instance are 36 X, 180 Y.

5. Verify on the Property inspector that the coordinates for the bottom instance are 36 X, 235 Y, then compare your image to Figure G-21.

6. Click the top button instance to select it, select the text in the Button Name text box on the left side of the Property inspector, type **starters**, then press [Enter] (Win) or [return] (Mac).

7. Select the text in the Text text box on the Property inspector, type **Starters**, then press [Enter] (Win) or [return] (Mac).

(continued)

FIGURE G-21
Duplicated button instances

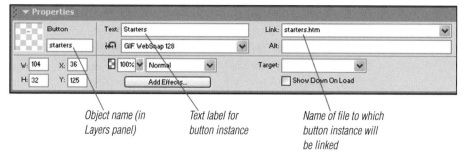

Object name (in
Layers panel)

Text label for
button instance

Name of file to which
button instance will
be linked

FIGURE G-23
Nav bar slices aligned

Align slices to avoid
extraneous slices

8. Click the Link text box on the Property inspector, type **starters.htm**, then compare your Property inspector to Figure G-22.

   TIP   In order to export an HTML file for the Down state of each page, the button name should match the link filename.

9. Repeat Steps 7 and 8 for the middle instance, changing the name of the button to **entrees**, the Text to **Entrees**, and the Link to **entrees.htm**.

10. Repeat Steps 6, 7, and 8 for the bottom instance, changing the name of the Button to **desserts**, the Text to **Desserts**, and the Link to **desserts.htm**.

You created duplicate instances and changed their properties.

Optimize and export the document and nav bar

1. Click the Show slices and hotspots button on the Tools panel, then align the slices of the nav bar until your image resembles Figure G-23. 🔲

2. Click the Hide slices and hotspots button on the Tools panel. 🔲

3. Click Window on the menu bar, then click Optimize.

4. Click the Settings list arrow, then click GIF WebSnap 128.

5. Click File on the menu bar, then click Export.

(continued)

6. Navigate to the drive and folder where your data files are stored, create a new folder named **recipes**, then open the folder (if necessary).

7. Click the Save as type (Win) or Save As (Mac) list arrow, click HTML and Images, then verify that your Export dialog box resembles Figure G-24.

8. Click Options to open the HTML Setup dialog box, verify that .htm is the Extension, click the Document Specific tab, verify that the Multiple Nav Bar HTML Pages check box is selected, then click OK to close the dialog box.

9. Click Save, open the file management tool that is on your operating system, adjust the settings to display extensions (if necessary), then navigate to the drive and folder where you created the recipes folder.

   The folder contains recipes.htm, and three html files that will show the Down state of the other buttons in the nav bar: starters.htm, entrees.htm, and desserts.htm.

10. Compare your image to Figure G-25, then close your file management tool.

You optimized and exported the document containing the nav bar, then viewed the associated export files.

FIGURE G-24
Options in the Export dialog box

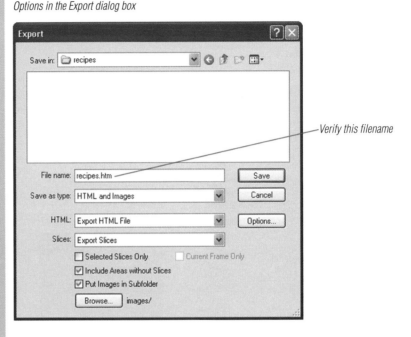

Verify this filename

FIGURE G-25
Exported nav bar files

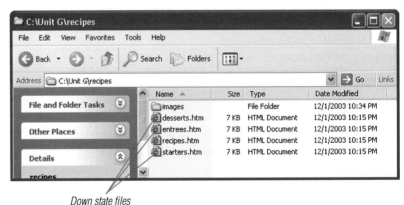

Down state files

FIGURE G-26

Previewing the nav bar in a browser

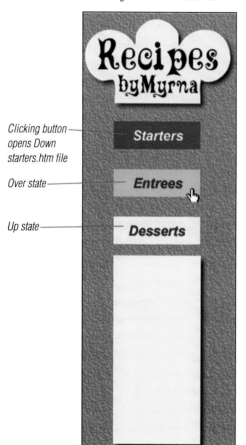

Clicking button opens Down starters.htm file

Over state ———

Up state ———

Preview the document and nav bar

1. Open your browser, then open recipes.htm.

2. Roll the mouse pointer over the Starters button, click the button, roll the mouse pointer over the Entrees button, then compare your image to Figure G-26.

   The starters.htm file opens in response to the mouse click and the Over state of the Entrees button responds to the rollover.

3. Roll the mouse pointer over the Starters button.

   The button turns blue, reflecting the Over While Down state.

4. Close your browser, save your work, then close recipes.png.

You previewed the nav bar in your browser.

INTEGRATE FIREWORKS
HTML INTO AN HTML EDITOR

What You'll Do

 In this lesson, you will learn about the basic relationship between the HTML code Fireworks creates when you export a document, and the HTML editor that will turn it into a Web page.

Understanding Web Page Structure and Basic HTML Code

A Web browser determines the appearance of a Web page by interpreting **Hypertext Markup Language (HTML)** code. In essence, HTML marks up the text in your Web page so your browser can read it. HTML consists of **tags** that describe how the text should be formatted when a browser displays it. The tags are used in pairs, as shown below, and contain data in between. For example, the tags *<title> Toy Parade </title>* include the Web page's title, Toy Parade.

HTML files are divided into two segments: a head and a body. The body contains the content of the Web page that the browser will display to the viewer. The head content is generally not viewed, except for the title. The head contains important information

that the Web page needs to function properly: the language encoding, JavaScript and VBScript functions and variables, and keywords and content indicators for search engines. JavaScript is a **client-side scripting language**, which means that it runs within a Web browser. It provides the interactivity in an HTML page—Fireworks automatically generates the JavaScript you need from the behaviors you add to a slice or hotspot. JavaScript generally sits inside the HTML page, between the open <script> tag and the close </script> tag. These script tags can be in the head or body section of the HTML, or both. JavaScript can also be in its own file, separate from the HTML document. In this case, the JavaScript file has the .js extension, and the HTML file will have a script tag that calls on the external file, such as the mm_menu.js file that Fireworks creates when you export a pop-up menu.

Using Exported Fireworks HTML

When you generate HTML by exporting files in Fireworks, you will probably want to integrate it and be able to edit it with the content you've created in an HTML editor, such as Macromedia Dreamweaver or Microsoft FrontPage. Depending on the kind of Web page you want to create, your HTML editor of choice, and your work preferences, you can accomplish this in several ways.

Fireworks generates two kinds of HTML code: one for an image map and one for a table for sliced images. An image map is HTML code that identifies hotspots in an image for linking. A table is HTML code that divides an area of the page into rows and columns for display. Every time you export slices in Fireworks, the program generates individual images based on your slices, and it must generate the HTML code for a table to re-assemble those images into a single unit. For example, when you export HTML and Images as the type, the code in <body> will contain an image map and/or table code, along with comments that allow you to roundtrip the code back to Fireworks from Dreamweaver.

Building a Content Page Around a Fireworks HTML Page

If your Fireworks HTML includes Fireworks-generated JavaScript, such as from behaviors you added using the Behaviors panel, you need to ensure that the HTML editor will recognize it. You can achieve this by using the following settings in the Export dialog box: verify that Export HTML File is the HTML selection, click Options to open the HTML Setup dialog box, and then select the HTML Style that matches your HTML editor, as shown in Figure G-27. JavaScript is inserted in between the open <script> tag and the close </script> tag.

QUICK**TIP**

You can also open the HTML Setup dialog box from the File menu.

When you export a document with HTML and Images as the type, you can open the HTML document that Fireworks generated in your HTML editor and then edit it as though you had created it from scratch in that program. Because HTML is an **open standard**, all HTML editors can read one another's code. However, some HTML editors, such as Dreamweaver, Adobe GoLive, and FrontPage, have special interfaces for creating and applying JavaScript interactivity.

FIGURE G-27
HTML Style export options

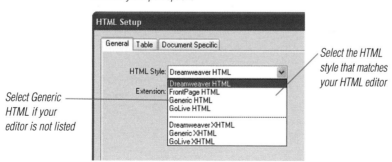

Select Generic HTML if your editor is not listed

Select the HTML style that matches your HTML editor

Figure G-28 shows the HTML code for different styles. JavaScript also appears differently depending on the style.

Inserting a Fireworks HTML Table into an Existing HTML Page

There will be many occasions when you need to insert a sliced image, image map, nav bar, or pop-up menu you created in Fireworks into the page layout of your HTML editor. For Dreamweaver, you can just place the insertion pointer where you want the element to appear and follow the directions in Dreamweaver for inserting Fireworks HTML. For other editors, you may need to be a bit more resourceful.

FIGURE G-28
Selected styles in HTML

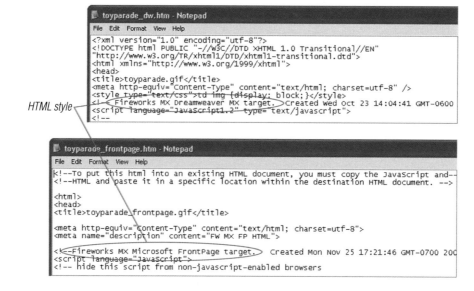

HTML style

For the HTML and JavaScript code, open the Fireworks HTML file, copy the open <script> tag and continue copying the code through the close </script> tag. Next, paste this code inside the head section of the new HTML page, right before the close </head> tag. To insert the body of the Fireworks HTML, copy everything between, but do not include the open <body> tag and close </body> tag, then paste it where it should appear in the new HTML page. Fireworks-generated HTML code may include comments that indicate when to start and stop copying, as shown in Figure G-29.

FIGURE G-29

Copy comments in HTML code

```
<!DOCTYPE HTML PUBLIC "-//W3C//DTD HTML 4.01 Transitional//EN"
<html>
<head>
<title>Toy Parade</title>
<meta http-equiv="Content-Type" content="text/html; charset=is
<!--==================== BEGIN COPYING THE JAVASCRIPT SECTION HERE
<script language="JavaScript1.2" type="text/javascript">
<!-- hide
function MM_findobj(n, d) { //v4.01
  var p,i,x;  if(!d) d=document; if((p=n.indexOf("?"))>0&&pare
    d=parent.frames[n.substring(p+1)].document; n=n.substring(
  if(!(x=d[n])&&d.all) x=d.all[n]; for (i=0;!x&&i<d.forms.len
  for(i=0;!x&&d.layers&&i<d.layers.length;i++) x=MM_findobj(n,
  if(!x && d.getElementById) x=d.getElementById(n); return x;
}

/* Functions that swaps images. */
function MM_swapImage() { //v3.0
  var i,j=0,x,a=MM_swapImage.arguments; document.MM_sr=new Arr
  if ((x=MM_findobj(a[i]))!=null){document.MM_sr[j++]=x; if(!
}
function MM_swapImgRestore() { //v3.0
  var i,x,a=document.MM_sr; for(i=0;a&&i<a.length&&(x=a[i])&&x
}

// stop hiding -->
</script>
<!--==================== STOP COPYING THE JAVASCRIPT HERE
</head>

<body>
<table width="640" border="0" align="center" cellpadding="0" c
  <tr>
    <td>
      <!--==================== BEGIN COPYING THE HTML ======
      <script language="JavaScript" type="text/javascript">
      <!-- hide
      if (document.images) {
```

Copy comments

Create a pop-up menu and submenu on the Content tab.

1. Open fwg_3.png, then save it as **literary_cat.png**.
2. Show slices, select the books slice, then open the Behaviors panel.
3. Add a Set Pop-Up Menu behavior to the books slice.
4. Add the following menu items with null link values in the Pop-up Menu Editor: Fiction, Biography, Kids, Coffee Table, and Hobbies.
5. Add the following submenu items to the Coffee Table menu item with a null value: Art, Nature, Travel.

Set the appearance.

1. Click the Appearance tab.
2. Select the HTML option and Vertical Menu as the orientation.
3. Enter the following font attributes: Font: Georgia, Times New Roman, Times, Serif; Font Size: 10; Bold, Left alignment.
4. Make sure that the text color is white and that the Cell color is black for the Up State and Over State.

Set table attributes and menu position.

1. Click the Advanced tab.
2. Enter the following cell attributes: Cell Width and Cell Height: Automatic, Cell Padding: 6, Text Indent: 0, Cell Spacing: 0, Menu Delay: 1000, select the Show Borders check box, then accept the default values.

3. Click the Position tab.
4. Set the menu position to the bottom of the slice and the submenu position to the top right of the menu.
5. Click Done to close the Pop-up Menu Editor.
6. Save your work.

Preview and test the pop-up menu.

1. Preview the document in a browser.
2. Test the pop-up menu and submenu, then close the browser.

Edit the pop-up menu.

1. Open the Pop-up Menu Editor from the Behaviors panel.
2. Add the following URL to the Biography link: **http://www.biography.com**, then set the target to _blank.
3. Click the Appearance tab, then change the Up State Cell color to **#FF9933** and the Over State Cell color to **#996600**.
4. Click the Position tab, then change the Menu position X coordinate to 22.
5. Click Done to close the Pop-up Menu Editor.
6. Save your work.
7. Test the pop-up menu in a browser, then close the browser.

Optimize and export the document.

1. Verify that no slices are selected.
2. Open the Optimize panel and make the Setting GIF WebSnap 128.

3. Open the Export dialog box, then create a new folder named **litcat**, then open the folder.
4. Verify the following settings: Save as type: HTML and Images; HTML: Export HTML File; Slices: Export Slices; and that the Include Areas without Slices and Put Images in Subfolder check boxes are selected.
5. Export the file, then save your work.
6. Preview the file in a browser, compare your image to Figure G-30, then close the browser and literary_cat.png.

Create a button symbol.

1. Open fwg_4.png, then save it as **technodude.png**.
2. Select the black rectangle on the canvas and convert it to a button symbol named **generic button**.
3. Edit the symbol in the Button Editor, select the Text tool with the following attributes: Font: Tahoma, Font Size: 13, Color: white, Bold, Center alignment.
4. Center the pointer over the cross hair, then type **MY LABEL**.
5. Select both objects, then align them vertically and horizontally.

Create other button states.

1. Click the Over tab, then click copy the Up graphic.

2. Add an Inner Glow effect to the rectangle that has default settings and make the glow color **#CCCCCC**.
3. Change the text color to **#00FF00**.
4. Click the Down tab.
5. Copy the Over graphic, then change the color of the rectangle to **#CC3300** and the text color to black.
6. Click the Over While Down tab, then copy the Down graphic.
7. Change the text color to **#00FF00**.
8. Click the Active Area tab, then make sure the slice covers the rectangle.
9. Click Done to close the Button Editor.
10. Save your work.

Create button instances.

1. Turn on Snap to Grid, if necessary.
2. Drag a duplicate instance of the generic button symbol instance to the right of the button instance on the canvas to form a horizontal bar.
3. Duplicate the button symbol instance.
4. Change the text of the left instance to **TECH SUPPORT**, the name of the button instance object to **techsupport**, and the Link text box to **techsupport.htm**.
5. Repeat Step 4 for the middle instance, changing the text to **PROGRAMMING**, the name of the button instance object to **programming**, and the Link text box to **programming.htm**.

6. Repeat Step 4 for the right instance, changing the text to **TUTORIALS**, the name of the button instance object to **tutorials**, and the Link text box to **tutorials.htm**.
7. Save your work.

Optimize, export, and preview.

1. Verify that no slices are selected.
2. Open the Optimize panel, then select GIF WebSnap 128 as the export setting.
3. Open the Export dialog box , create a new folder named **techno**, then open the folder.
4. Enter the following: Save as type: HTML and Images, HTML: Export HTML File, Slices: Export Slices, Include Areas without Slices

and Put Images in Subfolder should be selected.
5. Click the Options button and verify that the Extension on the General tab is .htm, that the Multiple Nav Bar HTML Pages check box on the Document Specific tab is selected, then close the HTML Setup dialog box.
6. Export the file, then save your work.
7. Open the technodude.htm file in a browser, then test the nav bar.
8. Compare your image to Figure G-30, then close your browser and technodude.png.

FIGURE G-30
Completed Skills Review

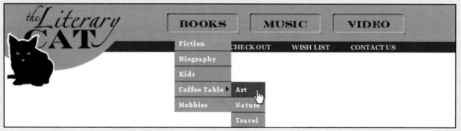

Some friends of yours own a successful specialty food delivery business, Snack of the Month. Business has been booming, so now they're ready to expand to more items. They've asked you to design their new Web site, Stuff of the Month.

1. Obtain images that will reinforce your food theme. You can obtain images from your computer, from the Internet, from a digital camera, or from scanned media. You can use clipart from the Web that is free for both personal and commercial use (check the copyright information for any such clipart before downloading it).

2. Create a new document and save it as **stuffomonth.png**.

3. Import the following file and the files you obtained in Step 1 into your document.
   ■ box.jpg

4. Create at least three buttons.

5. Create a pop-up menu and two submenus for at least one button.

6. Select the appearance of the pop-up menu items. Choose Image as the Cells type in the Appearance tab, then select styles of your choice.

7. Optimize and export the file.

8. Open the stuffomonth.htm file in a browser, then test the pop-up menu.

9. Save your work, then examine the sample shown in Figure G-31.

FIGURE G-31
Completed Project Builder 1

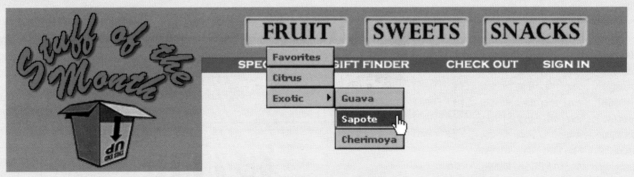

One of your good friends is a home project/crafts maven—she can transform any object into another object that someone will buy. You recently met someone who is a broker of large broken palette orders from discount and wholesale stores. Talking to her gave you the idea of starting a little side business: partner with your friend to buy up quantities of something and show how it can be transformed into a marketable item. You'll name the business Trash to Cash. You've already transformed your first item and

are ready to use your Fireworks skills to advertise the business. Your Web page will convey your message.

1. Obtain images of the bulk item or end product that will fit your theme. You can obtain images from your computer, from the Internet, from a digital camera, or from scanned media. You can use clipart from the Web that is free for both personal and commercial use (check the copyright information for any such clipart before downloading it).

2. Create a new document and save it as **trash2cash.png**.

3. Copy or import the files into your document and convert objects to symbols as necessary.
4. Create a navigation bar for the site.
5. Optimize and export the file.
6. Open the trash2cash.htm file in a browser, then test the nav bar.
7. Save your work, then examine the sample shown in Figure G-32.

FIGURE G-32
Completed Project Builder 2

DESIGN PROJECT

Typically, when you navigate a Web page, you only use the navigation bar to get to the next page or link. However, navigation bars and pop-up menus can easily become part the Web page design, and thus affect how you experience the site. Web sites are updated frequently to reflect current trends, so this page may be different from Figure G-33 if you open it online.

1. Connect to the Internet and go to *www.course.com*. Navigate to the page for this book, click the Student Online Companion, then click the link for this unit.

2. Open a document in a word processor, or open a new Fireworks document, then save the file as **navigation**. (*Hint*: You can also use the Text tool in Fireworks to answer the questions.)

3. Explore several sites, then, when you find one or two that interest you, answer the following questions:
   - What seems to be the purpose of this site?
   - Who is the target audience?
   - How is navigation used in the site? How many navigational elements are there?
   - How do the navigation system and pop-up menus fit the Web design? How are they configured?
   - Are navigation bars and pop-up menus subtle or obvious? Do you find them intuitive and useful? Do you like them? Discuss why or why not.
   - How would you change the navigation or pop-up menus at this site?

4. Save your work.

FIGURE G-33
Design Project

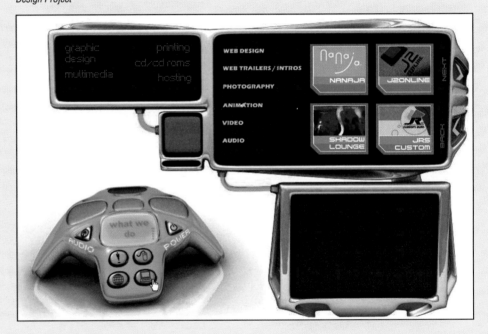

Your group can assign elements of the project to individual members, or work collectively to create the finished product.

You've been asked to determine how the study or work environment affects performance. You can examine the related variable of your choice, such as the neatness of a desk, aesthetic trappings, the quality of office supplies, and so on. Your group can choose the environmental variable of your choice and use your Fireworks skills to present a marketing solution.

1. Obtain images of the study or work variable you've chosen. You can obtain images from your computer, from the Internet, from a digital camera, or from scanned media. You can use clipart from the Web that is free for both personal and commercial use (check the copyright information for any such clipart before downloading it).
2. Create a new document and save it as **desktop_theory.png**.
3. Copy or import the files into your document.
4. Convert objects to symbols as necessary.
5. Create a pop-up menu and submenus.
6. Create a nav bar.

7. Optimize and export the document.
8. Open the desktop_theory.htm file in a browser, then test the pop-up menu and nav bar.

FIGURE G-34
Completed Group Project

9. Save your work, then examine the sample shown in Figure G-34. Note that part of the figure is a compilation of the nav bar and buttons in each state.

UNIT U
ENHANCING PRODUCTIVITY

1. Tailor and customize work.

2. Make global changes.

3. Integrate Fireworks with other applications.

4. Understand intellectual property issues.

UNIT U
ENHANCING PRODUCTIVITY

Making Your Job Easier

Inevitably, in the course of design, you are going to need to make a global change to one thing or another. Regardless of whom your client is (and especially if it's yourself), change might be necessary even after you think the project is complete.

Fireworks makes it easy to change many attributes in one or more documents using the Find and Replace feature and the Batch Process feature. You can perform a series of steps on one object, and then use the History panel to replay that series of steps on another object. You can also save steps as commands.

You can further tailor the Fireworks environment to improve your workflow by customizing keyboard shortcuts. Fireworks allows you to use shortcuts from other applications. Because Fireworks is a graphics

program, many of its robust (and cool) features take a hit on your system resources. You can adjust settings in the History panel and in the Preferences dialog box to change the way Fireworks uses system resources.

One of Fireworks' greatest strengths is its ability to interface with other programs. There are several features you can use to instantly integrate your documents with other programs within the Macromedia Studio suite and with other popular programs.

Finally, all Web content, whether it's something you view, download, or create, has some relationship with intellectual property law. Understanding the basic principles of copyright, trademark, and other intellectual property issues is essential to effective (and legal) Web page design.

Tools You'll Use

Undo marker

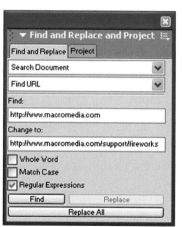

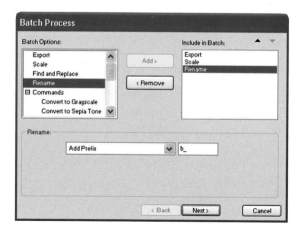

TAILOR AND CUSTOMIZE WORK

What You'll Do

In this lesson, you will duplicate a set of keyboard shortcuts, create a custom keyboard shortcut command, and then use the History panel to undo a step, replay steps, and save steps as a command.

Customizing Keyboard Shortcuts

The master set of Fireworks keyboard shortcuts shares common functions with other programs. For example, the copy shortcut, [Ctrl][C] (Win) or [command][C] (Mac), is found in other major software applications, including the Corel, Adobe, and Microsoft suites. However, some commands or tools do not have shortcuts, while others are Macromedia-specific. You can personalize your own set of keyboard shortcuts by creating or modifying the ones you want, or by using a set from another application with which you are familiar.

You can open the Keyboard Shortcuts dialog box from the Edit menu (Win) or Fireworks menu (Mac). Fireworks provides five default sets: Fireworks, FreeHand, Illustrator, Macromedia Standard, and Photoshop. If you want to use a shortcut set from another application, choose a set from the Current Set list. If you want to add a custom shortcut, you must first duplicate a default set, rename it, and then modify shortcuts as you wish. You cannot

replace or overwrite a default shortcut set, but you can modify custom sets. To view shortcuts, click an option from the Commands list: Menu Commands, Tools, or Miscellaneous. You can then change an existing shortcut or create one for a command that lacks one. Command shortcuts must include a **modifier key**: [Shift], [Ctrl], and [Alt] (Win), or [Shift], [command], [option], and [control] (Mac). Tool shortcuts cannot include a modifier key, only a letter or number.

> **QUICKTIP**
> You do not have to open a document to edit keyboard shortcuts.

Using the History Panel

The History panel records the steps you've recently performed for the currently open unsaved document. You can undo recorded steps using the History panel. You can also set the number of undo steps in the History panel by clicking Preferences on the Edit menu (Win) or on the Fireworks menu (Mac), and then typing a number in the Undo Steps text box on the General tab.

Figure H-1 shows steps in the History panel. The Undo marker points to the current step. You can step back into the history of your document by dragging the Undo marker up the step history in the panel, undoing each step beneath it. Undone steps are overwritten in the History panel by subsequent edits in the document; the History panel tracks results, not keystrokes.

You can also select one or more steps, select another object and replay the steps, or copy steps to the clipboard where you can use them to build a custom command

script to replay later. If you want to permanently save steps as a command, click the Save button on the History panel. The custom commands you create on the History panel appear at the bottom of the Commands menu.

Maximize Available Resources

Every graphics program you use is going to tap into the available resources on your computer to some extent, depending on the program and the operating system. As a general rule, PC users may find that Windows XP and 2000 manage resources better than Windows 98 or ME, while Mac users may find the same holds true for OS X over previous versions. You can search the system requirements Web page for your operating system on hints for optimizing your particular computer.

You'll use up more memory when you have several programs open at the same time and when you use Fireworks features that require more resources. For example,

creating text blocks requires fewer resources than applying effects to multiple objects.

Within the Fireworks environment, you can reduce the number of undo/redo steps that Fireworks stores by opening the Preferences dialog box from the Edit menu. Figure H-2 shows the General tab in the Preferences dialog box. You can also clear steps from the History panel by clicking Clear History from the History panel Options menu or by saving the document. Note that when you clear the history, you cannot undo that action; everything you've done in your document to that point is editable within the standard confines of the feature, but not undoable. For example, you can delete effects in the Effects section of the Property inspector to remove them, but you cannot undo the steps that created them.

FIGURE H-1
History panel

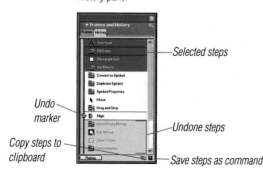

Selected steps

Undo marker

Copy steps to clipboard

Undone steps

Save steps as command

FIGURE H-2
General tab in the Preferences dialog box

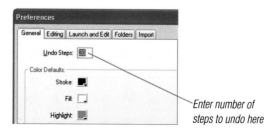

Enter number of steps to undo here

Create a duplicate keyboard shortcut set and custom shortcut

1. Open fwh_1.png, then save it as **rainbowtea.png**.

2. Click Edit (Win) or Fireworks (Mac) on the menu bar, then click Keyboard Shortcuts to open the Keyboard Shortcuts dialog box.

3. Click the Duplicate Set button at the top of the dialog box, type **MM Standard Copy** in the Name text box, as shown in Figure H-3, then click OK.

4. Verify that Menu Commands appears in the Commands list, click the expand icon next to View, scroll down the list, then click Slice Overlay to select it.

5. Click the Add a new shortcut button, press and hold [Shift], then type **S**.

   Fireworks automatically adds the modifier key, Shift, to the Press Key text box.

6. Compare your dialog box to Figure H-4, then click OK.

7. Verify that the rainbow.png window is active, press and hold [Shift], then press [S].

   The slices in the document are visible and the Show slices and hotspots button on the Tools panel is active.

8. Click the Hide slices and hotspots button on the Tools panel.

You created a duplicate set of keyboard shortcuts and added a custom shortcut.

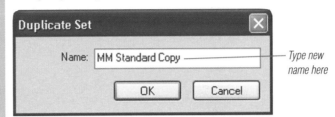

Type new name here

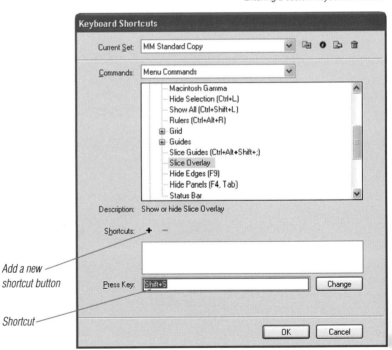

Add a new shortcut button

Shortcut

Move Undo marker up a step

Step to unbold text is grayed out

Undo a step in the History panel

1. Open the History panel from the Window menu.

   TIP You can also press [Shift][F10] to open and close the History panel.

2. Click the title text to select it, then click the Bold button on the Property inspector to unbold the text. **B**

3. Drag the Undo marker in the History panel up one step, then compare your image to Figure H-5.

   TIP When you undo an action from the Edit menu, the Undo marker moves up one step in the History panel.

You used the History panel to undo a step.

Managing Resources

To keep up with the latest developments, and for suggestions on conserving memory in Fireworks, search on "memory" on the Macromedia Online Forum for Fireworks site: http://webforums.macromedia.com/ fireworks and the Macromedia Fireworks Support Center Tech Notes site: http:// www.macromedia.com/support/search/. You can also open the Answers panel, display Tech Notes in the list, and then search the support site on "memory."

Replay steps in the History panel

1. Click the top stripe object on the canvas to select it, then click the Add effects button in the Effects section of the Property inspector. ✚

2. Point to Bevel and Emboss, click Inner Bevel, click the Bevel edge shape list arrow, click Smooth, then press [Enter] (Win) or [return] (Mac).

3. Click the Add effects button in the Effects section of the Property inspector, point to Blur, click Blur More, then compare your image to Figure H-6. ✚

4. Press and hold [Shift], then click the Set Effects steps in the History panel to select them.

   | TIP You must first select steps before you can replay them.

5. Click the bottom stripe object on the canvas, then click Replay on the History panel.

   The bevel and blur effects are applied to the object.

6. Compare your image to Figure H-7.

You selected and then replayed steps on the History panel.

FIGURE H-6
Effects steps in the History panel

Effects steps in the History panel and applied to object

FIGURE H-7
Replaying steps in the History panel

Click button to replay selected steps

FIGURE H-9
Command added to Commands menu

Commands

Manage Saved Commands...
Manage Extensions...
Run Script...

Creative ▶
Data-Driven Graphics Wizard
Document ▶
Panel Layout Sets ▶
Reset Warning Dialogs
Resize Selected Objects
Web ▶

Newly saved command ───── Bevel and Blur

Save steps as a command

1. Press and hold [Shift], then click the Set Effects steps in the History panel to select them (if necessary).

2. Click the Save button on the bottom of the History panel to open the Save Command dialog box. 💾

3. Type **Bevel and Blur** in the Name text box, as shown in Figure H-8, then click OK.

4. Click Commands on the menu bar, then compare your image to Figure H-9.

   The Bevel and Blur command appears on the Commands menu.

   | TIP To delete or rename a custom command, click Manage Saved Commands on the Commands menu, and then modify a command in the list.

5. Save your work.

You saved a command to the Commands menu.

Using Extensions

The Macromedia Exchange Web site contains a variety of JavaScript commands and Flash panels that you can add to the Fireworks environment. You can download extensions by first installing the Extension Manager from the Macromedia Exchange Web site: http://www.macromedia.com/exchange/em_download/, and then following the directions for viewing and downloading extensions. There are many third party sites that develop commands and extensions. You can link to these sites from the Macromedia Fireworks Support Center "Fireworks websites" TechNote, www.Macromedia.com\go\13187.

MAKE GLOBAL CHANGES

What You'll Do

In this lesson, you will find and replace text, and use the Batch Process feature to rescale several JPEG files.

Using Find and Replace

When you're working with any design, change is unavoidable and in many instances, welcome. However, learning when and how to call a project complete is an important skill, whether it's a Web site or a house design. Because Web content has both visual and experiential dimensions, the content that you can change is significant. A typical Web site can consist of hundreds of individual elements and images. While the question of whether you should change attributes and elements in a document remains subjective, Fireworks makes it easy to make those changes using the Find and Replace feature should you decide they're necessary.

Before you enter criteria to find and replace, you can determine how Fireworks will handle the affected files. When you open the Replace Options dialog box from the Options menu list, you can instruct Fireworks to close and save files after performing the find and replace, or to create backups of original files.

In many documents, the attributes you apply to vector and text shapes add to the overall design and give a document its unique look and feel. You can use the Find and Replace feature to change vector and text object attributes, as well as other elements. You can search a current selection, frame, document, project log, or a group of files. Once you select what you want to search, you can select what you want to find: text, font, color URL, and non-Web 216 colors. Each item has fields specific to it, as shown in Figure H-10. For text searches, in addition to preselected options, you can select the Regular Expressions checkbox to find patterns in text. A regular expression is a string of characters that tells Fireworks which pattern (string) to seek with and under what parameters. For example, the command `: %s/b[aeio]g/bug/g` will change each occurrence of "bag," "beg," "big," and "bog" to "bug."

Using Batch Process

Batch processing allows you to automatically apply the same modification to multiple files at the same time. You can run a batch process on any file that Fireworks can open. You can open the Batch Process dialog box from the Batch Process command on the Files menu. To run a batch process, you select the files you want, select the option(s), add them to the Include in Batch section,

adjust settings, click Next, and then click Batch. Figure H-11 shows sample settings in the Batch Process dialog box. Fireworks opens the files, makes the changes, and then closes the files. You can also save backups of original files and specify the destination location of the changed files.

You can run the following batch process options:

- **Export**—Select an export setting as you would from the Optimize panel, or click Edit to open the Export Preview dialog box.
- **Scale**—Choose to scale to size, to fit the area, or to a percentage.
- **Find and Replace**—Click Edit to open the Find and Replace panel, then select find and replace criteria.

- **Rename**—Rename files by adding a prefix, suffix, or by the file's original name.
- **Commands**—Run any or all of the JavaScript commands listed in the Batch Options section.

The Project Log can track the changes you've made to files by the Find and Replace and Batch Process actions. You can use the Project Log panel to organize the files associated with a document or group of documents, such as a Web site; track the changes you've made to documents; or to perform other actions, such as exporting the changed documents.

FIGURE H-10
Sample Find and Replace settings

What to search in

What to search for

What to find and replace

FIGURE H-11
Sample Batch Process settings

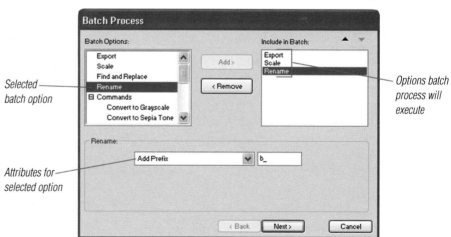

Selected batch option

Attributes for selected option

Options batch process will execute

Find and replace text

1. Open the Find and Replace panel from the Window menu.

   TIP   You can also press [Ctrl] [F] (Win) or [command] [F] (Mac), or click Edit and then click Find and Replace to open the Find and Replace panel.

2. Click the Search list arrow, click Search Document, click the Find list arrow, click Find Text, then enter the values shown in Figure H-12.

3. Click Find, notice that the word "Tee" is highlighted in the title, click Replace All, then compare your image to Figure H-13.

   Fireworks searches all the objects in the document, including each state of the button instances, and replaces "Tee" with "Tea." The dialog box tells you the number of replacements that Fireworks made.

   TIP   Fireworks does not search Library symbols that are not used in the document.

4. Click OK to close the dialog box.

   TIP   The results of the find and replace action may alter the alignment of objects on the canvas.

5. Close the Find and Replace panel.

You found and replaced text in the document.

Text settings in the Find and Replace panel

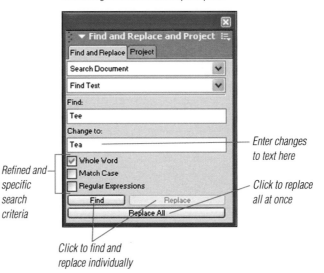

Enter changes to text here

Refined and specific search criteria

Click to replace all at once

Click to find and replace individually

Completed Find and Replace operation

Last replacement is highlighted

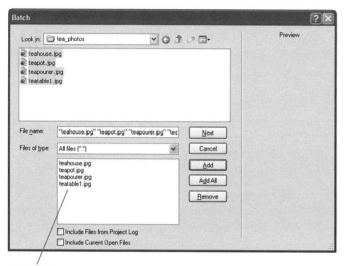

Selected files

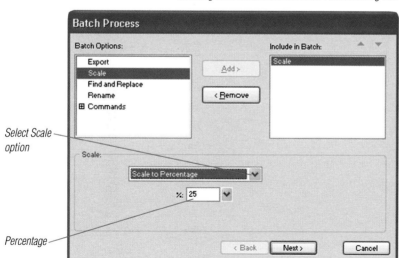

Select Scale option

Percentage

Run a batch process

1. Click File on the menu bar, click Import, navigate to the drive and folder where your data files are stored, then locate the tea_photos folder.

2. Import teapot.jpg, place the insertion pointer in the top left corner of the canvas, then click the mouse. ⌐

   The imported bitmap fills the canvas.

3. Delete the newly imported bitmap, click File on the menu bar, then click Batch Process.

4. Navigate to the tea_photos folder, verify that All files (*.*) appears as the Files of type (Win) selection, click Add All, compare your dialog box to Figure H-14, then click Next.

5. Click Scale in the Batch Options section, then click Add to add Scale to the Include in Batch section.

6. Click the Scale list arrow, click Scale to Percentage, double-click (Win) or click (Mac) the percentage text box, type **25**, compare your dialog box to Figure H-15, then click Next.

7. Verify that Same Location as Original File is selected in the Batch Output section, that Overwrite Existing Backups is selected in the Backups section, then click Batch.

   Fireworks opens and closes each file as it performs the batch process.

8. Click OK to close the Batch Process dialog box.

You ran a batch process on several files to rescale them at a set percentage.

View the results of batch processing

1. Click File on the menu bar, click Import, open the tea_photos folder (if necessary), click the View Menu button on the Import dialog box, click Details, verify that All readable files appears in the Files of type box (Win), then compare your dialog box to Figure H-16. ⊞▾

2. Note the file size for the files, open the Original Files folder, then compare the file size.

   The files scaled during the batch process are significantly smaller than the originals.

3. Return to the tea_photos folder, then double-click teapot.jpg to import it.

   (continued)

FIGURE H-16
Comparing file sizes

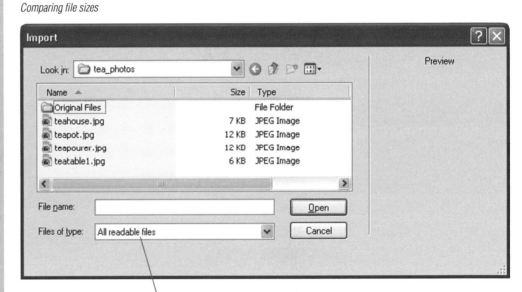

Verify this setting (Win)

FIGURE H-17
Scaled file imported into document

4. Position the insertion pointer in the top left corner of the canvas, then click the mouse. ⌐

   The imported file is much smaller and fits in a small portion of the canvas.

5. Type **20** in the X text box on the Property inspector, type **110** in the Y text box, click the Opacity list arrow, then drag the slider to **25**.

6. Click a blank part of the document window, then compare your image to Figure H-17.

7. Save your work, then close rainbowtea.png.

You compared the size of the original files and files scaled through batch process, and imported a scaled file.

INTEGRATE FIREWORKS
WITH OTHER APPLICATIONS

What You'll Do

In this lesson, you learn about the Quick Export feature and editing Fireworks files from Dreamweaver.

Using Quick Export

Before you begin work on a document in Fireworks, chances are that you know which application will eventually use the file. You can use the Quick Export button on the top right corner of the document window to export your document using the most common export options for the application of choice.

If the application into which you want to export is part of the Macromedia suite, you'll find that the program drop-down list contains export options specific to that program. For example, Dreamweaver options are HTML-based, such as exporting or updating HTML or copying it to the clipboard. Similarly, Macromedia Flash options allow you to export your document as a Flash SWF file (published Flash movies that can play independently of Flash), or to copy selected objects as vector objects.

You can also export your document to other popular applications, as shown in

Figure H-18. The Export dialog box opens and provides the relevant options for the program you've selected. For example, if you choose Export to Photoshop, you can select how the exported file will accommodate appearance, layers, objects, effects, and text. If you choose Export to FrontPage, an HTML editor, the export choices are HTML-based, or the same as exporting HTML to Dreamweaver.

Each of the Macromedia application options also includes a Launch command for that particular program. The application opens a new document; it does not open active Fireworks documents. However, you can easily import the file or edit a file created in Fireworks from the other application.

QUICKTIP

You can customize the Quick Export menu by creating JavaScript files that will appear as options on the menu.

Launching Fireworks from Dreamweaver

When you export a Fireworks document to Dreamweaver, you're actually exporting two files. In addition to the file exported in your chosen format, Fireworks creates a Design Notes file (.mno), which contains information about the source PNG file. Dreamweaver uses the MNO file to reference the source PNG file, which allows Dreamweaver to edit the image file in Fireworks from Dreamweaver.

You can use the Launch and Edit tab on the Preferences dialog box, shown in Figure H-19, to specify whether and how to use the source PNG file for editing and optimizing. You can choose one of the following options:

- Always Use Source PNG—automatically launches the designated source PNG file in the Design Notes and updates changes in both the source PNG file and the exported file.
- Never Use Source PNG—automatically launches and updates the exported file only.
- Ask When Launching—prompts you to indicate if you want to launch the source PNG file.

QUICK**TIP**

You must also set Fireworks as the primary external image editor in the Dreamweaver Preferences dialog box.

Once you've specified Fireworks as the image editor in Dreamweaver and inserted a file into a Dreamweaver document, you can edit the file in Fireworks by launching Fireworks from the Dreamweaver Property inspector. Figure H-20 shows the document window when Fireworks is launched from Dreamweaver. You can edit the file as you wish, and then click Done to return to Dreamweaver. You don't need to re-export or save the image file. You can also create a placeholder for an image in Dreamweaver, click Create on the Dreamweaver Property inspector, and then create an image file in Fireworks that matches the exact dimensions of the Dreamweaver placeholder. When you click Done to return to Dreamweaver, the image you just created is inserted in the proper location in Dreamweaver.

FIGURE H-18
Quick Export options

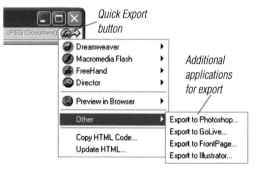

Quick Export button

Additional applications for export

FIGURE H-19
Launch and Edit settings in the Preferences dialog box

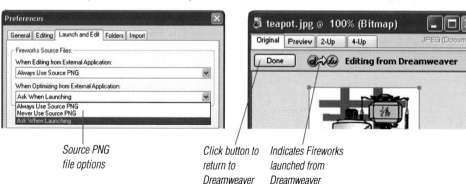

Source PNG file options

Click button to return to Dreamweaver

Indicates Fireworks launched from Dreamweaver

FIGURE H-20
Fireworks document window launched from Dreamweaver

UNDERSTAND INTELLECTUAL PROPERTY ISSUES

What You'll Do

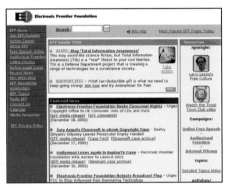

In this lesson, you will learn about intellectual and copyright property law and online privacy issues.

Understanding Intellectual Property

By definition, using multimedia in Web design involves combining content from several media: graphics, text, illustrations, HTML code, photographs, and other creative expressions of your ideas. The use and reproduction of all of these may be protected under one or more areas of law generally referred to as intellectual property. You can think of **intellectual property** as an idea or creation of a human mind. It also must have commercial value. Intellectual property is like any other property, except that instead of being *tangible*, like a DVD, it is *intangible*, like the songs or movie on the DVD. For comprehensive information on the concepts defining intellectual property law, visit the Electronic Frontier Foundation Web site: www.eff.org, shown in Figure H-21.

In the United States, intellectual property law involves four main categories.

Copyright law. A copyright arises upon an expression of an idea and thought, like Web page design or a new logo. Matter that is protected by copyright is referred to as a **work of authorship**, which includes the following:

- literary works (everything from mystery ebooks to sports manuals, and from clothing catalogs to computer source code)
- musical works and sound recordings
- dramatic works
- artistic and architectural works
- pictorial, graphic, and sculptural works (physical and digital)
- motion pictures, video games and tapes, computer and other audiovisual works
- broadcast and online transmission

Patent law. Under this "industrial" branch of intellectual property law, an inventor may apply for the protection of new, useful and "nonobvious" inventions and processes. For example, you can apply for a patent if you have devised a gene splicing technique for cancer, but not if you have designed a basic wastebasket.

Trademark law. Trademark law involves the protection of commercial identities and symbols. A **trade name** is the name of a business, corporation, company, and so on, which distinguishes one business entity from another. It can be a word, name, symbol, logo, or any combination thereof. A trademark must be adopted and used by an entity to identify their goods and to distinguish them from goods manufactured or sold by others. A *service mark* identifies the source of services instead of the source of goods, such as a restaurant chain.

Trade secret law. Protects information created by the expenditure of (often considerable) time or money. Trade secrets are naturally held confidential and not generally known in the trade.

QUICK**TIP**

Copyright protection extends to original work, such as a digital image, as soon as it's created.

One of the most important areas of general intellectual property is the idea of a public domain. **Public domain** indicates the status of any work or creation that was never protected by some form of intellectual property, or had protection that was lost through time or by legal events. You can use or copy public domain works at will. The prevailing assumption is that using works that are in the public domain should be encouraged because such use promotes competition.

In contrast, copyright infringement is taken very seriously. For example, you may recall one or two news items about Internet music file-sharing or radio sites. The penalty for

FIGURE H-21
Electronic Frontier Foundation Web site

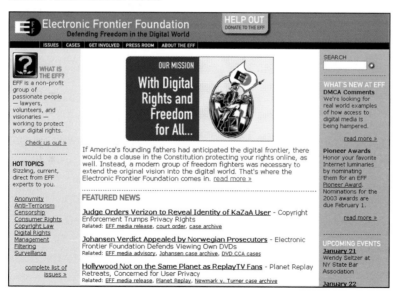

infringement of a registered copyright is up to $150,000 for each infringement. Even inadvertent infringement can lead to penalties, though not as strict.

The assumptions and burdens of proof governing copyright infringement are based upon civil law, not criminal law. Thus, there is never the need to show infringement beyond a reasonable doubt, and there may even be an assumption of guilt. For example, U.S. copyright law specifically prohibits removing a watermark from a photograph. If you are charged with removing a watermark, the attempt itself is viewed by the court as your willful intent to violate the owner's copyright. The assumption is that you are guilty and the burden of proof is on you to prove that you're not.

You can copy an "idea" of a work, but if you copy the "expression" of a work, that's a copyright infringement. The difference between "idea" and "expression" is a difficult concept in copyright law. Copying the expression of work is not limited to literal copying.

One limitation to copyright is **fair use**. Fair use allows consumers to copy all or part of a copyrighted work in support of their First Amendment rights. For example, you could excerpt short passages of a film or song, or parody a television show, all for noncommercial use. Determining if fair use applies to a work depends on the purpose of its use, the nature of the copyrighted work, how much you want to copy, and the effect on the market or value of the work. Fair use is used as the defense in many copyright infringement cases.

For information on international intellectual property law, visit the World Intellectual Property Organization (WIPO) at www.wipo.org, shown in Figure H-22.

FIGURE H-22
WIPO Web site

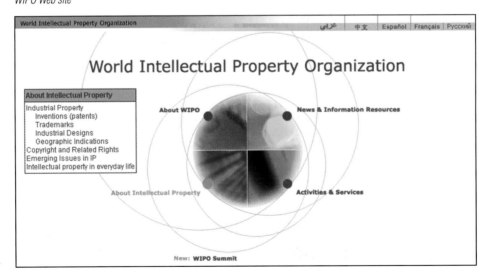

Original multimedia works are protected by copyright law and patent law. Other areas of law that intersect multimedia design are communications law and computer law. The products of the Web are literally intangible property operating in an intangible medium. As a result, the laws governing Web-based design are evolving.

Privacy as it Impacts Advertising and Marketing

Web advertising contains cookies and web bugs, which are used to track your browsing behavior, sometimes down to the keystroke. The essential questions about online privacy concern how information is gathered, the extent to which information is collected, and with whom it can be shared. For example, if you respond to a banner ad, your surfing history through that site can be stored, resulting in a browsing profile which can be sold to several buyers. When combined with other data, such as credit card purchases or surveys you've filled out, an aggregate profile of you is formed. That profile may or may not be accurate and may contain information you never thought would be disclosed. Privacy advocates are concerned that this information is collected, sold, re-assembled, and used to evaluate an individual without their knowledge or consent.

For information on cookies and Web bugs, visit the educational organization, Privacy Foundation, at www.privacyfoundation.org.

FIGURE H-23
Privacy Foundation Web site

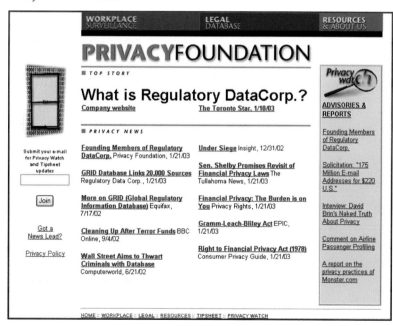

Create a duplicate keyboard shortcut set and custom shortcut.

1. Open fwh_2.png, then save it as **wrapit.png**.
2. Open the Keyboard Shortcuts dialog box from the Edit menu.
3. Duplicate the current shortcut set and change the name to **MM Standard Copy 2**.
4. Expand File menu in the Commands section, then select Batch Process.
5. Add a new shortcut to the Press Key text box: **Shift+B**.
6. Click OK.
7. Save your work.

Undo a step in the History panel.

1. Open the History panel.
2. Select the Wrap It text on the canvas. (*Hint*: Make sure that slices and hotspots are not visible.)
3. Delete the Inner Bevel on the Property inspector.

4. Drag the Undo Marker up in the History panel to undo the delete.
5. Save your work.

Replay a step in the History panel.

1. Add a Drop Shadow to the Bubbles bitmap with the following attributes: Distance: 5, Color: #000099, Opacity: 55%, and Softness: 6.
2. Select the Set Effects step in the History panel.
3. Select the bottom blue rectangle on the canvas.
4. Replay the Set Effects step.
5. Save your work.

Save the step as a command.

1. Verify that the Set Effects step is still selected in the History panel.
2. Save the step as a command. (*Hint*: Use the Save button on the bottom of the History panel.)

3. Name the command **Blue Drop Shadow** in the Save Command dialog box, then close the dialog box.
4. View the new command on the Commands menu

Find and replace text.

1. Open the Find and Replace panel.
2. Search the document for Bobble and replace it with Bubble.
3. Replace All instances, then close the dialog box.
4. Save your work.

Run a batch process

1. Import box2.jpg to top left corner of the canvas, then delete the object.
2. Press [Shift][B] to open the Batch Process panel.
3. Select all the .jpg files from the packing folder, then click Next.

4. Add Scale as the Batch Process, select Scale to Percentage, then set the percentage to **15**.

5. Click Next, verify that Same Location as Original File is selected in the Batch Output section, that Overwrite Existing Backups is selected as the Backups section.

6. Click Batch.

7. Save your work.

FIGURE H-24
Completed Skills Review

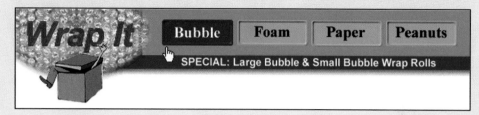

View the results of batch processing.

1. Open the Import dialog box, then compare the sizes of the original files to ones that were batch processed.

2. Import box2.jpg at the top of the Layer 1 layer, then move it beneath the title.

3. Compare your image to Figure H-24.

4. Save your work, then close wrapit.png.

You want to save steps that you perform frequently as commands. You can retrieve any solution file you created from previous Project Builders or Group Projects.

1. Open the document of your choice, then save it as **mydocument.png**.
2. If desired, obtain additional images that will reinforce your theme. You can obtain images from your computer, from the Internet, from a digital camera, or from scanned media. You can use clipart from the Web that is free for both personal and commercial use (check the copyright information for any such clipart before downloading it).
3. Add additional features, then save steps as commands and create additional keyboard shortcuts as desired.
4. Use the Find and Replace feature as necessary.
5. Add a new layer that you will use to record the names of the commands and shortcuts, then change the name of the layer to **commands**.
6. Use the Text tool to identify the name of the command and shortcut, then hide the layer.
7. Optimize slices as necessary.
8. Save your work, then examine the sample shown in Figure H-25.

FIGURE H-25

Completed Project Builder 1

You're helping an art gallery highlight their new exhibition on shapes and forms. So far, the shape photographs and images at the Web site don't do justice to the exhibit. They've asked you to design three picture frames in Fireworks that they can use to help accent the images on their Web page. You can pick the shape or form of your choice.

1. Obtain images that will reinforce your shape and form theme. You can obtain images from your computer, from the Internet, from a digital camera, or from scanned media. You can use clipart from the Web that is free for both personal and commercial use (check the copyright information for any such clipart before downloading it).

2. Create a new document and save it as **myframe.png**.

3. Import the images and create buttons or a nav bar as desired.

4. Create three or more frames for the shape images, saving the frame steps as commands.

5. Use the Find and Replace feature to change font and font color.

6. Add a new object on a layer that you will use to record the commands you created for each frame, then change the name of the object to **commands**.

7. Use the Text tool to describe each command, then hide the object on the Layers panel.

8. Save your work, then examine the sample in Figure H-26.

FIGURE H-26
Completed Project Builder 2

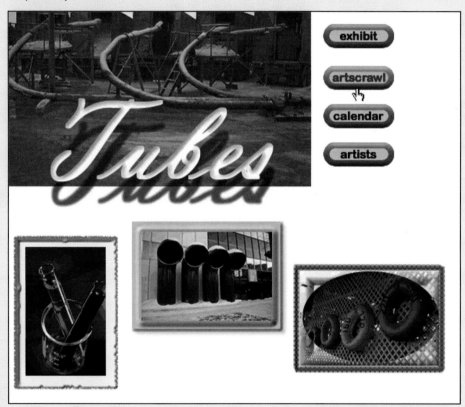

Intellectual property enters our lives from the moment we wake up and hear the custom sound we programmed into a clock, or smell the coffee that our coffee maker made at a preset time after automatically grinding the beans.

1. Select a product, process, or other intellectual property entity. (*Hint*: Just go through your normal day and notice something that fits the definition of intellectual property. Chances are, something you enjoy is someone else's intellectual property.)
2. Open a new Fireworks document, then save it as **ip_law.png**.
3. Identify your product or process, then obtain images of it. You can obtain images from your computer, from the Internet, from a digital camera, or from scanned media. You can use clipart from the Web that is free for both personal and commercial use (check the copyright information for any such clipart before downloading it).
4. Create an image of your selection, and show which parts are intellectual property.
5. Use the Text tool to identify the parts of your product or process affected by intellectual property. Split them into categories, and discuss each one. If there are any parts that don't obviously fall under intellectual property, try to explain why they don't.
6. Save your work, then examine the sample shown in Figure H-27.

FIGURE H-27
Design Project

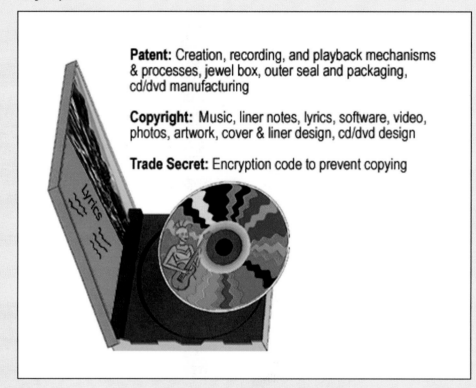

Patent: Creation, recording, and playback mechanisms & processes, jewel box, outer seal and packaging, cd/dvd manufacturing

Copyright: Music, liner notes, lyrics, software, video, photos, artwork, cover & liner design, cd/dvd design

Trade Secret: Encryption code to prevent copying

Your group can assign elements of the project to individual members, or work collectively to create the finished product.

Your group has been assigned to create a Fireworks document that contains many features and effects. You can choose the topic of your choice that celebrates something.

1. Obtain images of the topic you've chosen. You can obtain images from your computer, from the Internet, from a digital camera, or from scanned media. You can use clipart from the Web that is free for both personal and commercial use (check the copyright information for any such clipart before downloading it).
2. Create a new document and save it as **celebrate.png**.
3. Copy or import the files into your document.
4. Add multiple features, then save steps as commands or create additional keyboard shortcuts as desired.
5. Add a new layer, change the layer name to **commands**, then use the Text tool to identify the commands from steps, shortcuts, and find and replace commands you performed in the document.
6. Save your work, then examine the sample shown in Figure H-28.

FIGURE H-28
Completed Group Project

Read the following information carefully!

Find out from your instructor the location of the Data Files you need and the location where you will store your files.

■ To complete many of the units in this book, you need to use Data Files. Your instructor will either provide you with a copy of the Data Files or ask you to make your own copy.

■ If you need to make a copy of the Data Files, you will need to copy a set of files from a file server, standalone computer, or the Web to the drive and location where you will be storing your Data Files.

■ Your instructor will tell you which computer, drive letter, and folders contain the files you need, and where you will store your files.

■ You can also download the files by going to *www.course.com*. See the inside back cover of this book for instructions to download your files.

Copy and organize your Data Files.

■ Use the Data Files List to organize your files to a zip drive, network folder, hard drive, or other storage device.

■ Create a subfolder for each unit in the location where you are storing your files, and name it according to the unit title (e.g., Unit A).

■ For each unit you are assigned, copy the files listed in the **Data File Supplied** column into that unit's folder.

■ Store the files you modify or create in each unit in the unit folder.

Find and keep track of your Data Files and completed files.

■ Use the **Data File Supplied** column to make sure you have the files you need before starting the unit or exercise indicated in the **Unit** column.

■ Use the **Student Creates File** column to find out the filename you use when saving your new file for the exercise.

Macromedia Fireworks MX

Unit	Data File Supplied	Student Creates File	Used In
A	fwa_1.png		Lesson 1
	pool.png	my_blue_heaven.png	Lesson 2
	fwa_1.png		Lessons 3 & 4
	fwa_2.png elbow.gif		Skills Review
	none	crystal.png	Project Builder 1
	none	meandering_paths.png	Project Builder 2
	none	rocknroll	Design Project
	none	emoticon.png	Group Project

Unit	Data File Supplied	Student Creates File	Used In
B	none	fish.png	Lesson 1
	fwb_1.png		Lessons 2–5
	fwb_2.png		Skills Review
	none	remember_me.png	Project Builder 1
	none	impact_potion.png	Project Builder 2
	none	yoakum	Design Project
	none	classic_buckle.png	Group Project
C	fwc_1.png rocket.gif saucer.png book.eps		Lesson 1
	galaxy.jpg		Lesson 2
	astrocat.jpg		Lesson 3
	none	none	Lesson 4
	fwc_2.png smbottle.jpg sweet.png jelly beans.eps rings.png gumballs.tif		Skills Review
	button1.ai button2.ai	mybuttons.png	Project Builder 1
	none	roadtrip.png	Project Builder 2
	none	homecinema	Design Project
	none	mybug.png	Group Project
D	fwd_1.png		Lessons 1 & 3
	fwd_2.png		Lesson 2
	leaves.png		Lesson 4
	fwd_3.png fwd_4.png		Skills Review
	ship.jpg	treasure_hunt.png	Project Builder 1
	none	earthtrends	Project Builder 2
	none	imports.png	Group Project

Unit	Data File Supplied	Student Creates File	Used In
E	fwe_1.png		Lesson 1
	fwe_2.png		Lesson 2
	fwe_3.png		Lesson 3
	fwe_4.png		Lesson 4
	fwe_5.png fwe_6.png fwe_7.png fwe_8.png		Skills Review
	picture.jpg	geekchic.png	Project Builder 1
	none	maskgallery.png	Project Builder 2
	none	interactive	Design Project
	none	mytech.png	Group Project
F	fwf_1.png		Lesson 1
	fwf_2.png		Lesson 2
	fwf_3.png		Lessons 3 & 4
	fwf_4.png fwf_5.png fwf_6.png		Skills Review
	cake.gif candle.gif	birthdaycake.png birthdaycake.gif	Project Builder 1
	none	readbooks.png	Project Builder 2
	none	animation	Design Project
	none	mymoneymyth.png	Group Project
G	none	none	Lesson 1
	fwg_1.png	gmparts/gmparts.htm gmparts/mm_menu.js gmparts/assets/ folder	Lesson 2
	fwg_2.png	recipes/desserts.htm recipes/entrees.htm recipes/recipes.htm recipes/starters.htm recipes/images/ folder	Lesson 3
	none		Lesson 4

Unit	Data File Supplied	Student Creates File	Used In
	fwg_3.png	litcat/literary_cat.htm	Skills Review
		litcat/mm_menu.js	
		litcat/images/ folder	
	fwg_4.png	techno/techno_dude.htm	
		techno/techno_dude_1.htm	
		techno/techno_dude_2.htm	
		techno/techno_dude_3.htm	
		techno/images/ folder	
	box.jpg	stuffomonth.png	Project Builder 1
		stuffomonth/stuffomonth.htm	
		stuffomonth/mm_menu.js	
		stuffomonth/images/ folder	
	none	trash2cash.png	Project Builder 2
		trash2cash/trash2cash.htm	
		trash2cash/images/ folder	
	none	navigation	Design Project
	none	desktop_theory.png	Group Project
		desktop_theory/desktop_theory.htm	
		desktop_theory/mm_menu.js	
		desktop_theory/assets/ folder	
H	fwg_1.png		Lesson 1
	tea_photos/teahouse.jpg	tea_photos/teahouse.jpg	Lesson 2
	tea_photos/ teapot.jpg	tea_photos/ teapot.jpg	
	tea_photos/teapourer.jpg	tea_photos/teapourer.jpg	
	tea_photos/teatable1.jpg	tea_photos/teatable1.jpg	
		tea_photos/Original Files/ folder	
	none	none	Lesson 3
	none	none	Lesson 4
	fwh_2.png	packing/box1.jpg	Skills Review
	packing/box1.jpg	packing/box2.gif	
	packing/box2.gif	packing/box3.jpg	
	packing/box3.jpg	packing/box4.jpg	
	pakcing/box4.jpg	packing/Original Files/ folder	
	none	mydocument.png	Project Builder 1
	none	myframe.png	Project Builder 2
	none	ip_law.png	Design Project
	none	celebrate.png	Group Project

Absolute URL
A fixed URL starting with http:// used when linking to a Web page outside of your Web site.

Action
A response to an event trigger that causes a change, such as text changing color.

Alpha channel
The opaque area of the object.

Alternate text
Text that appears when you position the mouse pointer over a slice or hotspot.

Anchor points
Connect path segments in vector objects. They delineate changes in direction, whether a corner or a curve.

Animation
Created by rapidly playing a series of still images in a sequence, which creates the illusion of movement.

Animation handles
Handles on the animation path of an animation symbol: green (start), blue (frames), and red (end).

Animation symbol
An animation created from an object or instance on the canvas and stored in the Library panel. It has properties such as frame count, scale, opacity, and rotation.

Anti-aliasing
Blends the edges of a stroke, text, or pixel selection with surrounding pixels so that the edges blend into the background.

Behavior
A preset piece of JavaScript code that can be applied to a slice, hotspot, or button.

Behavior handle
A round icon that appears at the center of a slice or hotspot.

Bézier curves
The two-dimensional curves in a vector object.

Bitmap graphic
Represents a picture image as a matrix of dots, or pixels, on a grid.

Bitmap mask
A bitmap object used to mask other object(s).

Canvas
The area where you draw and manipulate objects and images.

Client-side scripting language
Computer code that runs within a Web browser.

CMY
Cyan, magenta, yellow.

Color depth
The number of colors in the exported graphic.

Color ramp
Creates and displays the range of colors in a gradient, including their transparency.

Composite path
The path created by the Join command when two or more open or closed paths are joined to form a single object.

Continuous path
The path created by the Join command if the two objects in the path are open.

Corner points
The square points of a path that has angles or is linear, such as a square, star, or a straight line.

Disjoint rollover
A rollover that swaps an image in a different part of the screen than where you triggered it.

Documents
The files you create in Fireworks.

Event trigger
An event, such as a mouse click on an object, that causes an action.

Fill
The color category (such as solid, gradient, or pattern) applied to an object, as well as its type and amount of edge.

Frame delay
The display time for animation measured in hundredths of a second—the default frame delay in Fireworks is 7/100 of a second.

Frame-by-frame animation
An animation process where you copy objects into different frames and then modify the objects in each frame.

Frames
Individual static images that make up an animation's image.

GIF
Graphics interchange format

Gradient
Two or more colors that blend into each other in a fixed design.

Hotspot
An area in your document that initiates a specific action, such as linking to a Web page or displaying an e-mail message pop-up window. A hotspot can also initiate a behavior in a browser, such as a swap image pop-up menu.

HSB
Hue, saturation, and brightness.

HTML
Hypertext Markup Language; HTML marks up the text in your Web page so your browser can read it.

Image map
The graphics and HTML containing information about hotspots and their URL links. Fireworks creates an image map when you export a graphic with hotspots.

Instance
A symbol on the canvas; a shortcut to its symbol.

Interactivity
Allows visitors to your Web site to affect its content.

Interlacing
Allows a file to download from the Internet gradually from low to high resolution.

JavaScript
A Web-scripting language that interacts with HTML code to create interactive content.

JPEG
Joint photographic experts group

Kerning
Adjusts the spacing between adjacent letters or a range of letters.

Layers
Layers divide and arrange the elements of your document in a logical front to back order. A layer can contain multiple objects, all of which are managed on the Layers panel.

Leading
Adjusts the amount of space between lines of text.

Library panel
Stores symbols for the current document.

Live Effects
Effects that are editable.

Looping
The number of times an animation will play after the initial playback in a Web page.

mailto URL
Opens an e-mail address window in a Web page.

Marquee selection
A flashing perimeter or dashed line around selected pixels.

Mask
Modifies the shape and transparency, including gradients, of an underlying image.

Mask object
A bitmap or vector object that masks another bitmap or vector object.

Mask thumbnail
Appears next to the object thumbnail on the Layers panel when you add a mask to an object.

Motion path
The animation trail in a document, consisting of animation handles. You can drag the handles to change the path of the animation.

Navigation bar
A group of buttons that link to different areas inside or outside the Web site.

Nested button symbol
A button symbol within a button symbol.

Objects
The individual elements in your document that are stored and managed on layers in the Layers panel.

Onion skinning
Allows you to view one or more additional animation frames while in the current frame.

Opacity setting
Determines if your image is completely opaque (100%), or completely transparent (0%). You can set opacity in 1% increments.

Open standard
Computer code, such as HTML, whose specifications are publicly available.

Optimize
The process that matches the format best suited for the type of graphic with the smallest file size that maintains image quality.

Path
An open or closed vector line consisting of a series of anchor points.

Path scrubber tool
Alters a path's appearance based on the pressure and speed with which you apply the stroke.

Patterns
Bitmap images that have complex color schemes and textures.

Pixels
Discrete squares of color values that can be drawn on a computer screen.

Plug-in
Adds features to an application. In Fireworks, plug-ins appear on the filters menu and the Live Effects pop-up menu.

PNG
Portable network graphics, the default file format in Fireworks.

Point handle
Corresponding to each anchor point, point handles are visible when you edit a curved path segment, but not when you edit a straight path segment. Also called a Bézier handle.

Pop-up menu
A menu that appears when you move the pointer over a trigger image in a browser.

Property inspector
Panel where you modify selected objects and set tool properties and other options. Depending on the activity or action you are performing, information on the Property inspector changes.

Relative URL
A link based on its location as it relates to the current page in the Web site's folder; use to link to a page within your Web site.

Reshape Area tool
Pulls areas of the path to a boundary.

Resolution
The number of pixels per inch in an image; also refers to an image's clarity and fineness of detail.

RGB
Red, green, and blue.

Rollover
A graphic element in a Web page that changes appearance when you trigger it with the mouse.

Sample
The color of a pixel or range of pixels picked up by the Eyedropper tool.

Slice
Used to attach a link or behavior to the image beneath it.

States
The four appearances a button can assume in response to a mouse action. They include Up, Over, Down, and Over While Down.

Storyboard
A visual script you use to show the action. It consists of a series of panels that plot the key scenes and illustrate the flow of the animation.

Stroke
A border applied to an object's edge consisting of attributes, including color, tip size (the size of the stroke), softness, and texture.

Styles
Preset attributes, such as size, color, and texture that you can apply to objects and text.

Styles panel
Where Fireworks manages pre-designed graphics and text styles.

Subselection tool
Tool used to move points on a path, or to select objects and paths within a group or composite path.

Symbol
Any text, graphic, button, or animation object saved in the Library panel. A way to reuse graphic objects, animations, and buttons in a document.

Tags
Determine how the text in HTML should be formatted when a browser displays it.

TIFF
Tagged image file format.

Tolerance
The range of colors the tool will select. The higher the setting, the larger the selection range.

Tools panel
Houses the tools you can use in the Fireworks work environment.

URL
Uniform resource locator, an address that determines a route on the Internet or to a Web page.

VCR controls
Buttons you use to preview animation on the Original and Preview tabs of the document window.

Vector graphics
Mathematically calculated objects composed of anchor points and straight or curved line segments, which you can fill with color or a pattern and outline with a stroke.

Vector mask
The vector shape through which the underlying object is viewed.

Web Dither
A Web Dither fill Approximates the color of a non-websafe color by combining two websafe colors.

Web Layer
The topmost layer on the Layers panel. It is a shared layer, meaning that its content appears in all frames.

Websafe colors
Colors that are common to both Macintosh and Windows platforms.

INDEX